Cross Chan

When a century ago the Entente Cordiale agreements were signed, no one could have realized how important a watershed it was to become. What began as a deal over various colonial issues became an increasingly close relationship in a world growing more dangerous. Ten years later it became a life-or-death alliance in World War I, and during the fraught interwar period a partnership attempting vainly to keep the peace. During World War II the two countries struggled together for the freedom of Europe and for their own survival. Since then, they have been leading partners in European politics and the chief representatives of Europe and defenders of its interests in the outside world.

This book tells the story of the triumphs and tragedies of this hundred-year relationship, as well as the everyday common interests and shared pleasures that give it substance. The actors include monarchs and politicians, soldiers and Resistance heroes, writers, artists, entrepreneurs, engineers, tourists, expatriates, sports stars and students.

Many hands have made light work of the story. Those who tell it have themselves contributed to history. They include the late Roy Jenkins, in a witty and personal view of Winston Churchill's relationship with France; Pierre Messmer, a companion of Charles de Gaulle during World War II and later Prime Minister; former Foreign Secretary Douglas Hurd, who remembers the historic meeting of Edward Heath and Georges Pompidou; Hubert Védrine, former French Foreign Minister, on future cross-Channel relations; and their successors Dominique de Villepin and Jack Straw.

Protagonists and witnesses are balanced by analysts and scholars from both Britain and France. Some are respected historians like Maurice Vaïsse and Christopher Andrew. They also include well-known writers ranging from John Ardagh, Miles Kington and Gillian Tindall to Maurice Druon, André Fontaine and Jean-Pierre Angremy. Their work has been welded into a coherent whole by the Franco–British editorial team.

What the book reveals, again and again, is the importance of looking beyond agreements and disagreements to the unspoken assumptions that underlie conscious thoughts and policies. Only thus, as experience shows, can the Entente be truly Cordiale.

Richard Mayne is an historian, writer and broadcaster. **Douglas Johnson** is Professor Emeritus of French History, University of London. **Robert Tombs** is a Reader in History at the University of Cambridge.

Cross Channel Currents

100 Years of the Entente Cordiale

Edited by
Richard Mayne, Douglas Johnson
and Robert Tombs

Published in association with the Franco-British Council

Routledge
Taylor & Francis Group

LONDON AND NEW YORK

First published 2004
by Routledge
11 New Fetter Lane, London EC4P 4EE

Simultaneously published in the USA and Canada
by Routledge
29 West 35th Street, New York, NY 10001

Routledge is an imprint of the Taylor & Francis Group

Typeset in Ehrhardt by Wearset Ltd, Boldon, Tyne and Wear
Printed and bound in Great Britain by TJ International, Padstow,
Cornwall

British Library Cataloguing in Publication Data
A catalogue record for this book is available from the British
Library

Library of Congress Cataloging in Publication Data
Cross-Channel currents : 100 hundred years of the Entente
Cordiale / edited by Douglas Johnson . . . [et al.].
p. cm.
Includes bibliographical references and index.
1. Great Britain–Foreign relations–France. 2. Great Britain–
Foreign relations–20th century. 3. France–Foreign relations–
Great Britain. 4. France–Foreign relations–20th century.
I. Johnson, Douglas, 1925–
DA47.1.C85 2004
327.41044'09'04–dc22
2004001265

ISBN 0-415-34661-4 (Hbk)
ISBN 0-415-34662-2 (Pbk)

Contents

CONTENTS

CONTENTS

Plates

Acknowledgements

The British and French offices of the Franco–British Council played a vital role in the production of this book. The editors would like to recognise the work done by the Secretary-General, Ann Kenrick, as well as Sylvie Blumenkrantz and Ruth Kitching. The French contributions were translated by Richard Mayne. Thanks are also due to Sir Peter Petrie who chaired the British Section of the Council from 1997 to 2002 and who gave his support to the initiation of this project. Finally we would like to acknowledge the financial support of Eurotunnel plc.

Forewords

Jack Straw and Dominique de Villepin

I

No two countries have a relationship so redolent of history as that between the United Kingdom and France. We are all made aware of this from an early age. British and French children are familiar with the same milestone dates – 1066, 1789, 1914 and 1945. They learn that their nations were not mere bystanders but participants in some of the key moments that have defined our continent and our world.

The importance of our relationship is inescapable to any British foreign secretary. During the war years, my official Residence in London was the home of General de Gaulle. His portrait adorns the wall to this day, a constant reminder of the bond forged between our countries during Europe's darkest hour.

This publication marks another historical milestone in UK–French relations – the hundredth anniversary of the signing of the Entente Cordiale. The Entente was very much a product of its time. Britain and France were then the world's two pre-eminent colonial powers. The Treaty represented a strategic decision by Paris and London to end their territorial rivalry in north Africa and beyond. But it also had a wider significance: it laid the basis for our military alliance through the last century, including in the two world wars.

Today the Entente Cordiale symbolises the enduring nature of UK–French relations and the fact that, irrespective of our occasional differences, our countries share an aspiration to extend the values of democracy, human rights and the rule of law across the globe. The Entente epitomises the sentiments expressed by President Jacques Chirac and

Prime Minister Tony Blair at the Le Touquet Summit in early 2003 that 'There is more that unites us than divides us.'

Today we are united on the need for a strong European Union that can deliver the jobs, security and prosperity our citizens expect. We agree that the Union should develop a stronger, more coherent voice in foreign affairs commensurate with its economic standing as the world's largest trading bloc. And following the agreement between the president and the prime minister at St Malo six years ago, we are working together to ensure that Europe learns from the tragic experience of the Balkans in the early 1990s by developing credible defence capabilities.

We are also united on the need to tackle the two great threats to collective security of the twenty-first century – international terrorism and the spread of weapons of mass destruction. Overcoming these threats will be a long and difficult task. But the UK and France can draw inspiration from our past when, together with our Allies, we faced down a no less formidable challenge to our way of life during the Cold War.

Our victory then was based on the supremacy of our values. Command economics and one-party rule ultimately proved no match for the combination of democracy, economic efficiency and social solidarity that had been the hallmarks of societies in Western Europe – particularly in the United Kingdom and France – for decades.

Our task today is to work together to ensure that these values are extended to other less fortunate parts of the world, including Africa, and to the great issues of the environment and sustainable development that face us all. The UK and France share a belief that humankind has an innate yearning for peace and prosperity. It is this belief more than any other that has underpinned the Entente Cordiale for the past hundred years. I am sure it will continue to do so over the course of the twenty-first century.

Rt Hon Jack Straw MP, Secretary of State,
Foreign and Commonwealth Office

II

Any historical event must be judged
in its totality.
Georges Clemenceau

Suggesting as it does the courtesy of a gentleman or a cultivated man, the term Entente Cordiale cannot fully reflect the profound change made to the history of France and Britain by the agreement reached in 1904.

In fact, there had been almost ancestral cross-Channel rivalry between the leading power on the continent and the queen of the seas. From the Hundred Years' War to 1815, not forgetting the confrontation between William of Orange and Louis XIV, our relationship had very often plunged Europe into misery and war, without a definitive victory on either side. Fontenoy, Yorktown, Trafalgar and Waterloo are all examples of battles in which our respective heroes distinguished themselves.

If the conflicts dividing us always seemed like fratricide, this is because we hold the same values. Alongside both our countries' thirst for glory and greatness, alongside our peoples' intense patriotism and our unconquerable desire for independence, other principles have united us. From Locke to Montesquieu, we have shared a demand for tolerance and a loyalty to fundamental liberties. Liberal thinkers in France from Benjamin Constant to Madame de Staël long looked to Britain for the example of a balanced political regime such as their own political masters had yet to achieve. And yet at Fashoda in 1898 our rivalry flared up again. No one doubted that a war was imminent, perhaps more fearful than any before. Mutual incitement was everywhere – in the press, in public opinion, in campaigns of hatred orchestrated by nationalist groups and by the 'colonial party'. There was a climax of tension between two peoples who then had only distorted pictures of each other. Prejudice and caricature held sway.

In these circumstances, to establish the Entente Cordiale was above all a triumph of political will and diplomacy. To resist the siren voices calling for war, the makers of the Entente needed great and passionate determination. Looking back, we can see how much they changed the course of history. The same theme of clarity, patience, independence and sense of history is what this book traces in the continuing relations between French and British statesmen. To identify points of disagreement and not evade difficulties – these were Paul Cambon's watchwords when he came to London at the end of 1898 with the firm resolve to deal with the problems of Egypt and Morocco. 'I believe that brevity and clarity of speech are more to the taste of people here than all diplomatic euphemisms': this sentence from his private correspondence pre-dated by five years the spirit of the Entente Cordiale. Better yet, it confidently shows us the path to follow a hundred years later.

Today, in Franco-British diplomacy, the search for agreement and the habit of dialogue are firmly entrenched. Protocol has evolved and the stakes are different, but one conviction endures. It was Delcassé's, and it is ours: for every dispute a solution can be negotiated. The great revolution that the Entente began was to ensure that our century of shared diplomacy has been marked by only 'friendly disagreements'. Because it has enabled the Channel to become that area of freedom and frankness that all dialogue needs, the Entente Cordiale deserves to be commemorated a century later. Its spirit has provided a context that still serves us well, as at St Malo in 1998 or in 2003 at the summit meeting in Le Touquet.

That spirit helped us both to survive the ordeals of the twentieth century. United in World War I, we shared the inferno of the trenches before achieving victory together. The French Resistance will never forget the debt France owes to Britain, whence came, on 18 June 1940, the first message of hope. Nor shall we forget Winston Churchill, the embodiment of survival in a Europe that many thought destroyed. France knows what it owes him, and to the British and other servicemen who lost their lives on the Normandy beaches and elsewhere.

If both our countries have thrown in their lot with Europe, they have not always had the same objective. Committed to historic reconciliation with Germany, France was the first to feel the need to bind its destiny to a united Europe. Britain long hesitated before joining an enterprise that it long viewed with prudence and mistrust. In our shared European venture, we have had disagreements. The impatience caused in France by Britain's reluctance to join the Euro has been equalled only by the annoyance caused in Britain by some of France's attitudes in the Atlantic Alliance. But, every time, we have been able to surmount these obstacles, thanks to the friendship that unites us, the values we share, and the historic experience we have lived through together.

The year 2003 was an illustration of this relationship, based on both frankness and necessity. During the Iraq crisis, we disagreed on fundamentals – whether to wage war or to go on pursuing disarmament through weapons inspection. And yet, during that same year, we showed our solidarity by taking a historic step in the building of Europe: recruiting ten new members to the European Union, and drafting its Constitution. In the field of defence policy, the initiative taken by France, Germany, Belgium and Luxembourg led to further controversy; but, there again, dialogue prevailed, and discussion showed the possibility of an accord. If each of us has managed to play our part, despite the differences we have never sought to minimise, it is because in the last analysis we share the same sense of responsibility.

The Entente Cordiale is celebrating its first centenary. To strengthen an *entente*, confidence must be solidly established, tended and developed. The most recent Franco-British summit, in London on 24 November 2003, was a good example. The deepening of our cooperation on defence, Africa or immigration, and the launching of new initiatives on health, research and the environment, all bear the mark of this mutual commitment. It was in this spirit that the French president hoped we should make the year 2004 that of 'cordial confidence', opening a new era in relations between Britain and France.

So the Entente Cordiale is more than a simple page in the history books. It has become a way of living together in a complex and sometimes difficult relationship, but one always rich in new possibilities. It remains the best witness of the fact that our two countries and peoples need to listen to each other. For it is by remaining ourselves, while yet hearing each other, that we French and British can carry our full weight in the future of Europe and, beyond that, in the affairs of the world.

Dominique de Villepin,
Ministre des Affaires Étrangères

Introduction

'That sweet enemy, France.' The phrase, from Sir Philip Sidney's *Astrophil and Stella*, dates from 1591, but after four centuries its hint of a love–hate relationship still touches a nerve. Like magnets, the French and the British feel mutual attraction: yet, the poles reversed, they grope for each other in vain, baffled by what forces them apart. As another poet, the Canadian Earle Birney, put it:

> We French, we English, never lost our civil war,
> endure it still, a bloodless civil bore;
> no wounded lying about, no Whitman wanted.
> It's only by our lack of ghosts we're haunted.

For a hundred years, the Entente Cordiale has sought to lay any lingering ghosts – with qualified success. This book surveys that century of Franco-British history and asks how the Entente fares today.

In doing so, it examines controversies and crises. At times these have involved real clashes of interest. Some disputes are indeed a zero-sum game. But not always. Increasingly, France and Britain resemble each other. Both were once world-class powers with extensive empires. Their political ideals have much in common and they share a broadly European culture. Each is endowed with a fine and sophisticated language. In the twenty-first century, both are uncomfortably dwarfed because neither is now a superpower. Each faces similar problems of immigration and globalisation. Both make common cause in the European Union, but each is concerned for its ancient nationhood.

Does such likeness make for like-mindedness or liking? It can, but frequently does not. Britain and France have been said to resemble *deux chiens de faïence*, china dogs staring at each other from either side of the fireplace, in identical but diametrically opposite poses, each the mirror image of the other. And the images are blurred – by language, mental habits, history, propaganda and folk memory.

Language raises not only linguistic problems (approximately solved by translation), but also semantic or hermeneutic complications. Most obviously, English, more than French, has Germanic as well as Romance roots. This makes ordinary French expressions seem 'abstract' or 'pompous' to unaccustomed British ears, while to French listeners some English expressions can sound curt or even 'brutal'.

Add the French habit of analysing problems as if from an administrative overview, putting principles first. This often clashes with the British habit of beginning with practical details and then (often reluctantly) seeing what pattern they make. The contrast, both linguistic and semantic, can be seen in two sentences: 'There is an increase in cross-border population transfers' versus 'More people migrate.'

History too – even recent history – has marked both Britain and France in similar but contrasting ways. So have propaganda and folk memory. No wonder their conditioned reflexes do not always tally. In the early days of the Entente Cordiale, for instance, memories of 1870 were still fresh in France, and Germany seemed a potential enemy. Britain, on the contrary, remembered France as a former rival.

A major concern of this book, then, is not simply to recount the past, but to learn from it – to look in particular for the hidden agendas and semi-conscious assumptions that have often underlain overt disagreements between Britain and France. Lack of mutual knowledge, unawareness of deep unspoken differences, and inadequate communication – all have caused quarrels that could have been avoided. They no longer provoke war, but they have scarred the Entente as they still sometimes sour the European Union. There was some degree of mutual misunderstanding, indeed, from the very beginning in April 1904.

I
A Century Ago

How the Entente Cordiale Began

Given that France and Britain have long been divided by a great deal of common history, it is not surprising that Franco-British relations are as much about the past as about the future. So it was with the Entente Cordiale, signed in the opening years of the twentieth century. That agreement between France and Britain was certainly not an alliance, nor even a treaty, both of which would have been forward-looking. Instead it was a hotch-potch of a convention and two declarations signed in London on 8 April 1904 whereby Britain and France settled a number of outstanding colonial differences over far-flung parts of their respective empires in Newfoundland, West and Central Africa, Egypt, Morocco, Madagascar and the New Hebrides islands. Rather than drawing the two empires together, it physically pushed them apart by establishing respective spheres of influence in Siam and West Africa. The agreements did not even contain a statement of general policy on friendlier relations. Only with hindsight was it clear that this was the starting point of an ever closer union between erstwhile rivals that would lead to alliance at the outbreak of World War I. That remarkable metamorphosis from enmity to amity took place in the space of only 15 years from 1898. During that period France and Britain shifted from being on the brink of war with each other to becoming wartime allies. How did this come about?

The 1904 Entente Cordiale was not the first of its kind between Britain and France (nor, for that matter, with others, as the term 'entente cordiale' was also used to describe the Anglo-American relationship in 1900). No more than its 1840s predecessor did the Entente end the traditional spirit of jealous rivalry that characterised Franco-British relations. Throughout the world French and British sailors, explorers, traders, even priests, met and competed, which was not surprising for the two greatest empires on the planet. The rivalry was punctuated by agreements such as that for the establishment of a condominium in the New Hebrides in 1887, the Constantinople Convention of 1888 neutralising the Suez Canal, and the 1890 Convention delimiting French and British spheres of influence in the Niger valley. But these agreements brought only local and temporary appeasement. Long-standing rivalries ran deep. In 1900 one embittered French colonialist noted: 'France gets colonies so that England may take them over.' On the other hand Britain's perception of the French derived from a curious combination of superiority and mystification, as the diplomatist Sir Robert Vansittart recalled: 'Victorian England was vaguely convinced that nineteenth-century France had too good a time; that Frenchmen laughed too much and cooked too well . . . More serious still, Victorian England suspected that the French put more into, and got more out of, sex than the English. Victorian England had not the vaguest idea of how this was done, but was sure that the advantage was not fair, and quite sure that it was not nice!'

Rivalry came to a head in 1898 at the interface of French and British imperial interests in Africa. France's dream was of a great French African Empire stretching south from Algeria in the north to the Congo in the south and from Senegal in the west to the Nile and beyond in the east. But realisation of that dream brought France into conflict with Britain's vision of its own African Empire. These competing visions created a nightmare for France in what became known as the Fashoda incident. In November 1898 a 150-strong French expeditionary force commanded by the plucky Captain Marchand attempted to penetrate into the Sudan and the Upper Nile Valley. Marchand's four-year-long trek from west to east suffered, if nothing else, from poor timing. At the small fort of Fashoda, Marchand came up against General Kitchener's army, fresh from its victory over the Mahdi. The British government demanded Marchand's withdrawal. A stand-off ensued. France contemplated war, but calculated that it was in no position to engage in a distant war with the greatest naval power in the world. The French government finally backed down.

War was averted, but Fashoda was a severe blow to French prestige. The incident, scarcely remembered in British historical consciousness, loomed large in that of France. A vociferous Anglophobia swept France, albeit mainly in Parisian circles, with the French manifesting their hostility to Britain by openly sympathising with the Boers during the Anglo-Boer War of 1899–1902. French volunteers left to fight alongside the Boers, while elegant ladies sported felt hats *à la Boer* and the élite

French military academy at Saint Cyr dubbed its 1900 cohort of graduates the 'Transvaal year'. French President Félix Faure told a Russian diplomat that Britain, not Germany, was France's true enemy. The anti-British propaganda of this time was so virulent that the Vichy governments of 1940 reprinted it with little modification (which partly explains why 'Fashoda' endures to this day). For their part the British élite took solace in the fact that from 1898 France was racked by the Dreyfus scandal.

When relationships have reached their nadir a fresh perspective often develops. Such an initiative came from France's foreign minister, the diminutive Théophile Delcassé, whose tenure of office opened with the humiliating necessity of the surrender of Fashoda. In the course of his six years at the helm of French diplomacy he was to carry out a bold reorientation of French policy. Increasingly suspicious of growing German power, he wanted the French to forget Fashoda and come to terms with Britain. Although Britain and France were arch-rivals abroad, in Europe, politically and commercially, there was no real reason why they should not be friends. But motive needed to be matched by opportunity.

Delcassé was helped in his quest because he understood that for all their differences, Britain and France had a common fear – growing German might. For France the prospect of simultaneous tension with Germany and Britain was to have one enemy too many. Germany's 1900 Navy Law confirmed Berlin's intention to build a fleet capable of challenging Britain's naval supremacy while posing an additional threat to French colonies. For Britain, long-standing isolation was becoming more dangerous than splendid.

Delcassé could also take heart from the fact that, for all the heat generated by Fashoda, Anglo-French relations had a more solid substratum of shared ideals and culture that allowed for bouts of mutual admiration. Many in the Parisian élite were sympathetic to Britain culturally, from the fictional English gentleman Phileas Fogg in Jules Verne's *Around the World in Eighty Days* to the more long-standing admiration for the works of Shakespeare or British political institutions. Large sections of the British élite were steeped in the traditions of French language, culture and literature. At a more mundane level financial interests in the City of London were sympathetic to better relations with France, while French colonialists (of whom Delcassé was one) felt that the French Empire could benefit from an arrangement with Britain on respective imperial interests. Barely three months after Fashoda, in February 1899, the colonial lobby group, the Comité de l'Afrique Française, which had been instrumental in securing Delcassé's nomination to the Quai d'Orsay, set about convincing their man of the need for a colonial agreement with London based on a barter of English influence in Egypt for French influence in Morocco. A sign that Franco-British differences were not insuperable came only four months after the Fashoda incident, when the two governments signed an agreement in London 'in a spirit of mutual good *entente*' specifying respective possessions and spheres of influence in the Nile Valley and West Africa. Even at the height of the Boer War by no means everyone shared the hysteria of the nationalist Paris press and its delectation at Britain's humbling 'at the hands of well-armed farmers in tall hats', even if few begrudged it its cathartic effect.

A measure of how superficial the Fashoda uproar had been in France was that barely five years later King Edward VII was invited to make a state visit to France. An officially inspired media had, in the intervening years, softened up public opinion, or at least that small element of largely Parisian opinion that took more than a desultory interest in foreign affairs. President Loubet's return visit to London two months later sealed the social side of the Entente, despite the minor diplomatic embarrassment of the representative of the Republic declining to don knee breeches for his audience with the king. The business deal was all that remained to be done.

Delcassé, and many of his colonialist supporters, longed for more widespread recognition of the preponderance of French interests in Morocco to complete France's North African Empire. Delcassé had already struck a deal with Italy on this in 1902; the opportunity to reach one with Britain was now at hand. Much of the groundwork for the settlement with Britain had been prepared by the French ambassador in London since 1898, Paul Cambon. On 8 April 1904 a comprehensive agreement was signed between the two countries. Other than the settlement of a number of long-standing imperial questions in various parts of the globe, in return for formal recognition of its position in Egypt, Great Britain gave France a free hand in Morocco. Although the words were not mentioned in any of the three documents, the agreement came to be known as the 'Entente Cordiale'.

The Conventions were welcomed on both sides of the Channel, despite murmurs about France surrendering to Britain in Egypt. Of greater importance was how either side interpreted the agreements. Delcassé wrote to a senior French foreign office official that the agreement 'should lead us, and I desire that it shall lead us, to a political alliance with England . . . If we could lean both on Russia and on England, how strong we should be in relation to Germany.' In Britain expectations were a good deal more muted. Though happy to have reduced imperial tensions with a rival, Britain was still not prepared to countenance the commitment of an alliance. Differing perceptions and expectations of the agreement partly explain French frustration and disappointment over the next decade in not being able to seal an alliance with Britain. It was a clear example of the cultural dissonance between French and British ways of negotiating. In 1904 the French were happy believing that they had secured the principle of closer relations with a potential ally; the British were pleased to have achieved the mere practicality of reduced tension with a former rival.

Although colonial rivalry between London and Paris did not cease altogether from this date, it was no longer the source of friction it had once been. But the great powers were already in the closing stages of the frenzied period of imperial expansion; the Entente Cordiale marked a more settled and stable approach to empire. Most of all it signalled the great powers' switch in focus from the imperial to the European scene. The rise of the German threat, described in Chapter II, disposed both governments to settle outstanding questions in order to have their hands free in Europe. Most important of all, the Entente Cordiale and the new-found Franco-British friendship signalled a new alignment of the great powers. It would soon be clear, not least to Germany, that Great Britain had definitely cast its weight on the European side of the balance of the Franco-Russian alliance. Europe was shaping up into two distinct – soon to be heavily armed – camps: on the one hand the Triple Alliance of Germany, Austria and (nominally) Italy; on the other the Triple Entente of France, Russia and Britain.

There now followed a second stage in the development of the Entente Cordiale, which was little known at the time – its progressive militarisation. In a desire to test the solidity of the Entente and simultaneously to pressure Paris into making concessions to Berlin over Morocco, Germany's aggressive behaviour at Tangiers in 1905 and at Agadir in 1911 encouraged Britain to take France's side against Germany. More importantly still, it institutionalised the Entente Cordiale by first initiating Franco-British defence cooperation and then deepening it.

The so-called First and Second Moroccan crises of 1905 and 1911 underlined the potency of the German threat and increased Britain's commitment to France. Although Britain had resolutely resisted a political alliance, from 1905 London agreed to secret military staff conversations with France – so secret that until 1912 most of the British Cabinet were unaware of their existence and would probably never have approved of them anyway.

Although the talks were in no way to bind the two governments, Paris saw in them firm and concerted British military support for France that was a step closer to an alliance. The secret General Staff talks were under way from December 1905 and were intended to map out possible joint action in a conflict in which both countries might become involved. Intended only as a temporary measure to provide for a possible conflict during the 1906 Algeciras conference, which had been called to settle the First Moroccan crisis between France and Germany, they became a key feature of the Entente – in effect its defence arm. Although the conversations lapsed from 1906 to 1910, they flourished when Brigadier-General Henry Wilson became director of military operations in August 1910 and fostered closer relations with the new French High Command in 1911. But what the French really wanted from such military talks was more the political symbolism of commitment than its military worth. Thus Britain's intervention in the first stages of the war was valued more in psychological than in material terms. When in 1909 Henry Wilson had asked General Foch: 'What would you say was the smallest British military force that would be of any practical assistance to you in the event of a contest such as we have been considering?' Foch replied immediately, 'One single private soldier and we would take good care that he was killed.' At times it seemed almost as if the French were less committed to the talks than the British. As late as August 1911 Wilson was obliged to admit to the Committee of Imperial Defence that he had no precise details of French war plans. But this was largely because the French were unclear themselves about what their war plans should be.

Prompted by the Agadir crisis with Germany, the new chief of the French General Staff, General Joffre, gave a greater place to Britain's assistance than his predecessors. His new plan contained detailed provisions for the concentration of the British Expeditionary Force of 150,000 men in northeastern France. Having secured the principle of the Entente in 1904, the French were now binding Britain in with detail. It was all very well for the British foreign secretary, the insular Sir Edward Grey – who had never set foot on the continent and spoke no French – to repeat ceaselessly to French Ambassador Paul Cambon (who spoke no English) that the secret talks in no way bound either country to come to the other's assistance in the event of war; that is not how the French read things. The British were saying one thing and apparently doing another. On the other hand, in choosing to ignore Grey's statements French diplomats and political leaders were deluding themselves as to the reality of Britain's commitment to France. Not for the first time the consequence of seeings things as France wished to see them produced frustration, disappointment and bouts of exasperation with Britain. The British Ambassador in Paris, Sir Francis Bertie, explained this to Sir Edward Grey as early as 1906:

One must take the French as they are and not as one would wish them to be. They have an instinctive dread of Germany and an hereditary distrust of England, and with these characteristics they are easily led to believe that they may be deserted by England and fallen upon by Germany.

Because the British did not believe that they were in any way betrothed to the French they saw no dishonour in the practicality of attempting to reduce tension with Germany following the Agadir settlement. The French, on the other hand, saw Britain's discussions with Germany to reduce naval rivalry in early 1912 as a dalliance that threatened their relationship. With the instinct of the scorned lover, France sought to draw its official partner back to its side by further engagements. Pandering to Britain's desire to reduce her naval commitments, Paul Cambon seduced Sir Edward Grey into a diplomatic agreement that further increased the militarisation of the Entente. In November 1912 Grey and Cambon exchanged letters to establish a Franco-British naval agreement whereby the French concentrated their main naval forces in the Mediterranean while Great Britain transferred part of its Mediterranean squadron to the North Sea to protect the French coastline. Although the British continued to insist that this in no way bound Britain to side with France in a conflict, and that it agreed only to consult in the event of a potential conflict, it certainly gave France a strong moral claim to British support should war break out.

The Grey–Cambon letters were a clear example of differing cultural values and attitudes that, not for the last time, would lead to misunderstandings between the two countries. Britain had insisted pragmatically that such an understanding could be merely verbal, as it did not commit either country to assist the other in the event of a conflict. The French accepted that, but insisted that it should be in writing. The rational French believed that what was written was more positive because it had the sanctity of text; as so often in French thinking, form was greater than substance. The British prime minister referred to the formula as 'a platitude', but there was no doubt that the French believed that they had secured a greater British commitment. The ultimate question as to what Britain's attitude would be in the event of war was, as Sir Edward Grey had repeatedly insisted to the French ambassador, dependent upon public opinion and Parliament. In the British Cabinet's view, this was still the case when on 1 August 1914, barely two days before France was at war with Germany, Paul Cambon insisted that Britain had a moral obligation to defend France's northern coastline because France had transferred its fleet to the Mediterranean. Not even Cambon's recourse to emotional blackmail paid off when he asked 'whether the word "honour" should be struck out of the English vocabulary'. But it does seem that the French had constrained Britain's freedom of action. As the First Lord of the Admiralty, Winston Churchill, had warned Prime Minister Herbert Asquith at the time of the exchange of the Grey–Cambon letters: 'Everyone must feel who knows the facts that we have all the obligations of an alliance without its advantages, and above all without its precise defini-tions.' In the end it was not the Entente with France that decided Britain's entry into war on 3 August 1914, but an almost forgotten treaty to uphold Belgian neutrality dating from 1839. Paul Cambon might well describe 2 August as 'the day through which I passed the darkest moments of my life'. Only the day before, he had spluttered to Sir Arthur Nicolson: 'They are going to ditch us. They are going to ditch us.' With the advent of war France finally got the official alliance it had so long craved in the Pact of London of 5 September 1914. It seemed that only in the desperation of war could the two states fully commit themselves to each other, as World War II would again demonstrate.

Since its inception the Entente Cordiale had been a fertile ground for misunderstandings and misperceptions between London and Paris. Each interpreted it from its own cultural vantage point and interests. Britain wanted all the benefits of an alliance without the obligations and failed to understand how France had drawn it into a moral commitment. Cambon and his political masters were so wedded to the idea of an alliance with Britain that they often mistook their desires for realities and ignored Britain's interests and *modus operandi*. Rose-tinted memories of the two countries fighting side by side in the ensuing war would, in the short term, expunge the memory of how at cross-purposes the two had been in the lifetime of the Entente. What is remarkable is that after the war neither side seemed to learn from the cultural experience of the Entente. France was all the more convinced that Britain needed to be tied down by a formal alliance, while Britain drew the opposite conclusion. As always, Franco-British relations seemed to be looking back to the future.

John Keiger

The Weight of History

Rudyard Kipling, in his stirring poem *France* (1913), made an eloquent attempt to turn history to advantage by portraying the centuries of conflict between Britain and France as a source of unique,
quasi-sexual, intimacy:

> Where did you refrain from us or we refrain from you?
> Ask the wave that has not watched war between us two!
> Others held us for a while, but with weaker charms,
> These we quitted at the call for each other's arms.

Although there was passion in plenty, 'cordial understanding' was
not so easy to conjure up from a turbulent past that provided both
countries with many of their great dates, places of memory, heroes
and sometimes villains: Hastings and Agincourt, Hereward the Wake
and Joan of Arc, Louis XIV and Marlborough, Blenheim and
Fontenoy, Wolfe and Montcalm, Napoleon and Wellington, even
Descartes and Newton. History has weighed heavily indeed: touchi-
ness, misunderstanding and suspicion were not effaced, and were
even aggravated, by alliance in two world wars and the subsequent
peace.

Yet long before Kipling there was no shortage of voices urging
cordial understanding, and giving powerful reasons. For most of the
nineteenth century, the two countries were the champions of European liberalism, parliamentary government and individual freedom.
Would not cooperation between the two advance the cause of
progress? King Louis-Philippe in his speech from the throne in 1843
used the phrase 'entente cordiale', first coined by the pacifist foreign
secretary Lord Aberdeen. Yet this entente failed. Fears remained in
Britain, voiced most vigorously by the ebulliently patriotic Lord
Palmerston, that France was not to be trusted, while Louis-
Philippe's attempts to be friendly made him despised by nationalists
at home. Napoleon III, despite the victorious alliance against Russia
in the Crimean War, aroused acute suspicions across the Channel.
The poet Tennyson wrote, 'we have got such a faithful ally, that only
the Devil can tell what he means', and Britain built ironclads, raised
a home defence force and fortified its south coast. France's defeat by
Germany in 1870–71 was something of a relief.

The French and British grew increasingly apart in their domestic politics after the 1848 Revolution. The former were periodically violent, and in the long run increasingly democratic and secular; the latter took pride in peaceful reform, piety and respect for tradition. France, in British eyes, seemed to be in a state of decadence and decline: a British publisher was jailed for publishing Emile Zola's 'obscene' novels, and British Protestant missionaries went to try to convert the French to Christianity. Although Francophilia was far from extinct, it focused on selected aspects of French culture – art, fashion, food, the countryside. Britain, in French eyes, was philistine, puritanical and dull. Even defeated revolutionary activists who took refuge in Britain criticised the manners, weather and cooking, and were repelled by what they saw as extremes of wealth and poverty, aristocratic privilege, and an eccentric constitution. Anglophilia was strongest among conservatives who were out of sympathy with their own country's development. It became common to define each nation in terms of its difference from the other. The leading philosopher and historian Hippolyte Taine, for example, concluded that 'the Englishman is stronger and the Frenchman is happier'. In short, there was little true meeting of minds or hearts in the second half of the nineteenth century.

This coolness would have been less important had it not been for intense imperial rivalry. This was inflamed by the British takeover of Egypt in 1882, which gave them effective control of the pride and joy of French engineering, the Suez Canal. By the turn of the century relations were frigid, and diplomats even worried about war. French enthusiasm for the struggle of the Boer republics (shared by both left and right) was matched by British sympathy for the persecuted Captain Dreyfus. On each side of the Channel, these episodes were taken to exemplify the worst aspect of the other: British greed and hypocrisy; French extremism and contempt for human rights. The brief and rather absurd military confrontation at Fashoda in the Sudan in 1898 (described above by John Keiger) provided a salutary shock: both sides drew back from open conflict. But at least one schoolboy remembered this French humiliation: Charles de Gaulle.

Yet with remarkable speed *entente* came, for reasons explained in the following pages. It owed less to a sudden blossoming of affection than to a pressing need to patch up colonial disputes and guard against the new dangers analysed in Chapter 2 by Christopher

Andrew and Paul Vallet. The cordiality of the entente was often more an aspiration than an achievement: episodic bursts of friendliness were balanced, if not outweighed, by chronic mistrust. It is true that British and French statesmen, soldiers and ordinary citizens often found – perhaps to their surprise – that they had more in common than they had supposed. Yet it remains a striking fact that a century of almost unbroken alliance, marked by shared dangers and common sacrifices, has not created a solid foundation of trust, affection or instinctive common purpose. The two societies are perhaps closer than they have ever been in their values, ways of life, levels of wealth and extent of influence in the world. The Iraqi crisis of 2003 showed the remarkable spectacle of a vocal element of the British public looking to Paris for a political lead – doubtless for the first time since 1792. But this only demonstrates the distance separating the two governments. There is less than ever a 'special relationship' or 'axis' across the Channel comparable with those that span the Atlantic and the Rhine. For this, the weight of history, ancient and modern, is largely responsible. Perhaps another hundred years will be enough to see the burden finally thrown off.

Robert Tombs

Vive notre bon Édouard!

Edward VII wanted Anglo-French cooperation. On his own initiative, not that of his ministers, he decided to make a state visit to Paris in May 1903. Winning over public opinion was essential. This was a risky venture at a time of violent Anglophobia, especially among nationalists, in France. The king had been the object of grossly insulting caricatures and vehement attacks in the press. If he were jeered and insulted in the streets of Paris, the whole project might come to a full stop. Some have credited Edward VII with the magical gift of turning public opinion from cool – even hostile – to warm and enthusiastic, but the reality was a little more complex: political calculation, commerce and the desire for a good time also played their part.

Nationalist groups were the main danger. Some asked 'bons Français' to wear badges of the Republic of Transvaal or to hang Boer flags from their windows. However, Paul Déroulède, the principal leader of the nationalists, had always put European politics before colonial issues, and he had decided that a rapprochement with Britain would strengthen France against Germany. His Ligue des Patriotes ordered its followers not to demonstrate, to remain calm and dignified and shout only 'Vive l'Armée' and 'Vive la France'. Although occasionally 'Vive les Boers' and 'Vive Fashoda' were heard, most nationalists followed orders, if often reluctantly, and there was no disruption.

At the other end of the political spectrum, the socialists too might have caused trouble, especially as the king was arriving on May Day, which then had a far more subversive connotation. He joked: 'It will interest him to see a revolution.' But the socialists did not demonstrate *en masse* either. Although some revolutionaries deplored the 'sheer stupidity of the masses neglecting their interests, preferring to watch a king go by', most socialist leaders welcomed the visit as a token of international peace and a proof that republican France was not 'ruined and humiliated in the eyes of other powers', as asserted by nationalist propaganda.

All official ceremonies – at the Élysée, the Quai d'Orsay, the embassy, the opera and the Vincennes parade ground – exceeded expectations. An effort was made towards culinary entente at the various receptions, with not only champagne, *homards à la parisienne*, *salade gauloise* or *sorbet à la Pompadour* being served, but also *crème Windsor*, *pudding à la Windsor*, oxtail soup, *oeufs à la Richmond* and *selle de mouton à l'anglaise*; the Quai d'Orsay achieved true bilateral communion by serving at lunch *jambon d'York truffé champenoise*. The king charmed and flattered his audiences in perfect French and without notes, repeatedly emphasising the importance of Anglo-French relations. He also managed to indulge in at least some of his favourite Parisian amusements: going to the races at Longchamps (John Bull aptly won) and attending the theatre, where he recognised an actress he had applauded in London, complimenting her on 'all the grace and *esprit* of France'. These words were repeated across Paris and reported in the press, contributing to his image as a true lover of France and as 'le roi parisien'.

The people of Paris turned out *en masse*, in a lavishly decorated and illuminated capital. The warmth of the welcome was boosted by large numbers of enthusiastic British tourists, and famous British stores were patriotically decorated. After the king arrived at the Bois de Boulogne station, a colourful procession of carriages crossed the Bois, the Champs-Élysées, the Place de la Concorde and the Faubourg Saint-Honoré, in a dignified atmosphere with few hostile cries. On the night of the Gala the Grands Boulevards and the Opéra district were flooded with onlookers, eager to see the king and the elegant *Tout Paris*. In the poorer districts, from Vincennes to the Hôtel de Ville, he was more cheered than in the elegant districts. The Place de l'Hôtel de Ville was invested by crowds, including 'socialistes, va-nu-pieds et pauvres diables'; ladders and folding chairs were for hire at strategic spots. The authorities had given permission for dancing in the streets and there were orchestras in public squares. Paris danced, especially workers on Sunday evening. The 'cakewalk' was a great success. The reception by the Paris Municipal Council, symbolically entitled in a newspaper 'Une cordiale entrevue', was revealing of the warm welcome for the king from unexpected quarters. A journalist recalled: 'The members of the Municipal Council were to a large extent ultra-radical, but any condescension on the king's part would, I felt, win them over. It did.'

Commercial exploitation contributed to the festive atmosphere, with street vendors supplying everything from 'cerise du roi' to Japanese handkerchiefs printed with the programme of the visit, walking sticks with handles carved with the king's head, and countless trinkets and postcards. New fashions were launched, for example a coat called 'Le King Edward', and there was an advertising campaign for English goods and restaurants connected with the celebrations. Café owners were keen to encourage the jollifications.

If royal charm was not – as myth has it – the only explanation for the success of the visit, it was certainly part of the story. Most French and English newspapers reported positively on the visit of 'the most Parisian of kings' – a reputation that Edward's frequent, and sometimes rather risqué, visits to Paris had won him. Some noted that royal prestige had dazzled the most austere Republicans. Thus the path towards public acceptance necessary to the 1904 Entente Cordiale was begun. The role of Edward VII was to be remembered in France. For example, in Marcel l'Herbier's 1939 film *Entente Cordiale*, Foreign Secretary Delcassé pays tribute to the king, 'le plus grand des diplomates'.

Isabelle Bussy

The White City, 1908

The Franco-British Exhibition of Science, Arts and Industries, held on a 140-acre site at Shepherd's Bush in west London, came to be known as the 'White City', owing to the brilliant 'fibrous plaster' applied to the pavilions and halls. The exhibition was considered the largest and most splendid event of its type ever mounted in London, with *The Times* going so far as to call it the 'most remarkable exhibition ever held in the British Empire'. It certainly proved a worthy successor to the 1900 Paris *Exposition universelle*. What was different in 1908 was that since 1904 France and Britain had been enjoying their Entente Cordiale: the exhibition was conceived to celebrate and promote the mutual understanding that appeared to have replaced the animosity between the two countries that had prevailed for so long.

The idea grew from proposals made in 1905 by the French Chamber of Commerce in London; after this, the project was taken up and endorsed by diplomats working for the governments on both sides of the Channel. King Edward VII himself, who had already done so much to promote better Franco-British relations, also gave his full backing to the primary aims of the exhibition, which, in the words of the official prospectus, were to increase 'the commercial intercourse between the two countries' and to strengthen 'their friendly relations'.

Work began on preparing the site in 1906. According to Imre Kiralfy, the commissioner of the exhibition and veteran organiser of such fairs, 'a bit of farm land lying half-forgotten at the very doorstep of London' had to be transformed by draining the whole area and 'improvising a complete modern city'. The exhibits were housed in 20 palaces and eight halls, devoted to Education, Science, the Fine Arts, the Liberal Arts, Engineering and Shipping, Transportation, Textiles, Social Economy, Women's Work, Sports, and French and British Colonies.

The 'Franco', as it was popularly known, was also conceived as a 'City of Pleasure', with its extensive gardens, restaurants, waterways, cascades and rides, including the extraordinary 'Flip-Flap' (so popular that it had a music-hall song written about it), the 'Canadian Toboggan' and the 'Scenic Railway'. Interestingly, some of the colonial and related exhibits tended to be treated as curiosities, or side-shows, such as the representations of a Ceylon 'village' (complete with snake-charmers), a French Senegalese village and an Irish village, 'Ballymaclinton'. A further attraction was the staging of the Olympic Games, for which a stadium was built capable of accommodating 150,000 people: this became the 'White City Stadium'. To service all this, the surrounding railway and underground network was extended, and it was estimated that 75,000 visitors could be conveyed to the site every hour.

The exhibition was opened on 14 May 1908 by the Prince and Princess of Wales, accompanied by diplomats and members of the organising committees from both sides of the Channel. The opening was spoiled by steady rain, and yet, although parts of the site remained unfinished, the exhibition was judged by all accounts to be worthy of high praise. One initial, minor, cause for concern – as reflected by letters printed in *The Times* – was whether the exhibition should break with English custom and open on Sundays, since to do so would suit French visitors to the site. There is some evidence too that in choosing exhibits French sensibilities were respected: in the review of the Fine Arts display, it was noted that paintings of military subjects had avoided topics that might – uncomfortably – have referred to British victories over their neighbours.

The political and international importance of the exhibition was underlined by the state visit of President Armand Fallières, who came to London amid great pomp and ceremony during the week 25–29 May 1908. As the president's ship – the cruiser *Léon Gambetta* – steamed into British waters, the Royal Navy's spectacular welcome seemed to emphasise the sheer scale of the hopes being placed in Franco-British *rapprochement*. As well as undertaking a lengthy tour of the exhibition in the company of the king, Fallières also attended a lunch at the Guildhall, visited the Royal Opera House, toured Windsor Castle and reciprocated by inviting Edward VII to an official dinner at the French Embassy. *The Times* – reporting in sometimes anecdotal detail how Londoners viewed their French guests – noted that the initials 'RF' emblazoned on tricolour placards adorning the route of the visit, were being interpreted not as 'République française', but as 'Real Friends'. For commentators at the time, the genuine enthusiasm extended to the French visitors was reflected in the warmth of the toasts made at the Buckingham Palace banquet. In proposing the health of the French president, the king stated: 'With all my heart I hope that this *entente* will also be a permanent *entente*, because it is necessary for the welfare and prosperity of our two nations and for the maintenance of the peace which makes for the happiness of the whole world.' In his reply, Fallières echoed these sentiments and stressed that Franco-British cooperation such as that displayed at the exhibition could only advance the cause of human civilisation.

The Franco-British Exhibition was conceived in an atmosphere of optimism and hope for international peace, although it was recognised at the time that both nations faced enduring political problems. The Boer War had discredited imperialism, and Edwardian Britain was dominated by issues such as the Irish question, reform of the House of Lords, social inequality and women's emancipation. In France, during July and August 1908, the Clemenceau government had to contend with widespread social unrest and strikes, which were violently put down. And both countries were constantly preoccupied by their triangular relationship with Germany; in diplomatic quarters, much attention was focused upon German reactions to the exhibition in particular and to the development of the Entente in general. Indeed, using the benefit of hindsight, one may say that the outbreak of the Great War in August 1914 – which put a sudden and murderous end to the hopes for international peace that had nurtured the Franco-British Exhibition – undoubtedly goes a long way towards explaining why it is that this huge and successful exhibition was so rapidly forgotten.

Martyn Cornick

II

Danger from the East

Contrasting views of what the Entente meant persisted – France believing, or hoping, that Britain was more deeply committed, and Britain concerned above all about sea power.

The German Threat

There is no single interpretation of the Entente Cordiale. At different times and to different people it has meant quite different things. President René Coty claimed on its fiftieth anniversary that 'the convention of 8 April 1904 embodied the agreement of our two peoples on the necessity of safeguarding the spiritual values of which we were the common trustees'. It was to something like this interpretation of the Entente that Winston Churchill appealed in 1940 when he made his famous offer to France of an Anglo–French Union. There were few statesmen on either side of the Channel in 1904 who shared so romantic a view. The convention of 8 April 1904 amounted, on paper, simply to a settlement of colonial disputes. 'In a word,' said the French ambassador in London, Paul Cambon, at the beginning of the negotiations, 'we give you Egypt in exchange for Morocco.'

Little attention was paid by most of the British Cabinet to Germany's likely reaction to the agreement. Even for those ministers, such as Balfour, who hoped that it might lead to a similar settlement with France's ally, Russia, there was no feeling that the Entente might be the beginning of a major diplomatic realignment. Balfour, according to a senior official in the Foreign Office, had no idea 'what may be expected from the Anglo–French understanding and would be ready to make an agreement with Germany tomorrow'.

Foreign Minister Théophile Delcassé, by contrast, regarded the agreement with Britain as the first step towards the Triple Entente that he had advocated twenty years earlier as the best guarantee of French security in Europe. 'His great desire', wrote the new British ambassador in Paris, Sir Francis Bertie, early in 1905, 'is, he says, to bring about a rapprochement between England and Russia, for if those two Powers and France acted together, peace would have a long reign.' That the transformation of the Entente desired by Delcassé did take place, however, was due far less to his own efforts than to the inept diplomacy of German Chancellor Bernhard von Bülow and his *éminence grise* at the Foreign Ministry, Friedrich von Holstein, the two architects of German foreign policy during the first Moroccan crisis in 1905. Time and time again in the years since unification German statesmen had shown that they could feel secure only in a world in which the other powers were prevented by their mutual hostility from combining against Germany. The sight in 1904 of England and France settling differences that the German Foreign Ministry had assumed to be permanent was more than either Bülow or Holstein could stand.

Germany had a good case for arguing that the Anglo-French agreement took no account of its own rights and interests in Morocco. But the protection of German interests in Morocco was only a secondary motive in the decision by Bülow and Holstein to provoke the first Moroccan crisis. Their main aim was the destruction of the Entente Cordiale: to prove to France that an agreement with Britain concluded without German consent was worthless. If France could be persuaded to submit the Moroccan question to an international conference, then Germany's aims would have been achieved. For, said Bülow, 'It is out of the question that the conference should result in handing Morocco over to France.' The Anglo-French agreement would thus have been shown to be worthless, and the possibility that the Entente Cordiale might one day become a coalition directed against Germany would have been destroyed.

The methods used by Germany ended by achieving precisely the transformation of the Entente that Bülow and Holstein were anxious to prevent. In March 1905 Germany began a war of nerves against France that culminated at the end of May and beginning of June in the threat of armed attack. This aroused an even more hostile reaction in Britain than it did in France. Even the cool-headed foreign secretary, Lord Lansdowne, warned the German ambassador that public pressure might force the British government to assist France against German attack. Although Lansdowne was unwilling to commit Britain in advance of war to more than diplomatic support for France, the French mistakenly believed in May 1905 that he had offered a binding commitment of British military assistance that would turn the Entente into an alliance. Cambon, it has been suggested, simply misunderstood the significance of a proposal by Lansdowne that the two countries begin 'full and confidential discussion ... in anticipation of any complications to be apprehended during the somewhat anxious period through which we are at present passing'. This explanation is, in itself, inadequate. The famous misunderstanding was possible only because a series of private assurances from British statesmen and service chiefs had already convinced the Quai d'Orsay that it could count on British support in a war with Germany. 'I know well what his reply will be,' said Cambon when told to raise with Lansdowne the question of British support against Germany. Certain of the answer he would receive, he did not doubt the significance of Lansdowne's proposal for 'full and confidential discussion'. It amounted, Cambon reported, to a proposal for the negotiation of 'a general agreement which would in reality constitute an alliance'.

When the French Cabinet discussed the question of British support against Germany on 6 June 1905 not a single minister expressed the slightest doubt about Britain's willingness to take part in a war with Germany. Indeed, some suspected that the British government might actually be anxious for the crisis to end in war. The belief that Britain had offered France a binding commitment of armed assistance against Germany continued to colour the French interpretation of the Entente Cordiale until World War I. Even in 1914 both the Quai d'Orsay and the French government believed that a formal commitment had been freely offered in May 1905, and that only the fall of the Conservative government at the end of the year had made it impossible to obtain that commitment thereafter.

Although the German war of nerves during the first Moroccan crisis ultimately defeated its own purpose, in the short term it was almost successful. With the solitary exception of Delcassé, who resigned, the French Cabinet agreed in June 1905 that, even with English support, it dared not run the risk of war with Germany. It decided instead to seek a compromise settlement. Maurice Rouvier, the French prime minister, offered Germany compensation in the Congo for French supremacy in Morocco, as well as cooperation in a variety of fields. Had Germany accepted these terms, the Entente Cordiale would have been destroyed and France might well have been drawn into a policy of continuing cooperation with Germany. The German government, however, found itself trapped by its own previous propaganda. Having publicly demanded an international conference and posed as the defender of Moroccan independence, it felt unable to back down and reach a bilateral agreement with France. By its own inflexibility Germany alienated those Frenchmen most anxious for agreement with it. Even Rouvier gradually recovered his nerve. In November he told one of his advisers: 'If Berlin thinks it can intimidate me it has made a great mistake. Henceforth, I shall make no further concessions, come what may.' A month later, he authorised the beginning of

Anglo–French staff talks to discuss cooperation in a war with Germany, as described in the previous chapter.

Under German pressure the colonial understanding of 1904 had come to imply a European understanding too. The new significance of the Entente as an informal, defensive coalition directed against Germany became clear as soon as the international conference on Morocco met at Algeciras in January 1906. The conference ended in a major diplomatic defeat for Germany. Contrary to Bülow's confident expectation, it was not France but Germany that found itself almost isolated. Throughout the conference France depended on British support. Sir Edward Grey, the new Liberal foreign secretary, dared not refuse that support even when he thought the French unreasonable. 'We can't', he insisted, 'press our advice on them to the point of breaking up the Entente.' If British support appeared to waver, Grey believed that France might well capitulate to Germany as it had almost done in 1905, and leave Britain isolated. Grey was careful never to raise French hopes that the Liberal government would ever give a *formal* guarantee of British support in a Franco-German war. Privately, however, he assured Paul Cambon on a number of occasions that 'in a crisis public opinion would oblige whatever British government was in power to march with France'. Cambon took the same view.

'An entente between Russia, France and ourselves', wrote Grey during the Algeciras conference, 'would be absolutely secure. If it is necessary to check Germany it could then be done.' In April 1906 he began the negotiations that led eventually to the conclusion of the Anglo-Russian agreement of August 1907. His motive in doing so was primarily fear and suspicion of Germany. He shared the view of one of his advisers that: 'If Great Britain and Russia do not very soon come to an agreement with regard to their respective interests in Persia they may find themselves confronted there with Germany very much as France did in Morocco.' Although Grey, unlike some of his advisers, was genuinely anxious to reduce the tension between Britain and Germany, he remained constantly afraid of taking any initiative that might endanger the understandings with France and Russia on which be believed British security depended. 'If we sacrifice the other powers to Germany,' Grey believed, 'we shall eventually be attacked.'

The possibility of a European war arising out of a Balkan, rather than a Moroccan, crisis arose for the first time in the twentieth century during the Bosnian crisis of 1908–9.

Until almost the end of the crisis Cambon remained uncertain whether British public opinion would take the same uncompromising attitude in a war arising out of Balkan rivalries that he did not doubt it would take in a war over Morocco. His doubts were resolved by the acceleration of the naval arms race between Britain and Germany. By the final stages of the Bosnian crisis in the spring of 1909 British public opinion appeared to Cambon (and to many others) to have been roused to a state of almost frenzied agitation by fears that, for the first time for centuries, British naval supremacy was in serious danger. Asquith's government, which had originally intended to build only four dreadnoughts (modern battleships) during the next year, was assailed by the slogan 'We want eight and we won't wait' and surrendered to it. 'This new situation', wrote Cambon, 'removes my doubts about England's attitude ... If we are drawn into a general European conflict, English opinion will not allow the government to stand aside; this must be obvious to Berlin.' Just as successive French governments (or, rather, the minority of ministers who paid serious attention to foreign affairs) had accepted Cambon's mistaken claim that Lansdowne had given a firm offer of support against Germany in May 1905, so they also accepted his over-confident assertion in 1909 that the British public would not allow their government to 'stand aside' if France were attacked by Germany.

The role of British public opinion was considered so important by the French government largely because of its lack of confidence in at least a section of the Liberal Cabinet. The French were well aware that some British ministers regarded the Entente, as interpreted by Grey, as the main obstacle to better relations with Germany. During the eight years before World War I the most frequent source of French anxiety about British loyalty to the Entente sprang from the influence of the radical wing of the Liberal Party and its Labour allies. The disquiet expressed by Jules Cambon (the younger brother of Paul) in 1909 was typical of the fears expressed by many French statesmen. 'I am not', he said, 'exactly alarmed about the Entente Cordiale, but I cannot get rid of the feeling that in certain quarters England is getting very German. I allude to a very large portion of the Liberal Party and especially to the Labour Party, who seem to be gaining influence and power.'

The influence of British radical politicians tended, as in the case of Jules Cambon, to cause disquiet rather than real alarm in Paris. When a radical statesman publicly advocated better relations with Germany, Paul Cambon invariably reported that his views were not those of the British people. While Edward VII remained on the throne, his influence was regarded as an important additional safeguard against radical reorientation of British foreign policy. Edward's state visit to France in May 1903 had been interpreted by Delcassé as proof of British willingness to conclude the Entente. Like Cambon and Delcassé, French ministers had a wildly exaggerated confidence in the king's ability to determine the course of his country's foreign policy and regarded his presence on the throne as a 'guarantee' of British loyalty to what they believed were Britain's obligations under the Entente Cordiale. Their illusions were strengthened by Edward's own tendency to depart from his role as a constitutional monarch during meetings with French statesmen. 'Tell us what you want on each point,' the king told Cambon during the Algeciras conference, 'and we will support you without restriction and reserve.' Edward's (in reality inconsequential) private visit to Paris in the spring of 1906 was treated by the Ferdinand Sarrien government as of major diplomatic significance. The illusions even of the usually hard-headed Georges Clemenceau (prime minister from October 1906 to July 1909) about the king's role in British policy-making were illustrated by his decision to interrupt Edward's 'cure' at Carlsbad in August 1907 by a meeting to urge on him the desirability of the British introduction of conscription. Edward's death in 1910 was widely regarded in France as a considerable blow to the Entente. George V, Cambon regretted, would never have 'the same authority' in foreign affairs. Bertie frankly informed the Quai d'Orsay that, like his Danish mother, Queen Alexandra, George was rather dim: 'None of the princes in the Danish royal family is intelligent and the Prince of Wales is no better than his mother.'

With Edward's death, Cambon gloomily concluded that there was not a single statesman of real stature left in England. Only Lloyd George and Winston Churchill, he observed prophetically, really possessed the gift of leadership, but for the moment they were still *trop nouveaux venus* and inspired too little trust. What was particularly disturbing for the future was that both these men were widely regarded as friends of Germany and enemies of the Entente. In December 1908 Bertie warned the Foreign Office that it would be disastrous for Churchill to visit France: 'He would not be believed whatever he might say.' Stephen Pichon, the French foreign minister, strove to explain Lloyd George's friendship for Germany to the French cabinet on the grounds that he was 'a Celt and not an Englishman'.

One of the most surprising and reassuring aspects of the Agadir crisis in 1911 from the French point of view was that it transformed both Lloyd George and Winston Churchill into firm friends of France. Lloyd George's conversion was particularly dramatic; Churchill later suggested that it took even Lloyd George himself somewhat by surprise. In July 1911, at the height of the crisis, Lloyd George, hitherto considered the most pro-German member of the Liberal government, suddenly delivered the strongest public warning to Germany so far given by a British statesman. This warning was interpreted throughout Europe as a clear promise to France of British armed support against German attack. 'Messrs Lloyd George and Winston Churchill', said Cambon when the crisis was over, '...have been enlightened by events. They are now second to no-one in their support for the Entente Cordiale and they play a decisive role within the cabinet.' Agadir, Cambon confidently declared, had once again demonstrated the truth of Grey's assurance that, in a crisis, British opinion would force its government to stand by France.

Hardly had the Agadir crisis been concluded, however, than fears revived in France of a new German attempt to undermine the Entente. The first to raise the alarm was Sir Francis Bertie. No British diplomat in modern times has had a more remarkable view of the role of an ambassador. He was, as Sir Robert Vansittart (who served under him in Paris) euphemistically observed, 'wholly disinclined to scrape a second fiddle or to become one of the mouthpieces which Foreign Office and Government have now made their agents'. In the spring of 1912 Bertie called at the Quai d'Orsay to put Poincaré on guard against the policy of the British government. There was, he said, a serious danger that, in order to limit the naval arms race, Britain might be persuaded by Germany to give a formal undertaking not to take part in an aggressive war against it: an undertaking phrased in such a way as to create possible obstacles to British intervention in a war forced on France by Germany. 'We are dealing', said Paul Cambon, 'with very devious people. The German aim, remorselessly pursued for the last eight years, is to create a breach between ourselves and the English which will gradually widen, until it leads sooner or later to a complete separation.'

Although all prospect of an Anglo-German agreement disappeared within a few weeks of Bertie's warning, his alarmism led to a new French attempt to secure a formal promise of British support against German attack. Cambon rightly believed that if the Conservatives returned to power such an undertaking could be obtained. Both Balfour and Austen Chamberlain urged Grey to conclude a formal alliance. Sir Arthur Nicolson, the permanent under-secretary at the Foreign Office, privately assured Cambon that the Liberals were 'at the end of their tether' and would soon hand over power to the Conservatives. Although Nicolson's prophecy proved to be mistaken, the survival of Asquith's Cabinet had one significant advantage that the French failed to perceive. Under a Liberal government, radical and Labour opposition to the Entente, especially in Parliament, was far more restrained than it would otherwise have been. Between the Agadir crisis and the eve of World War I there was scarcely a single full-dress Commons debate on foreign policy. Grey and Asquith had to cope with hardly more than a few 'inconvenient questions'. Had a

Unionist government come to power, the left-wing challenge to the Entente would scarcely have been so muted.

Cambon believed that Grey himself was willing to give a formal under-taking of British support against Germany, but was prevented from doing so by his radical colleagues. The Liberal government did, however, agree to an exchange of letters in November 1912 which, though reserving the freedom of action of each government, provided for immediate consulta-tion in a crisis. If joint military action was thought necessary, it was to be on the basis of arrangements made by the General Staffs, described in Chapter I by John Keiger. Asquith, like Grey, was privately convinced that, if it came to war, Britain would be bound to support France against German attack. The phrasing of the exchange of letters, however, enabled them to assure both Parliament and their radical colleagues that Britain was bound by no commitment of any kind. Neither Grey nor Asquith was capable of conscious, deliberate deception. But it is difficult to avoid the conclusion that, in stressing Britain's entire freedom of action, they were taking refuge in a legalistic formula that disguised the moral obligation to France that both felt that Britain had incurred.

Even on the eve of war in August 1914 neither Asquith nor Grey was fully conscious of the ambiguity of his own position. Asquith wrote in his diary on 2 August: 'Happily I am quite clear in my mind as to what is right and wrong.' He then added a number of points that revealed anything but clarity of mind: '(1) We have no obligation of any kind either to France or Russia to give them military or naval help... (3) We must not forget the ties created by our long-standing and intimate friendship with France.' Exactly the same contradiction was apparent in Grey's famous speech to Parliament a day later on the eve of British entry into World War I. 'This remarkable speech', wrote Lord Loreburn later, 'began with an elaborate effort to prove that the House of Commons was perfectly free to deter-mine either for peace or war. It ended with a passionate declaration that this country would be disgraced if we did not declare war...'

The Foreign Office view of the significance of the Entente Cordiale during the July crisis that preceded World War I was summed up in a memorandum by Sir Eyre Crowe, the assistant under-secretary:

The Entente has been made, strengthened, put to the test and celeb-rated in a manner justifying the belief that a moral bond was being forged. The whole policy of the Entente can have no meaning if it does not signify that in a just quarrel England would stand by her friends. This honourable expectation has been raised. We cannot repudiate it without exposing our good name to grave criticism.

This was the French view also of Britain's obligations under the Entente Cordiale. It was shared by the Conservative and Unionist Party, and by many Liberals. But it was not, as Grey and Asquith discovered, the view of a majority of their colleagues in the Cabinet. Even British public opinion did not at first give France the decisive support that Grey had led the French to expect. There was a feeling in Britain, Grey believed, that if France went to war, 'It would . . . not be in any quarrel of her own at all; it would be because she, as Russia's ally, had the misfortune to be involved in a Russian quarrel, in which France had no direct interest and which did not arouse feeling in the French people.'

The July crisis in 1914 revealed in a more acute form the divisions within the Liberal Cabinet over the obligations of the Entente Cordiale that had shown themselves during the Agadir crisis three years before. Until the end of July the Cabinet, though deeply divided in its attitude towards France, was able to agree on a common policy of trying to avert the war. Once war became inevitable on 1 August, however, the divisions within the Cabinet could be no longer concealed or reconciled. Grey and Asquith were resolved to resign unless the Cabinet agreed to give France armed support. Without the German attack on Belgium there is little prospect that the Cabinet would have done so. Had Germany made its attack directly across the French frontier, Asquith's government would almost certainly have fallen. Whatever the action taken by the next British government, there would then inevitably have followed a period of bitter recrimination not merely between France and Britain but also within Britain itself over the failure of the Asquith Cabinet to stand by France. At the beginning of August the recrimination seemed already to have begun. Cambon in London angrily demanded of the Foreign Office if Britain any longer knew the meaning of honour. Bertie in Paris felt 'sick at heart and ashamed'. He wrote in his diary of the French crowds cheering outside his embassy in the confident expectation of British support: 'Here today it is "*Vive l'Angleterre*"; tomorrow it may be "*Perfide Albion*".' 'It fairly makes one gasp', wrote Neville Chamberlain a few days later, 'to think that we were within a hair's breadth of eternal disgrace . . .'

In the summer of 1914 there was a general conviction in Paris that Britain had acquired a moral obligation to support France against German attack. In Britain, however, the approach of World War I revealed a remarkable confusion over what the Entente Cordiale really meant. Some, such as Lansdowne, believed that the Entente was actually 'stronger than an alliance', because, unlike an alliance, it was not limited to specific cir-cumstances. Others maintained that, on the contrary, the Entente Cordiale was no more than a phrase that carried with it no obligation of any kind.

Until the July crisis, French diplomats and ministers, who mistakenly believed that they had been offered British military assistance as far back as May 1905, failed to grasp the extent of Britain's confusion over its obligations to France. Appropriately, perhaps, it was Germany that ended the confusion and resolved the crisis in the Entente Cordiale on the eve of World War I. It was Germany's hostility to the Anglo-French agreement of April 1904 that had made that agreement the beginning of a major diplomatic realignment. And it was Germany also that succeeded, by its invasion of Belgium in August 1914, in overcoming the divisions within Asquith's government and transforming the Entente Cordiale into a war alliance.

Christopher Andrew and Paul Vallet

Crisis in Morocco

The Entente Cordiale had no sooner been formed than it faced a surge of international tension. The first Moroccan crisis (31 March 1905 to 7 April 1906) was the first test of the new relationship established between France and Britain on 8 April 1904. The Entente Cordiale emerged from it strengthened and deepened. Furthermore, the crisis revealed a new pattern in the balance of power in Europe, confirmed in August 1914 with the outbreak of World War I.

The crisis arose from a clash over Morocco between France and Germany. France, which had been established for 75 years in Algeria and more than 20 in Tunisia, wished to extend its influence over the weak and unstable Sherifian Empire.

To enjoy as much freedom of action as possible, French Foreign Minister Théophile Delcassé made extensive diplomatic preparations. In 1902, France appeased Italy by recognising Italian interests in Tripolitania and Cyrenaica. It put an end to its colonial rivalry with Great Britain by abandoning its own claims on Egypt in exchange for freedom of action in Morocco, where it also persuaded Spain to grant it a dominant position. Considering that Germany was not a Mediterranean power, and therefore unconcerned by the situation in Morocco, Delcassé omitted Berlin from his diplomatic preparations, but merely 'informed' the Germans of the Franco-British agreement.

The crisis was sparked off by Germany, which felt slighted by being sidelined from so important an international development. Berlin believed that its own position was strong. The Russo-Japanese conflict had weakened the military alliance between Moscow and Tokyo. Great Britain, as Japan's ally, felt no sympathy for the Empire of the Czars. Paris, therefore, was somewhat torn between its alliance with St Petersburg and its Entente with London.

In Morocco itself, the French mission to the Sultan in Fez was pressing hard for a programme of reform that would have given France a dominant position. But the Sultan was playing for time, in the belief that Germany would support him. To this end, during an impromptu stop at Tangiers on 31 March 1905, Kaiser Wilhelm affirmed in his usual flamboyant style the absolute independence of Morocco, and proposed an international conference to consider what reforms the Sultan should undertake.

Rather late in the day, Delcassé sought to open negotiations with Germany about the future of Morocco. But Berlin did not respond, and tension grew in Europe, while the French mission in Fez had to acknowledge that it had failed. Delcassé opposed an international conference: he believed that Germany was bluffing, and that Great Britain would back France to the point of concluding a formal alliance. He overestimated both France's influence over the Sultan and Britain's willingness to get involved. At no time had Lord Lansdowne, the British foreign secretary, ever envisaged a formal alliance with France. This is clear not only from his diplomatic correspondence but also from his private papers.

The crisis came to a head at a Cabinet meeting in Paris in 6 June 1905, when Delcassé, isolated in the face of Prime Minister Maurice Rouvier and his colleagues, was obliged to resign. But his fall did not immediately lead the French government to accede to an international conference, inevitable as this was. The word in Paris was that 'Without prior agreement with Germany such a conference would be dangerous, while with prior agreement it would be useless.'

Nevertheless, France ably exploited Germany's desire for a conference. It managed to negotiate an agreement with Germany that barred the conference from considering France's traditional policy and earlier Franco-Moroccan agreements about the frontier with Algeria. Franco-German accord on these points extended also to the reform of the police, notably the port police, and to an 'open door' in matters of trade.

The negotiation was led in Paris by Paul Révoil, former governor-general of Algeria, for France, and by Dr Rosen, for Germany. France had the advantage of knowing what it wanted, while Germany knew only what it did not. Agreement was reached on 28 September. France accepted the international conference, but its laborious diplomatic preparations proved their worth. On 29 August Russia had signed a pact with Japan. By the time of the Morocco conference, the international situation once more favoured France.

The conference began at Algeciras on 16 January 1906. Thirteen countries, including the United States of America, took part. France failed in its attempts to negotiate bilaterally with the Germans and, despite constant support from the British, the other participants began to lose patience and to suggest solutions that would have limited France's freedom of action and imposed some kind of international protectorate.

A *faux pas* by Germany's ally, the Austro-Hungarian Empire, prevented this outcome. It was an attempt to make the impasse official. The delegates to the conference had already realised that France's draft proposal of a Final Act had no chance of success, and Austria took the opportunity to propose adjourning the proceedings. In response, Paul Révoil for France and Sir Arthur Nicholson for Britain called for a procedural vote under which the conference would resume work the next day. There were ten votes for the motion and only three against (Germany, Austro-Hungary and Morocco), confirming that Germany was isolated and that France had in effect won, although the details were not settled until 7 April 1906.

The end of the crisis not only strengthened the Entente Cordiale. It also built, around the Entente, a new balance of power in Europe.

In the first place, the French and the British had been able to gauge the solidity and seriousness of their Entente while at the same time realising its limits: Delcassé had been mistaken in taking Lord Lansdowne's words as promising a formal alliance. The British Cabinet, concerned at the growing strength of Germany, had judged France to be a loyal and stalwart partner.

Russia, for its part, although weakened by its failure *vis-à-vis* Japan, had remained faithful to its alliance with France despite seductive overtures from the Kaiser when the two emperors met at Bjorkö. Meanwhile, paradoxically, the renewal of the Anglo-Japanese alliance, this time guaranteeing India's north-west frontier, encouraged Anglo-Russian rapprochement. This led in 1907 to the Triple Entente linking Britain, Russia and France.

Finally, the United States, which had no material interests in Morocco, for the first time took part in a European conference, alongside France and Britain.

Thus took shape, on 7 April 1906, the constellation that, around the Triple Entente, was soon to face the Central Powers and overcome them in 1918.

Jean-Marie Le Breton

A Somewhat Subtle Mathematicians' Entente

It may have been simple politeness on the part of the German Mathematical Society, which was playing host, but on Thursday 11 August 1904, a French and a British lecturer spoke in succession at the plenary session of the third International Mathematicians' Congress in Heidelberg. If so, it was the politeness of the powerful. The learned German society was regarded as the leading mathematical body in the world, both in size and in output. But it may have been more than coincidence that the two speakers – Paul Painlevé '*aus Paris*' as the official proceedings put it, and A. G. Greenhill '*aus London*' – gave the same importance, in their successive contributions, to the problems of reality and nature. This was all the more remarkable in that throughout the nineteenth century European countries had developed the idea of mathematics as 'pure science'. The expression 'pure mathematics' may be surprising, in that no one refers to 'pure physics' or 'pure philosophy'. But it had prevailed, almost as dogma, in Germany.

The situation at the beginning of the twentieth century can be better understood by looking at the mathematical geography of the time – a question of linguistic areas rather than nations. There was mathematical science in German, seen as an intellectually autonomous world, well represented by the periodical *Mathematische Annalen*. Its French counterpart, founded in Paris in 1836, was the *Journal de mathématiques pures et appliquées*, home of Francophone mathematics, partly the heir of the Enlightenment and of positivism, but somewhat abashed by the feeling that France had declined since the Franco-Prussian War. Finally, there was a mathematical science expressed in English. This could be considered imperial, but only in the sense that it was self-sufficient. British mathematicians at that time rarely took part in international gatherings. Europe's other mathematical publications, in Sweden or in Italy, while producing respectable work of their own, drew more or less equally on French and German influences.

The Franco–British coincidence of views noted above was less than an *entente*. But, like the diplomatic Entente Cordiale of that same year, it had an unnamed common opponent as well as allies to convince. The mathematician who was their Aunt Sally had abandoned Natural Philosophy, as practised by the Enlightenment and by

Newton, in favour of mathematical abstraction for its own sake and formalism as the supposed spur to innovation. Here is the heavy irony employed by Greenhill, the British speaker at Heidelberg in 1904, to describe the analytical obfuscation of the theta functions used to explain the movement of a child's spinning top:

> I will be so bold as to offer an heretical opinion in the presence of Drs Königsberg, Krause, Krazer, and other authorities on the subject, that the theta-function by itself is not the expression of any important physical law; and that to begin elliptic function theory with the theta-function ... is deterrent to a student of Natural Philosophy.[1]

The names of the German mathematicians mentioned by Greenhill ranged from his host at Heidelberg to the Karlsruhe professor in charge of collecting and publishing the Proceedings – all 'top' people, echoing the word that Greenhill preferred to use when discussing gyroscopes. The theta function, although derived from the elegant theory of elliptic functions brilliantly established in the nineteenth century on the basis of German contributions, was only an artifice for the spinning top, whatever the claims of the German mathematician Felix Klein. That artifice was suspect, thought Greenhill. He took a realist position, and was glad to do so, since it enabled him to explain reality without recourse to pedantic and complicated language. The mathematics of an object that turns on itself should not be over-complex, because even the child sees the top revolving roughly on its own axis, and because mechanics is a well-developed, mature science, and therefore naturally simple. Greenhill thus neatly combined Anglo-Saxon empiricism with Cartesianism.

As with the Entente Cordiale, the concordance of Painlevé and Greenhill may at first sight seem rhetorical. Certainly, the play of irony was not identical on either side of the Channel. But on closer inspection a shared mentality can be seen. Painlevé is no doubt better known for having combined the roles of prime minister and minister

---

1 A. G. Greenhill, 'The Mathematical Theory of the Top Considered Historically', *Verhandlung des dritten internationalen Mathematiker-Kongress in Heidelberg von 8. bis 13. August*, herausg. Von A. Krazer, B. G. Teubner, Leipzig, 1905, p. 106.

for war in the autumn of 1917. As a young man, in 1900, he had become a member of the Académie des Sciences, and five years later a professor at the École Polytechnique. At the 1904 Congress he defended analytical mathematics, or calculus, at least in so far as this was 'natural' or 'physical' and did not create artefacts that could not be observed. To justify the mathematician's healthy imagination, Painlevé metaphorically invoked the necessary transition from the real to the imaginary – both in their precise mathematical sense. Imaginary numbers, like real numbers, were expressions introduced into algebra by René Descartes, in order to find systematic ways of resolving polynomial equations. The transition to imaginary numbers was also the great advantage of the elliptic functions referred to by Greenhill. That so French a thinker as Descartes should have discussed the 'imaginary' in 1637 proved the objective quality of human imagination and the rational validity of algebra, despite its dealing with symbols or fictions. Imaginary numbers, in fact, had received realistic validation or physical confirmation in 1873 in the very British James Clerk Maxwell's work on electricity. Painlevé stressed this, and his irony about the scholastic spirit was a vindication of the mathematician, whose task was to make natural what had been abstract – or at least to naturalise it, making it mimic nature, as taxidermists 'naturalise' a stuffed animal to display it in a museum.

> The introduction of imaginary numbers was very much in the nature of things. It was not a caprice that led mathematicians to resort to them: nor was it in order to disguise, under absurd scholastic complications, their inability to deal with real problems.[2]

Theta functions, the transition to imaginary numbers – technical terminology is employed here simply to situate Franco-British complicity in its mathematical context. It is important not to stray too far from it. Less specialised, more stereotyped language would distort the facts. This is what a French author wrote at that time:

---

2 Paul Painlevé, 'Le problème moderne de l'intégration des équations différentielles', *Verhandlung des dritten internationalen Mathematiker-Kongress in Heidelberg von 8. bis 13. August*, herausg. Von A. Krazer, B. G. Teubner, Leipzig, 1905, p. 89.

Nothing is more diametrically opposed to German thought than British thought. In the latter, there is no desire for rigorous reasoning which might involve judgement; there is no quest for systematic, artificial order; in a word, there is no geometric spirit. Instead, there is a prodigious capacity to see, clearly and distinctly, a multitude of concrete objects, while leaving each of them in the place it has been assigned by a complex and shifting reality. Nothing, therefore, seems better fitted to counterbalance the exaggerated influence of German thought than the influence of British thought.[3]

Such a political caricature would have been as misplaced in the proceedings of a congress of the 'scientific international' as in the report of a diplomatic meeting. Its author, Pierre Duhem, was a physicist, scientific academician, and historian of scientific ideas from the ancient world onwards. He made his remarks to the students of the Catholic University of Bordeaux in 1915. The date alone explains the nationalist *parti-pris* and the implication that French thought was perfectly balanced between the two opposites. Britain was the effective ally – but the only advantage of the empiricist, utilitarian positivism that Duhem ascribed to the British was as a counterweight to the German system, and it was essential to avoid both extremes. For Duhem, a theory in physics was only a framework designed to 'safeguard the appearance of phenomena without pretension to absolute truth'. Duhem regarded the development of science in terms of Christian apologetics. Franco-British complicity in 1904 was far less than dogmatic in this sense, but also more than merely conventional. Mathematicians of both countries aimed at objective truth as it was the truth of Nature itself. An anecdote may avert another possible misreading of the situation. In 1916, the logician Bertrand Russell, then a fellow of Trinity College, Cambridge, stood before his judges, who condemned him as a conscientious objector to military service, after which he lost his fellowship. He affirmed that in France, if conscientious objectors were shot (as the law permitted) 'it would let loose a veritable storm of protest from bishops, nonconformist leaders, and members of parliament'. Even if the remark is flattering to France, it does not denote Franco-British complicity about

---

3   Pierre Duhem, *La Science Allemande*, A. Hermann, Paris, 1915, p. 91.

pacifism, but illustrates Russell's admiration for the 'intellectuals' influencing French public opinion.

Positivism carries responsibilities. Mathematicians in France were not seen as 'intellectuals' in the full sense, except when they expressed themselves as philosophers, like Henri Poincaré. But they were regarded as masters of intellectual exactitude, whose task was to express the regularity of how the material world worked. The professional basis of Franco-British complicity was the joint recognition that mechanics was the supreme science. It was because it was both theoretical and based on the real, material world that both Painlevé and Greenhill called themselves 'mechanicians'. Less mathematical considerations, deriving from thermodynamics as with someone such as Duhem, were put in second place. In this way, deductive mechanical science, traditionally bound to the natural world by mathematical interpretation, remained almost neutral *vis-à-vis* religion. It employed determinism as an effective hypothesis, but as Isaac Newton had used the law of dynamics, without claiming to prove it or its *raison d'être*. Mechanics suited the pursuit of 'natural theology', then dominant in Cambridge, as well as it accorded with the laicism soon to be adopted by the Republic in France. In 1904, all this favoured the Franco-British complicity evident in the speeches by Greenhill and Painlevé.

That complicity did not follow naturally from the previous history of the two mathematical communities. The British tradition had been formed in and by universities whose tasks had included producing honest administrators for the Empire. The French had evolved in the Grandes Écoles, designed to prepare the future and train technocrats. Even so, the emergence of similar thinking by French and British mathematicians was not fortuitous. It bore witness to shared experimental rationalism, to use Gaston Bachelard's later expression, confident of its ability to face the crisis afflicting science at the beginning of the twentieth century. It was against the word 'crisis' that the two communities were most agreed. Not because they refused to see the difficulties raised by treating all scientific problems in terms of mechanics, but because they were not daunted by them. Their past mastery of reasoning seemed a guarantee of the future.

So they preferred to investigate reality mathematically in order to understand and master it, rather than to investigate mathematical thought for its own sake, analysing its bases, its logic, and the possible interplay of axioms – a tendency thought to be Germanic. In French and British eyes, the 'monsters' produced by formalistic mathematical thinking were 'pathological' aberrations from the elegant regularity of the analytical explanations themselves. Yet the most serious path along which the analysis of mathematical thought and its coherence evolved – pursued by, among others, the eminent David Hilbert at Göttingen – insisted on the radical autonomy of mathematics.

But there was also, in a sense different from but analogous to Hilbert's work, the logical analysis of the young Bertrand Russell and Alfred North Whitehead in Cambridge. As a result, Franco-British agreement about the aim of mathematics was not unanimous, although it was a favourite theme of mathematical orators on both sides of the Channel when they spoke to an international audience. This established a kind of diplomatic *entente* in the growing 'scientific international'. It could involve accepting only the French point of view, provided it was expressed by a great mathematician. One instance was the great intellectual dispute over the scope of mathematics between Henri Poincaré, born in 1854 and based in Paris as a member of the Académie des Sciences, and the German David Hilbert, born in 1862. They were both giants: each dominated all the mathematical disciplines, and neither was restricted to a single specialist field. Their dispute continued from one international congress to another. In Paris in August 1900, Hilbert foresaw the future of mathematics in a logic of formal rigour while Poincaré replied by addressing the congress in Cartesian terms, insisting on mathematical intuition and inner sense, but also on the role of physics proper. His full response came eight years later, at the Rome congress in 1908, when he stressed the ability of mathematics to offer analogies making it possible to approach the complexity of reality rationally, and thereby impose order on it. But such order was useful only if it involved innovation.

What has been said shows how pointless it would be to try to replace the free initiative of the mathematician by any kind of mechanical procedure. To obtain a result of real value, it is not enough to grind out calculations or to use a machine to put things in order. It is not order as such that matters, but unexpected order. My machine may grind away at brute facts, but it will never grasp the soul of things.[4]

Poincaré's ontological order opposed both the arbitrary or ideological order of classification and the prescriptive order of Hilbert. On the contrary, in one of his last writings in 1912, he said he believed it was possible to deduce mathematically, by analysing human sensations, that physical space was indeed three-dimensional. So much so that he deployed against the nominalists the same irony as Greenhill.

> But when all is said and done, there are many ways of classifying everything; a good librarian always finds plenty to do, and every new classification has something to teach the philosopher.

The sting was in the tail. The last phrase was a dig at scholastic or Kantian philosophy. There again, French and British mathematicians had the same attitude, called positivist in France, and in Britain known as 'natural philosophy'. The proof of their apparent *entente* came at the Fifth International Congress of Mathematicians, held in Cambridge at the end of August 1912. The astronomer and geophysicist G. H. Darwin, son of the evolution theorist, sang the praises of applied mathematics, which he said had always been honoured at Cambridge. This was an allusion to Isaac Newton, the founder of celestial mechanics, which had brought prestige to mathematical thought by proving that pure calculation could predict the existence of previously unseen planets such as Neptune. Darwin naturally went on to praise Poincaré for reviving celestial mechanics and recalled what he had said in Rome. Darwin concluded by declaring how difficult applied mathematics was, but how useful and moral, since it involved 'honest attempts to unravel the secrets of the universe in which we live.'[5]

There was certainly irony in the implication that in some *a priori* way there might be 'dishonesty' in the abstract! But the remark also

---

4 Henri Poincaré, 'L'avenir des mathématiques', *Atti del IV Congresso Internazionale di Matematici*, pubblicati per cura di Castelnuovo, Roma, *Academia dei Lincei*, vol. I, 1909, p. 169.
5 Proceedings of the Fifth International Congress of Mathematicians, Cambridge, at the University Press, 1913, p. 36.

expressed the modesty of mathematicians in the face of what was still unknown.

These Franco-British scholars might be blamed for failing to point out, in their cross-Channel rapprochement, that Einstein's relativity theory, first published in 1905, continued the constructive line of Newton's natural philosophy.[6] It was a revolution, but in the sense in which the stars revolve, returning to the same thoughts but at a deeper level. Poincaré foresaw the basic criticism that could be made of the hypothesis that space and time were absolute, but he still let others mock such doubts. The tiny minority of French and British intellectuals who were mathematicians were then so accustomed to being ironical about theory for theory's sake, and about the dominance of mathematics over thought in general, that they perhaps failed to realise how cordial their *entente* was. It became explicit before 1914 in the publication of Godfrey H. Hardy's *A Course of Pure Mathematics*, a book still in print long after World War II. For although the mathematics invoked by Hardy was described as 'pure', it showed not so much a 'geometrical spirit' as a 'spirit of finesse'.

The *entente* was cordial in that it almost naturally involved a way of applying the ancient science of Euclid, thoroughly renewed at the turn of the century. Mathematicians were quietly working. The earlier triumphs of Newton and Laplace made it possible to contemplate with confidence the pursuit of rationality, with all its possible contradictions. This was not a Faustian quest, a desire to explain everything, like Hilbert declaring 'Wir sollen wissen, wir werden wissen.' Hardy, more modestly, saw mathematics as a reservoir of 'patterns', of forms that the physicist could adapt as needed – 'models' such as a fashion designer adapts to the taste of the client.

Jean Dhombres

---

6 Françoise Balibar, *Galilée, Newton, lus par Einstein. Espace et relativité*, PUF, Paris, 1984.

III
World War I, 1914–18

World War I was the *Entente*'s first major challenge. In retrospect, and in view of history, its response was striking.

Testing the Entente Cordiale

In the course of their long history before the twentieth century, the French and the British had fought side by side only rarely. In the nineteenth century the only instance was the siege of Sebastopol in the Crimean War, when alongside 90,000 French soldiers there were only 20,000 British. The tradition was rather for 'Joan of Arc, Waterloo and Fashoda', and at the turn of the century the idea of war between France and Britain was not unthinkable. In 1901 the son-in-law of General Boulanger, Commandant Driant, who wrote military novels under the pseudonym of 'Captain Danrit', published *La guerre fatale*, about an invasion of England by French troops.

The Franco-British atmosphere certainly changed with the Entente Cordiale in 1904, but this was not an alliance. It involved neither diplomatic nor military cooperation. However, in November 1912 French Ambassador Paul Cambon and British Foreign Secretary Sir Edward Grey exchanged letters saying that, if war threatened, the two governments would study what measures to take. Since 1907 there had also been talks at General Staff level, although without commitment, and in 1912 it was decided that in the event of war the French fleet would keep watch on the Mediterranean and the British fleet the Channel and the North Sea.

In fact when the July 1914 crisis began, it seemed highly unlikely that Britain would intervene. At the eleventh hour, when France's involvement in war seemed more and more inevitable, and general mobilisation was decreed on 1 August, the constant concern of French President Raymond Poincaré was to know what Britain would do. 'Until the last moment,' he wrote in his *Memoirs*, 'the French government had no idea what line Britain would take.' He had been right to worry, because Britain had not

47

decided. British public opinion was deeply peaceable, if not pacifist. Sir Edward Grey was a man of peace, but he believed in the balance of power and was quite soon convinced that it was in Britain's interest to fight.

He believed, however, that it would not do so unless public opinion were first persuaded that it was necessary. This was what he repeated to Paul Cambon on 30 July – but it was not what happened. When German troops invaded Belgium on Monday 3 August, the British were still enjoying the long bank holiday weekend, and the public knew nothing of the invasion. Whether to declare war was decided not by the public but by the Cabinet, which on the morning of the 3rd decided to make the attack on Belgium a *casus belli*. Grey was determined to intervene, but the invasion gave him the decisive argument.

He was backed by Prime Minister Herbert Asquith. Four members of the Cabinet resigned, but two withdrew their resignations. The following day, however, saw quasi-unanimity. The *Manchester Guardian*, which had led opposition to war, threw in the sponge. It regretted the fact, 'but all disagreement is now at an end. We have a united front.' As the American historian Bernadette Schmitt has written:

All available evidence confirms this verdict. Sir Edward Grey might have secured the consent of Parliament to the undertaking to protect the northern coasts of France against German attack. But without the Belgian issue, he would not have had behind him an enthusiastic House of Commons or a united country. The neutrality of Belgium was not the only reason, perhaps not the principal reason, why the British foreign secretary advocated the intervention of Great Britain, but it was the reason which persuaded public opinion of the necessity and justice of that course.[1]

Conservatives, Liberals and Labour were practically unanimous in voting credit for the war; and for the British historian John Keiger, this was why the most divided nation on the eve of the war developed one of the most cast-iron *unions sacrées* of all the belligerents.[2] In fact, it was not the Entente Cordiale that had led the United Kingdom into war, but awareness of Britain's interests.

---

1 Bernadette E. Schmitt, *The Coming of the War, 1914* (2 vols), Charles Scribner's Sons, New York and London, 1930.
2 John Keiger, 'Britain's "Union sacrée"', in *Les sociétés européennes et la guerre de 1914–1918*, ed. Jean-Jacques Becker and Stéphane Audoin-Rouzeau, Université Paris X, Nanterre, 1990.

Nevertheless, waging war required an army, and the British army was very small. General mobilisation could not be decreed, because there was no compulsory military service. For the time being, and apart from its sea power, Britain could contribute to the war only four infantry divisions and one of cavalry, a total of about 100,000 soldiers, whereas Germany and France had at once mobilised millions of men. Nor could Britain really do more for some months, although everyone expected the war to be short. A British Expeditionary Force (BEF) was rapidly sent to the continent, however, under Sir John French, who to the surprise of many in France bore the title of marshal. When this small, irascible man went to fight alongside the French it was never for a moment imagined that his small force would be placed under French command.

Franco-British cooperation could be conducted only by talks between the two commanders-in-chief. For the French command, the arrival of British soldiers was nevertheless very welcome, because – having taken a long time to realise the importance of Germany's advance through Belgium – it had few troops in place to oppose it. The British Expeditionary Force, having landed from 11 August at Boulogne, Rouen and Le Havre, came in on the left of the French Fifth Army under General Lanrezac, who launched the Battle of Mons on 23 August. The British, who were professional soldiers and good marksmen, inflicted heavy losses on the German troops. They and the British disagreed about who had won; but because Lanrezac, to the right, was beaten on the River Sambre and forced to withdraw, the British had to do likewise. The great retreat began, involving battles like that at Le Cateau, where British troops came under very heavy pressure.

Lanrezac and French got on badly. French, despite his name, spoke little French. Lanzerac, like Joffre, spoke no English. But that was not the essential problem. French suspected Lanzerac of having put him in a difficult situation, leaving him to his fate by beating a retreat. Lanzerac, one of France's most brilliant generals, thought the British were useless.

His unhappy relationship with French, among other things, was to cost him his command. But the most extraordinary thing was that the British Expeditionary Force, retreating by forced marches, disappeared from the front. French, in fact, envisaged returning to the Channel ports and re-embarking for Britain. British War Minister General Kitchener had to come to France to give him the order to cooperate with Joffre, even at the risk of losing his army. As French said, 'My confidence in the ability of the heads of the French Army to fight this campaign is declining rapidly.' Only after a dramatic meeting with Joffre did he agree to continue to take part in the battle. The BEF was reintegrated with the French, between the

Sixth and Fifth Armies, and in the Battle of the Marne it found itself facing the breach that had separated the First and Second German Armies. Advancing – cautiously – into this breach, it played its part in the German retreat.

Britain's role in the beginnings of World War I had perforce been limited, but Kitchener was one of the first to realise that the war would be lengthy, and that there would have to be a sizeable British army. The appeal for volunteers, and the astonishing response – 500,000 by mid-September and 3 million by the end of 1915, before a slowdown in 1916 made necessary gradual conscription – enabled British forces to play a considerable role. When the continuous front was established from the North Sea to Switzerland, it was logical for the British to hold its northern section, from Picardy to Flanders; and in 1916 it was on the Somme, where the French and British armies met, that General Joffre and General Douglas Haig (who had just replaced French) decided to conduct a large-scale joint offensive. Their plan had to be changed after a German surprise attack at Verdun in February 1916, and owing to the gradual reduction of France's role the Battle of the Somme was predominantly fought by the British. It cost vast numbers of British lives: Kitchener's troops were slaughtered. The first day of the battle, 1 July 1916, was 'the bloodiest day' in British history, with 60,000 casualties, 20,000 of them fatal. Although it continued for months, the battle won little ground for the Allies. In the French subconscious, the Battle of Verdun predominates: in the British subconscious it is the Somme and, later, Passchendaele – a name almost unknown to the French. In the war fought jointly but separately by the French and the British, 1917 was an important landmark. The new British prime minister, David Lloyd George, agreed for the first time to put British troops under French command 'for the duration of the battle' that was in prospect. Their commander Douglas Haig protested vehemently, appealed to the king, and threatened to resign, but finally had to give in. The new leader of the French army, General Nivelle (whose mother was British and who spoke perfect English) had made great efforts to please his allies, and had succeeded. He had promised 'a splendid harvest of glory for the British and French armies'. But the experiment ended badly. The British had some successes on their part of the Front, but the French suffered a serious defeat on the Chemin des Dames, worsened by the mutinies that followed it.

Douglas Haig seized the opportunity to recover his independence and convince Lloyd George that the war must be continued by fighting a major battle in Flanders. He believed that the Germans were so weakened that the British army could now win the war by itself. The result was one of the most appalling battles of the war in the mud of Flanders. After months of fighting, the British managed to seize Passchendaele, but that was all.

Not until 1918 did the French and the British stop fighting side by side, separately, and begin to some extent to fight together. This was the result of Germany's March offensive and its breakthrough in Picardy. Defeat was clearly looming when, on 26 March, the British political leaders and their generals, including Lloyd George and Douglas Haig, met their French counterparts Clemenceau, Foch and Pétain at Doullens, a little village on the Somme. The situation was so nearly desperate that national considerations took second place. General Foch was entrusted with 'coordinating the action of Allied armies on the Western Front'. Even this was not enough. On 3 April he was given 'strategic command' of military operations, and on 14 May he became 'commander of the allied armies in France'. It had taken almost four years of war for the French and the British to fight under a single command, each nevertheless still keeping their own stretch of the front. They had to fight on other fronts, too, where the division between the two great allies was less obvious. The Dardanelles was very largely a British-led operation; and in general the British government believed that the eastern Mediterranean was a zone of British influence. At the same time, the troops of various nationalities, including French and British, who made up the army of the East were under French command.

In the absence of true *entente* between the two allies in the field, did the Entente Cordiale influence their war aims? In reality, it was somewhat by chance that the two powers found themselves fighting side by side. They simply had a common foe: there was no detailed commitment. The London Declaration of 5 September 1914, whereby France, Britain and Russia promised not to make a separate peace, was negotiated while the Battle of the Marne was raging. Later there were various agreements with Russia and Italy, and about the Near East, but virtually none as regards the essential – Germany. To take just one example, the recovery of Alsace-Lorraine was for France a permanent and primordial war aim, but not until very late in the day, on 5 January 1918, did Lloyd George declare his will to fight for it, at the same time as for the restoration of Belgium, which was nothing new.

Whether in the military field or in others the Entente Cordiale was not a 'cordial misunderstanding', but in World War I it only partly justified its name. Small wonder, then, that this is how it is remembered, at least by historians. There has been much mention of the low opinion some French soldiers had of British troops. On the other side, British historians have often been a little scathing about the French army. David Shermer, for example, has written that after the Chemin des Dames, 'it became more and more obvious that "*les armées gauloises en loques*" had to remain on the defensive until American forces arrived on the continent'.[3] Another British historian, Tim Travers, wrote at the end of a recent work that the Expeditionary Force and its allies won the war in 1918.[4] Here, the French army seems to have been reduced to auxiliary of the BEF.

Certain particular speeches made after the war recall the feelings of comrades in arms, but it is surprising to find no trace of them in histories of the war, whether British or French. They do not deny such feelings: they simply ignore them. There is scarcely ever a paragraph on the subject.

Yet even if *entente* between the two peoples is seldom mentioned, one can nevertheless believe that it remained deeply engraved on their subconscious. It forged a new relationship between Britain and France. The Great War helped to efface a past most often marked by mutual antagonism. But even so fearful a shared ordeal could not by itself create a new tradition.

One reason is probably their differing conceptions of the war. For the French, it was *their* war; but they did not fully realise that for the British, too, it was *theirs*. But Clemenceau above all, and the French too – whatever they might have said – knew very well that they would not have won the war without the British . . . and without the Americans.

Jean-Jacques Becker

---

3   David Shermer, *La Grande Guerre*, Éditions Cathay, Paris, 1977.
4   Tim Travers, *How the War was Won*, Routledge, London, 1992.

So, even in war, different perceptions continued. Britain still emphasised sea power, and France the war on land. Different battles, too, entered each nation's folk memory – Verdun in France, the Somme and Passchendaele in Britain. But, whatever the contrasts, two great leaders complemented each other: Kitchener and Foch.

Winning the War: Kitchener and Foch

The Entente's successful war effort in the Great War represented the triumph of improvisation in the face of novelty. As a joint endeavour, the coalition struggle was poorly managed until the final year of victory. France sought the dénouement in military victory, Britain in economic strangulation: two often incompatible methods that reflected the nations' different histories. France feared defeat on its own soil, Britain on the high seas, and hence their broader strategic policies were frequently at variance. War aims too diverged, as each state looked to secure its own advantage in the post-war power vacuum which would follow the overthrow of Germany and its allies. Too often in the day-to-day formulation of policy personal differences and national rivalries undermined the effective pursuit of the common goal, the destruction of German power. Fortunately the Entente was to find two leaders, a British soldier-administrator and a French professor-general, who learned to look beyond limited national horizons. The thoughts and actions of Field Marshal Lord Kitchener, British secretary of state for war from August 1914 to June 1916, and General Ferdinand Foch, ultimately Allied generalissimo in 1918, furnished the Entente with the means and method of victory.

Although joint military planning for war began in 1905, neither Britain nor France planned for the war they were actually to fight, individually or together. The French expected their long-cultivated élan to sweep them quickly to a decisive military victory, aided to a limited extent by the small British regular army, and to a great extent by the Russian behemoth. The British, from centuries of practice, expected the French, with a small token reinforcement, to hold the line, while their naval strength slowly crushed Germany's economic challenge and forced it to the peace table.

In the event, neither military spirit nor naval supremacy ultimately won the war. Mobilisation and attrition, factors that were not apparent in 1914, were the keys to Allied victory. Those who managed the Allied war effort had therefore to find a way to win this new sort of war, while at the same time struggling with its day-to-day management. One Englishman and one Frenchman had the vision and energy to bring the Entente through the maelstrom to triumph.

Only one man on the Entente side, Britain's hastily appointed secretary of state for war, appreciated the nature of the war from the start, and how it would be won – although he did not live to see the fruits of his insight. In his first interview with the press in August 1914 Kitchener made it clear that in his opinion the Entente was facing a long war, and that the war would be won by the side that fielded the last man and the last gun. On this basis he took the decision that sustained the Entente's military effort through a three-year trench stalemate. Kitchener began to mobilise Britain's huge potential for a lengthy war of attrition. It would be a long and contentious process. His call for volunteers produced the British empire's first citizen army, equipped and sustained by a prodigious industrial and financial effort. Events on the battlefield in France and Flanders ultimately proved Kitchener's sagacity.

After the first massive yet indecisive clash of arms on the Franco-German frontiers, France's brave but ill-directed army recoiled into the interior of France. Unbeaten, it fought the invader to a standstill but could not reconquer the sacred soil of *la patrie*. General Foch, a brave and dynamic leader of men, made his reputation in this massive bloodletting. But the rising star of the French army was as nonplussed as his fellow generals when it came to the new style of warfare. It would be three years before he found the key to unlocking the military stalemate of the Western Front. Then, in the summer and autumn of 1918, Foch was to direct the Allied armies in the greatest military offensive yet witnessed, delivering the long-sought decisive victory that overthrew German imperial power. Kitchener's citizen army, honed through three years of attritional trial and error to the peak of military efficiency, were in the vanguard.

The Entente began the war ill-organised and impatient. Pre-war planners such as the French commander-in-chief, General Joseph Joffre, expected the war to be short and sweet. Things turned sour, however, almost immediately, as the Anglo-French armies were forced into headlong retreat behind Paris and military liaison broke down. Before a month had passed the alliance was on the verge of collapse. The Cabinet despatched Kitchener to Paris to save the Alliance and Britain's reputation by effectively ordering the disillusioned British commander-in-chief, Sir

John French, to march to the sound of the French guns. The Allied armies held together in the face of adversity, and reversed their initial misfortunes on the Marne. Defeat had been avoided, but military victory was nowhere near; the invaders were driven back to the River Aisne, where they dug in on the Chemin des Dames for a long stay. The French remained impatient. As stalemate set in in November 1914 Kitchener met Joffre and Foch, now Joffre's right-hand man, to discuss the military situation. 'During my conversation with Lord Kitchener,' Foch recollected after the war, 'I was struck by the accuracy of his conceptions in what concerned the war, which he already saw would last a very long time.' The Frenchmen wanted more men immediately; they contended that Britain's barely trained and ill-equipped volunteers should be rushed to the front. Kitchener would not yield: 'On July 1st 1915 you will have one million trained English soldiers in France. Before that date you will get none, or practically none,' he informed the disappointed Frenchmen. The scene was set for a battle of wills between the British secretary of state and the French high command.

Kitchener saw the war as a whole, while his allies were mesmerised by the German army entrenched on French soil. To drive out the invader Joffre wanted to attack with all available forces as soon as possible. Kitchener countered that the real fighting should not begin until the summer, when Britain's new armies were ready. Then the Entente would face a three-year war of attrition. Meanwhile the Entente should seek easier victories away from the Western Front. The limited forces at Britain's disposal were to be used to force the Dardanelles, to open up a direct sea route to Russia and refuel the spluttering steamroller. The key to military victory in the west, he argued, should be a well-organised and adequately provisioned offensive all along the front. In 1915 the Allies lacked the means, and their limited offensives barely dented the solid enemy glacis. But in 1918 it was to be this method, on a much grander scale, that Foch used to storm the enemy's linear fortress and force victory.

Kitchener, diplomat as well as military organiser, was eventually forced to give in to increasingly strident French demands, although not without fighting a lengthy rearguard action in an attempt to maintain a strategic reserve and gain advantages away from the deadlocked Western Front. But by the summer of 1915 he was forced to accept that the solidity of the Alliance must come first. He agreed that Britain's fresh new armies should come to the Western Front to sustain flagging French resolve and support their offensive operations, even though, as he informed his Cabinet colleagues, he was 'far from sanguine that any substantial military advantage would be achieved'. This was the one key lesson he passed on to General

Haig, who was to direct his new armies in the field. Again and again, against his better judgement, Haig deferred to the French in the interests of Alliance solidarity. One year later he launched Kitchener's army in its first fateful offensive on the Somme – a premature attack to sustain the hard-pressed French.

By the summer of 1915 a more far-sighted and sombre mood overtook the Allies, as they woke up to the political and economic reality of modern industrial war. There would be no quick victory, and greater care would have to be taken to avoid defeat and regain the initiative. The home front would have to be properly managed, the better to sustain the fighting front. The leisurely *ancien régime* methods of departmental management of the first year of war – 'procrastination and muddle', as Lord Esher derisively commented – had produced disagreement and mistakes, none greater than the hastily organised and ill-managed Dardanelles expedition. Replacing them was, however, to be a slow and contentious task. Inexperienced but in earnest, the British and French prime ministers finally met for the first time in July 1915, after nearly a year of war, to resolve the acute tension between Kitchener and Joffre. This first Allied strategic conference was hastily organised, and its conclusions were uncertain compromises. Nevertheless, Joffre got what he wanted – a commitment of Britain's New Armies to the Western Front. Allied strategy and policy remained at loggerheads through the failed autumn offensive on the Western Front that followed, and the tardy and ineffective Salonika misadventure of the autumn. The strategic impasse of 1915 had severely compromised Allied relations, and steps were taken to streamline the coalition's military directorate. Regrettably the visionary Kitchener, not the stolid Joffre, found his strategic responsibilities pared down.

As acknowledged strategic leader of the coalition in 1916, Joffre sought the solution to the stalemate in better coordination and greater effort rather than more subtle military method. The offensive was to be renewed in greater scale by the Anglo-French armies side by side astride the Somme. More force would puncture the hole that had not been made in 1915. Britain's New Armies, large and enthusiastic but with no military experience, would for the first time take the lead. Haig reluctantly agreed as the French wavered under the grinding pressure at Verdun. His armies were not yet ready for the decisive push, but keeping the coalition together had to come first. By 1916 Britain had a great army with no real military experience. This would have to be gained on the battlefield, with inevitable mistakes and losses.

Tragically drowned on his way to Russia, Kitchener did not live to see his New Armies crippled on 1 July 1916, and ground down in the months that followed. Foch, directing the French armies on their flank, saw only too well that his old pre-war philosophies of offensive war were inapplicable in the modern struggle of man against machines. But pure attrition, the unimaginative and alienating solution of commanders on both sides in 1916, did not suit the dynamic General Foch. Nor did it suit the politicians in London and Paris. David Lloyd George, Britain's new and determined war leader, and Aristide Briand, France's increasingly insecure premier, sought to dissociate themselves from the mistakes of the past without really appreciating the real nature of the war they were fighting. Joffre and Foch were found new and less responsible billets, while the Allied governments asserted their control over strategy. They looked for a new man with promise. They found a man who made promises.

The resulting 'Nivelle experiment' set back the cause of Allied military relations and nearly destroyed the coalition. General Robert Nivelle, master of the dominant artillery arm and victor of Verdun, promised a decisive breakthrough on the Western Front within 48 hours. Half-English and bilingual, this proto-Napoleon could speak the politicians' language, although he did not convince the realists. The usually compliant Field Marshal Haig, personally resentful of the upstart French general but understandably doubtful about his over-ambitious plan, had to be brought to heel by his own prime minister. Lloyd George's formal subordination of the British high command to French authority for the duration of the coming offensive was perhaps the most misguided and harmful incident in Anglo-French relations of the whole war. Nivelle's own war minister, Paul Painlevé, listening to Foch's wiser counsel, threatened to cancel the offensive before it began. It was allowed to proceed in April 1917, and duly failed to live up to Nivelle's extravagant promise. Worse, it precipitated a crisis in French government and high command that threatened to break the coalition and lose the war.

British ministers too found themselves in a prolonged struggle with their military advisers on the strategy and policy of the war. While the generals still believed that continuing pressure on the German army on the Western Front would eventually produce a military victory, pessimism gripped the British governing classes. The war could not be won without compromising their pre-war values of liberalism and paternalism and bankrupting the nation – events in Russia had demonstrated what happened to a ruling class that lost control of its people. Better to secure the empire and arrange a compromise peace, than continue sacrificing British lives for France and risk social upheaval. The more phlegmatic Lloyd George determined to see it through, although try as he might he could not offer any way out of the strategic impasse in the face of military intransigence. In the short term the generals won through, and Haig's war of attrition continued through 1917. Elsewhere, greater imagination was at work.

While General Nivelle tried and failed to break the stalemate, the former Professor Foch was on sabbatical in Limoges. 'This period of rest was not without some value,' he noted in his post-war memoirs, 'for it enabled him to meditate upon the lessons and the future problems of the War, and thus prepare himself for the tasks awaiting him.'[1] Foch concluded that the Allies needed three things: matériel, as an alternative to the expenditure of increasingly scarce lives; real leadership of the united Allied armies, rather than the conditional and intermittent coordination that currently existed; and operational methods that would break the stalemate. The Nivelle experiment over, Foch's common sense and long-term perspective began to prevail. Back from disgrace, appointed by Painlevé as French chief of staff and technical adviser to the French government in May 1917, he began to prepare the means. A massive armaments programme, backed up by American money and manpower, was initiated, to bear fruit in 1918 and 1919 and furnish the material base for the final victory, if the Allied armies could hold out that long. Leadership and method would follow.

While Foch planned and prepared, Kitchener's armies, their voluntary enthusiasm tempered by the reality of combat and level-headedness of conscript drafts, mastered the modern battlefield. The French, under General Pétain's pragmatic leadership, recovered their spirit. It was not that the Allied armies could not win battles: they demonstrated increasingly sophisticated and effective combined-arms techniques as 1917 progressed, 'biting and holding' the key German defensive positions along the Western Front – Vimy ridge; the Messines ridge; the heights of Verdun; the Menin Road ridge; the Malmaison plateau. The Allied armies had the method to win battles, but not yet the war. The strategic breakthrough remained elusive – Passchendaele was a ridge too far.

Under conditions of linear siege warfare strategic breakthrough was not possible, as Foch realised through careful study of these operations. Exploitation could not be carried forwards; the inertia of the modern deep battlefield prevented that. The enemy would have to be defeated by other means. Lateral exploitation was the realistic alternative, using Allied mobility and matériel predominance to the full. In 1918 for the first time the allies would have the men, tanks, aeroplanes and guns to prepare the whole front for the offensive, and be able to shift the main front of battle rapidly when inertia slowed the advance. There would be no decisive knockout, but a succession of rapid body blows, from which the enemy would have no time to recover. A surprised British foreign secretary, Arthur Balfour, received an animated practical demonstration as Foch delivered a succession of 'violent pugilistic gestures first with his fists and then with his feet', as they strolled together in the gardens of Versailles. A succession of powerful waves would break against the enemy's front, throwing him off balance and driving back his line. Foch now had the method, Kitchener's suggested method, to go with the military means – a massive arsenal and effective experienced armies – but he did not yet have the authority or the opportunity. The final requirement would be centralised control of the Allied forces, without which such concerted blows would not be possible.

Foch was the most experienced coordinator on the Allied side. He had worked on pre-war plans for Anglo–French military cooperation. In autumn 1914 he had directed the French, British and Belgian armies in the crucial defensive battles. He had coordinated British and French offensive effort on the Western Front throughout 1915 and 1916. In 1917 he had worked closely with his opposite number in London, Sir William Robertson, to coordinate wider Allied military effort. He had arranged for the deployment of the American Expeditionary Force in France. Lloyd George had even looked to him for military advice as an alternative to the unpalatable truths he was receiving from Robertson and Haig. He had coordinated Anglo–French support for the hard-pressed Italian army at the end of 1917. He had joined the new Allied Supreme War Council as military adviser and chairman of its military arm, the Executive War Board. Foch was trusted by all the Allied leaders, both soldiers and politicians. He was the only man who could run an Allied war effort.

His time came in March 1918, when in the face of imminent breakdown in military liaison and defeat in detail he assumed the task of coordination, and soon afterwards, command, of the Allied armies on the Western Front. First Foch had to earn the trust of his multinational subordinates, French, British, American, Belgian and Italian. His calm conduct of the defensive battle in the first half of 1918, his willingness to lead rather than command, and his brilliant seizure of the initiative on the Marne in July 1918 produced a rapid and effective acceptance of central military authority. His final task was to convince his subordinates that the tide had turned and it was time to attack. 'Tout le monde à la bataille,' he preached, with customary vigour, in the summer of 1918. In no doubt that the decisive moment had finally come and his lengthy attrition of the enemy was finally to pay dividends, Haig willingly rallied to the cry. French, British, Americans and Belgians swept forward in an unstoppable armed tide. In the final hundred days of the war Kitchener's citizen army mounted an unbroken series of nine brilliant but sadly forgotten offensives. From the opening of the victory march at Amiens on 8 August – Ludendorff's 'black day' of the German army, when he admitted that the war was lost – through the storming of the supposedly impregnable Hindenburg position on 29 September, to the liberation of Mons on Armistice Day, Haig's veteran army, pre-war regular soldiers, Kitchener's volunteers and later conscripts showed what a properly trained, well-equipped and well-led citizen army was capable of on the modern battlefield.

Two British field marshals – for Foch too was awarded that rank in recognition of his military genius – should wear the laurels of 1918. John Terraine has written:

> Kitchener was one of the few men whose vision was large enough to embrace the whole War; but the War itself was too large to be dominated by any one man. Vision is one thing, control another; the great unanswerable question is whether, had he lived, Kitchener might have found, in the second half of the War, a means of imparting his vision through a proper machinery of control.[1]

It was to be Foch, indirectly inspired by Kitchener's vision, who was ultimately to achieve that control, through perseverance and force of personality. 'I am conscious of having served England as I served my own country,' reads Foch's epitaph on his statue in London, erected by a grateful Allied nation. But he could not have achieved what he did without the foundations laid by Kitchener. Kitchener's epitaph, 'the organiser of victory', was different but equally deserved. Kitchener was the armourer and strategist of the Entente, while Foch was the leader and field commander. Their complementary efforts brought the Entente through four years of strain to military victory. Separately – and without Kitchener's untimely death it might have been together – they did more than any other men to win the war for the Entente.

William Philpott

---

1 John Terraine, *Douglas Haig: The Educated Soldier*, Hutchinson, London, 1963.

Turning-point: The Somme

The 1916 Battle of the Somme, journalistic shorthand in Britain for futility and slaughter, was the turning point of the war, militarily, socially and politically. For the British and French armies it was their largest common battle before their 1918 victory. It was the graveyard of old methods, and the nursery of new armies. For both nations it was a defining social and cultural experience. The disaster of the first day, 1 July, when 20,000 men were killed, still stands in Britain as a metaphor for all that was wrong with the war, and has occluded the real achievements of Britain's citizens led by soldiers in that battle and afterwards. On the Somme the French old guard exhaled their last gasp. Britain willingly seized the baton of military leadership. A new international union was constituted, which was to endure beyond the war's end. Belligerent John Bull would chivalrously support shell-shocked Marianne through the remaining years of conflict. Both partners had now to lead their awakening masses, who would no longer follow blindly.

Conceived in the winter of 1915–16 as the decisive battle that would win the war, with the experienced but tired French army leading their fresh but untested British allies to victory, the conception of the battle and the war had changed by 1 July 1916. Attrition, the solution to the strategic stalemate introduced by the German commander Erich von Falkenhayn, had tempered Allied optimism. The French, bled almost white at Verdun, called desperately for relief. In the opinion of their chief, Sir Douglas Haig, the partly trained British divisions were not ready to attack. Yet politically he could not refuse the brave yet failing ally. The British would take the lead on 1 July; the French would do what they could.

Better versed in the methods of industrial war, the French caught the Germans by surprise south of the River Somme, achieving a striking success on the first day of the battle. North of the river the British army had more mixed fortunes. On the right flank, alongside the French, they made progress, but further north unharmed German defences checked the British attack, inflicting massive losses. With the element of surprise gone, the Allied armies were left to make the best of a clear yet indecisive initial success.

Four and a half months of grinding attrition followed. The casualty lists were long on both sides of the line; both weary *poilus* and keen imperial volunteers felt that they had been ill-used by their leaders. In future they would question the methods, if not the object-ives, of their elders' war. Their generals were temporarily non-plussed, groping for an alternative to the sacrifice of human life. Haig and Ferdinand Foch, directing the Allied armies, realised that the nature of war had changed. Modern war was a war of industries and technology, not of individual heroes. Their methods would be refined accordingly. The seeds of their 1918 victory were sown in the fields of Flanders in 1916. In future the machines of modern war – artillery, tanks, aeroplanes, machine-guns – would lead; the brave, loyal, skilled but pragmatic infantry would follow.

The high ground astride the River Somme was the graveyard of optimistic young men from both empires. The chatter of machine-guns and the boom of artillery sounded the death-knell for any hope of an easy victory and a return to political and social normality. Yet within the strategic parameters of attrition, anathema though that concept has subsequently become, the battle was a clear victory. As Lord Esher was later to write, it 'settled the inevitable issue of the war'. The Somme was also the graveyard of the imperial German army, whose morale never recovered from their systematic ejection from successive carefully constructed defensive positions. Falkenhayn, hoist by his own strategic petard, was relieved of command. His suc-cessors, Paul von Hindenburg and Erich Ludendorff, brought realism to German headquarters. They tightened their belts in anticipation of more of the same, withdrawing their depleted divisions to stronger defensive positions and putting out feelers for a negotiated peace.

The battle turned the war and those who fought it. Their common suffering and achievement finally cemented the Anglo-French alliance, while a new social contract was forged in the fire and mud of this unremarkable corner of the French countryside. Britain and France were to see the war through together, although with a very different spirit, and with much more realistic expectations, than in the spring of 1916. Pessimism gripped the Allied leaders, and disillu-sionment and self-preservation overtook their surviving soldiers. A year of strain followed, before political and military dynamos – Lloyd George, Clemenceau, Haig and Foch – inspired their patriotic but war-weary citizens on to victory.

William Philpott

An Anglophile

Shortly after Georges Clemenceau became premier of wartime France in November 1917, the veteran British ambassador to Paris, Lord Bertie, described him to the Foreign Office: 'You know how much superior he is to his predecessors in largeness of views and in quick decision. He is at times irritable and is inclined to see offence when none is intended; but he is straight and that is a quality which is not a common one in France and he is as pro-British as any honest Frenchman can be.'

This rough sketch touched upon the paradoxical nature of the 'Tiger's' complex relationship with Britain. Following in the Anglophile tradition of the French Enlightenment, his father, in 1865, took him to visit the British philosophers Herbert Spencer and John Stuart Mill, a trip that inspired him to translate Mill's *Auguste Comte and Positivism* into French. As the most prominent radical leader in France after 1871, Clemenceau went on to meet many British liberals, republicans, positivists and radicals, including William Gladstone, John Morley, John Bright, Sir Charles Dilke and Frederic Harrison. Of these early encounters, the most important political contact was with Joseph Chamberlain. He described Clemenceau in 1882 as 'an able man' whose 'opinions are very much those of any sensible English radical'. Inspired in part by the positivist idea that liberal Britain and France were natural European partners, Chamberlain and Clemenceau contemplated the formation of an Anglo-French alliance as early as 1891. This idea proved to be premature and the two later fell out over Chamberlain's imperial politics. Clemenceau nevertheless maintained a strong personal connection with England through his friendships with the headstrong and opinionated family of Rear Admiral Frederick Maxse and the idiosyncratic social democratic leader H. M. Hyndman. Maverick critics of their own government, they encouraged him to blend sincere Anglophilia with a deep-rooted distrust of Britain's political classes.

As premier of France from 1906 to 1909, Clemenceau strove to convert the Entente Cordiale from a colonial agreement into a working combination on European questions. Specifically, he hoped to solidify Britain's military commitment to fight with France in the event of war with Germany. While this strategy obviously benefited

France, Clemenceau sincerely believed that it was also the best course of action for Britain's strategic and moral interests. With these concerns in mind, the French army under his government dropped its mobilisation plans for war against Britain and began secret staff conversations with the War Office in 1907 for the deployment of a British Expeditionary Force (BEF) on the northwestern flank of the French army. Later, in 1910, Clemenceau personally toured the Belgian frontier with one of the future commanders of the BEF, General Sir John French. In his ongoing effort to fight 'Little Englandism', he even joined Lord Robert's National Service League in 1911 on the grounds that a strong English army was essential for the European balance of power.

The outbreak of World War I indicated Clemenceau's fear of German militarism, but the dispatch of the BEF to the continent deepened his faith in the Entente. Building upon his relationship with the Maxse family, he became a fervent admirer of the British fighting man. His relations with Whitehall, however, were never easy. In the Allied strategic debates, he consistently opposed the dispatch of French and British forces away from the Western Front to overseas 'sideshows'. As a leading French senator and as president of the Inter-Allied Parliamentary Committee (1916–17), he worked against the advocates of the Salonika campaign. As premier of France after November 1917, he opposed the British campaign in Palestine and pushed London to increase its recruiting efforts in order to maintain the BEF's strength. On the Western Front, he worked for closer Anglo-French cooperation. He first supported Field Marshal Haig and General Pétain in their effort to control the inter-Allied strategic reserve, but when the German offensive in March threatened to split the Allied armies, he backed the elevation of General Foch to Allied generalissmo. In a departure from Pétain's southward strategy, Clemenceau supported Foch's risky deployment of French reserves behind the BEF during the remainder of the German spring offensives. The 'Tiger's' stature was so great at this point that many British leaders, including Haig, General Sir Henry Wilson and Lord Milner, considered him to be the dominant Allied personality.

Clemenceau's overall wartime record mitigated difficulties between the French army and the BEF while increasing tensions between London and Paris. At the Paris Peace Conference, his overriding objective was to maintain the wartime alliance of France, Great Britain, the United States and Italy. Of these powers, British cooperation was the most important ingredient in his vision of a just and secure peace. He thus had to repair relations with London, but this necessitated working with Prime Minister David Lloyd George, whom he considered to be an untrustworthy politician rather than a true statesman. In order to maintain Anglo-American support Clemenceau made numerous, albeit grudging, concessions on French claims, ranging from Palestine to the question of an independent Rhineland to the French occupation of the Saar. However, he was unable to overcome Lloyd George's traditional British reticence towards a continental commitment. Although Lloyd George proposed an Anglo-American treaty to guarantee French security, the British prime minister first excluded the Dominions from this agreement, and then made the British pledge contingent upon approval of the American Senate. When Woodrow Wilson lost the battle for treaty ratification, Britain's commitment to France became void. Clemenceau thus retired from politics in January 1920 with his security strategy for France in ruins.

Clemenceau's visit to Britain in 1921 summed up the clash between his unusual Anglophile intellectual roots and conventional Anglo-French relations. After receiving an honorary doctorate from the Oxford University, he visited Parliament at Lloyd George's request. Here he asked the British prime minister why he had become an 'enemy of France', to which Lloyd George candidly replied: 'Well! Isn't that our traditional policy?' This failure to bridge culture and diplomacy was one of the great tragedies of Clemenceau's life.

Robert K. Hanks

Sacrifice or Memory

When Napoleon came to power France was by far the most populous country in Europe, with 33 million inhabitants to England's 15 million. Even huge Russia had only 39 million, while little Prussia (whom Napoleon was to defeat in two lightning battles) had no more than 6 million. As a consequence of Napoleon's wars, France lost a total – staggering at that date – of over 2 million men.

Then came Bismarck's defeat of Louis Napoleon's Second Empire in September 1870, and the resultant loss of Alsace-Lorraine, two of France's fairest provinces. In 1900 France awoke to the dreadful realisation that it was now outnumbered by 15 million in population [41 million to 56 million] by the virile nation across the Rhine that had, inevitably, become its natural enemy. And as the new kaiser's imperial Germany seemed increasingly aggressive, so the demographic disparity between France and Germany grew, approaching nearly 20 million by 1911.

If France was ever to achieve a stable balance of power in Europe, let alone regain the lost provinces – to which every French politician was dedicated – by the beginning of the twentieth century it was painfully clear that it would have to enlist new allies. It looked first to Russia, and then – in 1904 – to Britain.

Nevertheless, when World War I came in 1914, because of the sheer power of the German military machine and the shortcomings of its new Allies, and indeed of its own war plan, France was still to bear the highest proportion of losses of any of the major combatants. After the first five months of the war alone it had lost 300,000 killed (nearly as many as Britain's total dead in World War II), with another 600,000 wounded, captured or missing. By the end of 1915 France had lost 50 per cent of its regular officers. The terrible battle of Verdun the following year cost it another 400,000 casualties. Lasting ten months, with a hideous intensity of slaughter hitherto unseen on any battlefield, Verdun rightly went down in French annals as one of the greatest epics of national glory. It ended in victory, but a Pyrrhic victory in every sense. In the following year, 1917, the bloodshed brought the French army to the brink of mutiny and beyond. With Russia out of the war and gripped by revolution, Pétain, the hero of Verdun now nominated commander-in-chief, recognised that the brunt of the fighting henceforth would have to be borne by British – and fresh American – troops.

But the insidious effects of France's heroic 'victory' at Verdun were felt long after 1918. A whole generation, exhausted by war, grew up with the belief that 'we could not do Verdun again'. The Maginot Line, defensive in concept, was a symbol of this; the defeatism that preceded the defeat of 1940 its end result. Then, even in this brief Blitzkrieg campaign, disproving the legend that the whole of the French army simply did not fight, over a hundred thousand French soldiers were killed; while almost the same number escaped at Dunkirk to fight again. In defeat, two million Frenchmen went to German POW or labour camps, for the next five years. A statistic deeply shocking to French pride, but not incomprehensible under the circumstances, shows that before the end of 1943 85,000 French women had had illegitimate children by Germans – the humiliation of being occupied an experience from which Britain was mercifully spared.

Shamed but unbowed, France resurgent returned to life again under de Gaulle in 1944. Yet, almost immediately, it found itself caught up again in war – first in Indochina, then in Algeria. The first came to cost France's army more lives than America lost in Korea, while Algeria added another 23,000 deaths to the century's total.

These losses in colonial wars were something that, again fortunately, Britain never experienced. Again, they left their mark in France. Closely allied in French minds to the Algerian War, the disastrous Suez débâcle of 1956, on which Britain foreclosed, reminded many Frenchmen all too vividly of the downside of Dunkirk in 1940. In a crisis, '*les anglo-saxons* will always pull out' was a cry widely heard. It could be seen leading in a direct line, first to de Gaulle's 'NON' to Harold Macmillan's application for British entry to the EEC in January 1961, and – three years later – to France's withdrawal from NATO.

Deep down in many French hearts that particular reading of Dunkirk – for the British a triumph, for many Frenchmen a desertion – will always remain a latent poison. In this celebration of the centenary of the Entente Cordiale it is, therefore, also perhaps proper to consider just what glory, sacrifice and memory have meant to France over these hundred years.

Alistair Horne

IV
Between the Wars

After World War I, France's concern over Germany was more widely shared. But Britain still did not share France's priorities. Paris wanted security: London pursued disarmament. They disagreed about reparations, and even the Locarno Treaties looked different on either side of the Channel.

The 1920s

France and Britain had fought World War I together. Peace divided them. Yet they had a common interest in maintaining their solidarity: to build a lasting peace, restore economic prosperity, recover their status as world powers, stand up to nationalism in their colonies, stem the Bolshevik revolution, and avoid the recurrence of war. But peacetime found them disunited. Old disagreements were far from disappearing, revived by disputes over the peace settlement or over sharing out the spoils. Everything seemed destined to set them apart, but one question dominated all the others: relations with Germany. On this they no longer saw eye to eye. In the 1920s, Britain feared the power of France as much as it had feared that of Germany before the war. So the German question was now the real bone of contention between France and Britain. The British believed that Germany was too weak to wage another war. France, fearing German revenge, did not intend to disarm unless its security was solidly guaranteed. Britain, for its part, feared French militarism. Stories were even published in which London was attacked by squadrons of French aircraft.

All this began while the Treaty of Versailles was being negotiated. At the peace conference, France called for the autonomy of the left bank of the Rhine as a defence against any further German aggression. Woodrow Wilson and David Lloyd George opposed it, citing the need to avoid creating a new Alsace-Lorraine. The impasse was total. But in March 1919 Lloyd George made a remarkable proposal to Georges Clemenceau. If France, he said, would give up the left bank of the Rhine, the United States and Britain would agree to sign a defensive alliance with it – and, he added, to build a Channel tunnel to enable British troops to reach France more quickly. But because the Franco-British treaty of guarantee was integrally linked to the Franco-American treaty, the British withdrew their guarantee when, on 19 March 1920, the American Senate rejected the Treaty of Versailles.

From this time onwards, therefore, 'entente cordiale' was no longer on the cards. Disagreement between the two countries became general. The question of reparations was the pretext, and the Ruhr crisis was the symbol, but there was a deeper reason and a divergence of national interests. The crux was the British tradition of the 'balance of power'. Before 1914, the British policy of opposing the strongest power on the continent had focused on Germany. In 1919, the British believed that the strongest power was France: hence the change in perspective.

The divergence of interests was obvious enough. Britain, keen to recover its role as a dominant economic power, sought a rapid economic revival in Germany as an export market. This was why the main dispute between the French and the British was over reparations – a terribly complex problem, made all the more so because it was linked to that of war debts.

Unlike the French, who had suffered great destruction in the north and the east, the British brought into the reparations equation the factor of military pensions. At the Spa Conference on 16 July 1920, they secured agreement that their share in German reparations should be 22 per cent against 52 per cent for France. But there was beginning to be significant evolution in the British state of mind, under the influence of the economist John Maynard Keynes. In November 1919, having been a member of the British delegation at the Peace Conference, he published a best-seller, *The Economic Consequences of the Peace*. His argument was simple: to restore the health of the European economy, Germany's prosperity must be revived, allowing it to play a key role in international trade. The prerequisite was to annul – at least in part – German reparations. So to encourage economic recovery the British proposed to cancel both war debts and reparations, whereas the French wished to write off only the debts. France owed a debt to Britain – less than it owed to the United States, but still amounting to some 13,000 million gold francs. It believed that while Britain and the United States had made a greater financial effort than France, it had made a greater human effort. It therefore sought either an across-the-board cancellation of war debts or at least their substantial reduction and a long period for their repayment. If all war debts were not written off, France wanted their reimbursement to be conditional on payment of German reparations – i.e. that France should pay its debts only if Germany paid its reparations.

Positions hardened. The French wanted to 'make the Boche pay': the

British – for commercial reasons – were anxious to avoid the total ruin of Germany. They also wanted what they received in reparations and debt repayments to reimburse their own debts to the Americans. Finally, in 1921, Germany was forced to accept that the sum total of reparations be fixed at 132,000 million gold marks. This was far too much, all the more so since Western Europe, and Germany in particular, underwent a serious economic crisis at the beginning of the 1920s. In fact, negotiations were resumed in the autumn and winter of 1921–22. In December 1921, Lloyd George approached Aristide Briand with an offer to guarantee the French frontier in exchange for a reduction in the amount of reparations. France refused. Britain's proposal of a moratorium was rejected by the militant postwar Chamber, which was determined to see the Versailles Treaty carried out to the letter. From the summer of 1922 onwards, Raymond Poincaré (who incarnated this attitude) decided on the so-called 'productive pledges' system. Accordingly, in January 1923, France decided to occupy the Ruhr basin. This was probably one of the tensest moments in relations between France and Britain, since France's policy was in direct opposition to the interests of Britain, with whom Germany was a major trading partner.

The occupation of the Ruhr, condemned by British Prime Minister Stanley Baldwin, profoundly strengthened the popular conviction that France and Britain were radically opposed to each other. The British press denounced French imperialism, which it said tended 'to make law for others . . . and to suppose it had a monopoly of political wisdom'. A caricature in *Punch* on 10 January 1923 showed Poincaré and Bonar Law looking at a goose wearing a dunce's cap. Their conversation is a dialogue of the deaf:

> Mr Bonar Law: 'This poor bird cannot lay eggs without a long moratorium.'
> M. Poincaré: 'And I say it can. A goose that can lay, but won't, must be forced to, even if I have to wring its neck.'

The French financial and monetary crisis, however, obliged Raymond Poincaré to seek international aid to support the franc, and in November 1923 he had to agree to remit the question of reparations to a committee of experts chaired by the American banker Charles G. Dawes. This put forward its conclusions in April 1924: a provisional plan, valid for five years, which was adopted by the London conference in the summer of 1924 and notably reduced the reparations figure foreseen by the 1921 state of payments. As a result, the French government agreed to evacuate the

Ruhr in the summer of 1925, in exchange for guarantees about German disarmament.

Between November 1923, when France agreed to re-internationalise the problem of reparations (which eventually meant evacuating the Ruhr), and July 1926, when it signed treaties on debts with the United States and Britain, the country suffered from serious ministerial instability, which explains the time the settlement took.

At the end of August 1925 the French and the British finally agreed on the sum that France should pay to Britain, but the final accord, which included a suspension clause (in case of serious crisis) and a safeguard clause (if German reparations were not paid) was not reached until July 1926.

It took three more years (until July 1929) for these agreements to be ratified. During that time, the British press gave free reign to its irritation: 'France must pay.' It was only after a total of ten years' ceaseless debate that a definitive solution was found. In the summer of 1929 the Dawes Plan was replaced by the Young Plan (named after the American Owen D. Young), which fixed the payment of reparations until 1988, again reducing the total.

But the problem of reparations was not the only issue over which France and Britain were at odds. Throughout the 1920s, the question of security was omnipresent. Despite grand proclamations of faith in collective security, the League of Nations remained a frail institution. It was not universal (America was absent in particular), and it lacked armed forces to impose its decisions. It failed on what was thought to be its very *raison d'être*: the reduction of armaments. Britain's dislike of permanent commitments in continental Europe explained its refusal to go further in giving security guarantees to France. This, again, was a face-to-face clash.

The British wanted disarmament first. The French wanted security first. For the British, who were convinced that Germany was no longer a threat, disarmament would ensure lasting peace. The French, mistrustful and afraid of German revenge, believed that in the absence of any other valid guarantees of collective security their safety depended on the superiority of their army and the disarmament of Germany. The League of Nations tried to achieve collective security, but without great success. Outside the League, moreover, Britain and America organised the Washington Conference (November 1921–February 1922) to discuss disarmament. France managed, by the skin of its teeth, to prevent the conference from tackling land forces. However, on naval disarmament it found itself facing an Anglo-American common front that imposed a new hierarchy of naval powers in which it found itself reduced to the same level as Italy.

Britain sacrificed its own supremacy, accepting parity with the United States, but ensured its superiority over other European fleets.

On 27 September 1922, in the vain quest for collective security, the League of Nations adopted Resolution XIV, which made arms reduction conditional on a defensive agreement for mutual assistance. When such a treaty came up for discussion in 1923, the French and British points of view again clashed. The French insisted on security, the British on disarmament. British Prime Minister Ramsay MacDonald in particular thought it vital to lay down precisely the reduction of armaments. The failure of the treaty for mutual assistance was a body blow for the League.

To break the vicious circle of security and disarmament, could arbitration help? In September 1924 the Assembly of the League studied the draft presented by the Czechoslovak Foreign Minister Edvard Beneš of a 'Protocol for the Peaceful Settlement of International Disputes', which introduced a third option: obligatory arbitration. Under this system, all international disputes would be submitted either to the Permanent Court of International Justice or to arbitration. If one of the parties in the dispute refused this procedure, the Council of the League could by a two-thirds majority vote ask members of the League to apply sanctions. In exchange for this very powerful commitment on security, the states signing the Protocol pledged themselves to work for a reduction in armaments. If this was not achieved, the Protocol would become null and void. Was this at last a solution? The fact that Ramsay MacDonald and Édouard Herriot were in power at the same time was an opportunity to be seized. The Franco-British resolution was adopted unanimously on 2 October 1924. Ten states, including France, ratified the Protocol. But in November 1924 its British supporter Ramsay MacDonald was defeated in the general election. The Conservative government that succeeded him was against the project, and was confirmed in its hostility by the United States (which saw the Protocol as a new Holy Alliance), by the Dominions (which wanted no part of it), and by Mussolini's Italy (which held aloof). On 12 March 1925, in a statement to the Council of the League, the new foreign secretary, Austen Chamberlain, announced that Britain was rejecting the Protocol. This new conflict did considerable damage to the system of collective security. Yet from 1925 onwards France and Britain were no longer frontally opposed to each other, and from 1925 to 1929 there was even a certain convergence in their diplomacy. There were several reasons for this. Economic stability and prosperity had returned; Aristide Briand's long tenure of the French Foreign Ministry from 1925 to 1932 put a premium on the policy of conciliation, which pleased those in charge of the British Foreign Office; and the German policy of seeking moderate revision of the peace treaties, as pursued by Gustav Stresemann, coincided with Britain's inclination for political realism and its desire to avoid any new continental commitment. The British believed that they could thereby guarantee Germany's western frontiers and the demilitarisation of the left bank of the Rhine. But the Locarno Treaties clearly reflected contrasting points of view.

Unlike France, which saw the Treaties as a first step in organising security, the British saw them as its guarantee. Still, Locarno, became the symbol of peace, and in 1926 Germany was admitted to the League of Nations. Two years later, in a solemn declaration, the leading states in the world formally renounced the use of war. This was the Kellogg–Briand Pact of 27 March 1928. It seemed to make possible a peace relying on agreement by all the parties concerned, not on some form of *diktat*.

Was this the dawn of collective security? No, because the British still stubbornly opposed any guarantee of Western Europe's frontiers and would make no alliance with any other power. Disarmament, put back on the agenda by the League of Nations, was once again paralysed by Franco-British disagreement.

This divergence of views, as much on the sociological aspect of armaments as on how to disarm, in fact concealed a far deeper disagreement about the maintenance of peace in Europe after Versailles. For the British, arms were the direct cause of wars. To reduce armaments was to lessen the number of men able to fight. To place a direct limit on the weapons of war was to make war less possible, to delay its outbreak, and to prevent its prolongation. Disarmament meant security. For the French, it was insecurity that made defence and armaments necessary. Disarmament meant depriving peaceful nations of the weapons that would deter possible aggressors. This contrast between the British and French positions derived from a fundamental difference of attitude towards security. With the enemy defeated and the German fleet destroyed, Britain in its island shelter could not understand the need for security felt by continental nations, which seemed obsessive. Unlike the French, who felt insecure, the British believed that their own security had been ensured by victory, so they pressed for disarmament. True, British disarmament also reflected the need for economy, but it was based on assessment of the facts. In the Imperial Defence Committee, at the beginning of the 1920s, political leaders told the heads of the armed forces that they need not expect a major conflict for some ten years. As a result, the British army quickly demobilised and its numbers regularly diminished. The air force failed to modernise adequately and the Royal Navy accepted parity with the USA under the Washington agreements, as well as a general ceiling as agreed in London.

In practical terms, peace had to be secured by sanctions and by force. Were the Versailles Treaties to be revised? If so, a priority objective was disarmament, putting an end to military disparities. In addition, the pacifist tendencies shown by British public opinion, hostile to continental commitments perpetuating an unjust territorial settlement, confirmed British statesmen's reluctance to accept any binding obligations or to become the policemen of the League.

Two successive blows at the end of the 1920s brought an end to these peacemaking efforts. On 24 October 1929 – 'Black Thursday' – came the New York Stock Exchange crash and the beginning of the world economic crisis. In May 1930 the Briand Memorandum came before the League of Nations, embodying a proposal for European Union that its author had launched in September 1929. The majority voted against it. Among them, significantly, were the British. They rejected it because the Dominions did not wish to see Britain form part of such an association.

To sum up, there was scarcely any *entente cordiale* in the 1920s. On the eve of the terrible 1930s, there was defiance on both sides of the Channel. And in 1930, again, a British White Paper rejected the proposal of a Channel tunnel. This provoked a symptomatic lament from a French daily newspaper, *Le Journal*, on 11 June 1930: 'At the prospect of digging a modest tunnel under the sea, the British – although they are governed by socialists, pacifists, and internationalists – throw up their hands in horror. No, no, we prefer to remain in our splendid isolation! It's a little discouraging for those who believe in the inevitable onset of universal brotherhood.'

Maurice Vaïsse

Problems multiplied as the 1920s turned into the 1930s. Both France and Britain were shaken by the 1929 crash, but they reacted differently. And if they both, at first, misread Adolf Hitler's intentions, here too their responses were coloured by past experience.

The 1930s

Towards the end of the 1920s, even before the world economic crisis that began in 1929, the atmosphere in Europe grew gloomier and both Franco-British and Franco-German relations grew more tense. At the international conference in The Hague in August 1929, the British pressed Aristide Briand, against his will, to agree to early evacuation of the Rhineland, part of which was still occupied by the 'former Allies' under the Treaty of Versailles. This clearly revealed the divergence between Britain and France. British policy sought to restore Germany to the concert of Europe by gradually returning to it the rights withdrawn by the Treaty of Versailles, while French leaders were still mistrustful of Germany and were keen to retain the maximum guarantees of security, such as the occupation of the Rhineland. It was evacuated in 1930, but on the condition that it was permanently demilitarised.

In October 1929, in the United States, came the great economic crisis that affected all of Europe in the following months and years, and seriously troubled international relations in the 1930s. It struck Britain more rapidly than France, which until 1931 preserved the illusion of being an enclave of prosperity in the middle of Europe. The crisis impelled Britain to turn more towards its dominions and its empire, led France to accumulate a large stock of gold, and encouraged Germany to seek a privileged economic position in Central and Eastern Europe. It in no way incited the partners in the Entente Cordiale to draw closer to each other. German pressure towards Eastern Europe more and more ran counter to the interests of France, which had several allies in that region, notably Poland and Czechoslovakia, whereas Britain considered that Eastern Europe was not one of the areas in which it had interests.

At the beginning of the 1930s, France and Britain continued to disagree about disarmament and security. This was true of naval disarmament which was the subject of difficult negotiations before the Disarmament Conference. Britain wanted to extend the Washington Treaty of 1922 to all categories of naval vessel in order to maintain its superiority over other European fleets. France refused to accept limits on small ships and submarines and called for very large figures for global tonnage so as to maintain superiority over the Italian fleet in the Mediterranean. At the Naval Conference in London in the spring of 1930, there was no real agreement, and Briand more than once clashed with Ramsay MacDonald. In 1930–31, the British tried to reduce Franco–Italian naval rivalry while safeguarding their own interests, but the French navy (in general not Anglophile) resisted, and sought to preserve its autonomy and its unrestricted capacity to build more ships. Altogether, on the eve of the World Disarmament Conference, Franco-British relations were fairly tense. Disagreement on naval matters weighed heavily and helped discourage the British (who barely understood France's need for security) from backing French requests on land armaments in the Conference itself.

During the Conference, which began in Geneva in February 1932, Franco–British relations had their ups and downs. One of the essential issues was Germany and its future rights. Germany, which claimed it had disarmed, called for either equal rights or the disarmament of other nations. France was reluctant to reduce its own armaments, believing that Germany had not disarmed and was still a danger. Britain, meanwhile, continued to rely on its balance-of-power principle, which led it to support part of Germany's requests without making an enemy of France. French diplomats and negotiators at the Geneva conference were alarmed, and objected to Britain's acting as an arbiter between France and Germany. In the face of Germany's ever greater demands in the course of 1932, it was British pressure, backed by that of the American delegation, that in December led Édouard Herriot, French prime minister and foreign minister, to concede 'equal rights'. Part V of the Versailles Treaty was abrogated, and Germany obtained the *de facto* right to rearm if there was no disarmament agreement. A few weeks later, the French and the British found themselves dealing no longer with the Weimar Republic, but with Adolf Hitler, who became German chancellor in January 1933.

Hitler's coming to power did not immediately change all the elements of international relations – or, at least, the people concerned did not immediately realise the difference that it made. In Britain, the impression was that Hitler was no more than an exemplar of extremism such as had existed in German politics since Bismarck's time; sooner or later, it was thought, he would collide with a more moderate faction. In France, likewise, few people at first understood the true nature of the Nazi regime: there was little more mistrust of Hitler than there had been of the last leaders of the Weimar Republic. And in 1933, although France still enjoyed a position of strength *vis-à-vis* Germany, it neither stood firm against German demands nor undertook direct negotiations with the Third Reich. The lack of support from Britain was one reason for this policy vacuum, but not the only one.

Thus, when in October 1933 Germany quit the Disarmament Conference and the League of Nations, there was no coordinated Franco-British reaction. From then on, Germany could consider itself free to ignore international rules and rearm as it thought fit. Disarmament questions were not buried, however: part of Britain's diplomatic effort at the end of 1933 and the beginning of 1934 was aimed at ways to bind Germany in a Convention it could freely accept, combining limited rearmament for itself and a degree of disarmament by the other countries, notably France. In France, where Gaston Doumergue's government had come to power after the anti-parliamentary riots of 6 February 1934, Britain's January 1934 proposals were hotly debated. The diplomats of the Quay d'Orsay and their Minister Louis Barthou favoured the proposed Convention, which in their eyes would contain Germany within rules that it accepted, with a number of safeguards. But the majority of the government and most military leaders rejected the idea of an agreement that would rearm Germany and disarm France. In a celebrated Note of 17 April 1934, the French government declared that its priority was to ensure France's security and that it therefore refused Britain's proposals for a disarmament convention. This was indeed the end of all hopes of disarmament, even if a few attempts were later made by both France and Britain to relaunch the idea of a convention that would bind the various nations, Germany included.

France's rejection of Britain's proposals in April 1934, and differing views on how to deal with Germany, briefly disturbed the countries' bilateral relations. This was evident at Geneva in a number of clashes between French Foreign Minister Louis Barthou and British Foreign Secretary Sir John Simon. Barthou, who was anxious to affirm the autonomy of French foreign policy and no longer mainly to react to British initiatives as his predecessors had done, was nevertheless convinced that close relations with Britain were valuable, if not vital. He was therefore careful not to endanger them. Since Japan and Germany had left the League in 1933, and in the absence of the USA and the USSR (although the latter joined in September 1934, after French efforts half-supported by the British), the League's survival and its basic policy of collective security depended more than ever on Franco-British accord.

Another more general factor may help to explain the weakness of Franco-British relations in the first half of the 1930s. This was the difference between France's and Britain's political systems and leaders, which caused a degree of psychological alienation. Britain had a very stable political system. Ramsay MacDonald was in power from 1929 to 1935, first in a Labour government and then in a coalition. During those years most of Britain's leaders, beginning with the prime minister, were scarcely pro-French. In France, by contrast, governments succeeded one another rapidly, lasting between six months and a year. This led to a lack of thrust in foreign policy as in domestic affairs. After Briand's departure, there was instability also in the Ministry of Foreign Affairs. Between France and Britain there was sometimes mutual disdain, or at least a difference of perception: they did not always realise that in the face of German revisionism their national interests tallied. The British tended to scorn France's unstable governments, and at the beginning of the World economic crisis envied France's wealth, which contrasted with Britain's unemployment and hunger marches. The French reproached Britain for its balance-of-power policy, which was enabling Germany to recover elements of its power: they thought it was too easy for an island nation to underestimate the threat from Germany. What was more, the League of Nations, which worked largely thanks to Franco-British cooperation, was beginning to show signs of weakness. It failed to carry out Briand's plan for European union; it could not propose concerted remedies for the economic crisis; and it could not halt Japan's aggression against China (the Manchurian conflict, autumn 1931 to spring 1933).

In the mid-1930s, then, there was a general impasse in Franco-British relations. The various points of disagreement between France and Britain crystallised in 1935, one of the lowest points of the Entente. It was marked by three key events: Italy's war in Abyssinia, Hitlerite Germany's reestablishment of conscription in March, and the Anglo-German naval agreement in June. When Mussolini's Italy attacked independent Abyssinia, finally annexing it in 1936, France and Britain agreed on the basic principles of their response, but acted differently. They both held that the League of Nations should apply economic sanctions to Italy. But the France of Pierre Laval was less critical of Italy than were the British, all the more so because it felt threatened by Germany. So France was slow to decide on and then apply sanctions to Italy, because it was unwilling to alienate a neighbour that might support it in any conflict with Germany. (The year before, it had been Italy's firm reaction that had caused Hitler to withdraw from his attempted *Anschluss* with Austria; and the Rome–Berlin Axis was not formed until 1936.) British public opinion sided with the

League and with Abyssinia; and when in December 1935 Laval concocted with British Foreign Secretary Sir Samuel Hoare a secret agreement (the abortive Hoare–Laval Pact) to offer Italy a large part of Abyssinia, the British public was outraged and Hoare had to resign.

The Abyssinian war only indirectly concerned Germany, which was no longer a member of the League. But the attitudes of France and Britain *vis-à-vis* Germany influenced their reactions to Italy. Moreover, in so far as the war in Abyssinia tended to divide France and Britain, it served German interests. Britain at that time did not feel threatened by Germany, and without consulting France it even signed an Anglo-German naval agreement authorising Germany to have a fleet equal to 35 per cent of Britain's – in effect revoking the naval clauses of the Versailles Treaty. The French were shocked by this unilateral British action, which they regarded as contrary to the Entente Cordiale, and which gave Germany (now strengthened by a conscript army) advantages in exchange for no corresponding concessions.

Germany's remilitarisation of the Rhineland in March 1936 sparked off a crisis that showed how limited was France's and Britain's willingness to resist Hitler. France was weakened by the economic crisis; French public opinion was pervaded by pacificism and a kind of resignation; and the country was led by a transitional government. It was unwilling, therefore, to go to war in defence of the demilitarisation of the left bank of the Rhine, although this was one of the last guarantees of its security surviving from the Treaty of Versailles. The British, who felt less directly threatened by Germany's breach of the Treaty, made no attempt to encourage a firm reaction by the French. However, they reaffirmed their guarantee to France, although the Locarno Treaty was now superseded. Some French leaders later sought to invoke Britain's lack of support as a pretext for their own inaction, but it remains clear that France failed to take the chance to react when its security was directly threatened.

The second half of the 1930s was a crucial time for Franco-British relations. The two countries more and more clearly represented the democracies as against the Fascist and Nazi dictatorships, and gradually drew closer, becoming re-accustomed to the idea of going to war together if need be. But the process was slow, and its price was French acquiescence in the British policy of 'appeasement' – making further concessions to Germany – until the return to resoluteness in 1939. At the time of the Popular Front in France and the beginning of Neville Chamberlain's premiership in Britain, Franco-British relations were marked by the debate about appeasement. Should concessions be made to Hitler's demands, in order to deflect his lust for power towards Eastern Europe and delay any war with Germany (hoping even that this might make it impossible)? This was essentially Chamberlain's strategy in 1937–38. But for the British it was no great novelty. Offering concessions to Germany in the hope of reintegrating it in the European system and preventing the return of war had already been Britain's policy for several years before and after the advent of Hitler.

The improvement in Franco-British relations coincided with the period of the Popular Front in France. Léon Blum and Foreign Minister Yvon Delbos were very pro-British, and set out deliberately to reinforce the Entente Cordiale. They were encouraged by senior Foreign Ministry officials, notably Secretary-General Alexis Léger (the poet Saint-John Perse), a famous Anglophile. And on the British side Anthony Eden, foreign secretary from December 1935 to February 1938, was more open to French views than his predecessors Simon and Hoare. To strengthen cross-Channel links, French leaders had to tune in to British preoccupations. It was very largely to avoid a clash with Britain – and also to avoid too serious internal dissensions – that the Popular Front government adopted (and had Britain endorse) the policy of non-intervention in the Spanish Civil War. Blum's first impulse would have been to help the Spanish Republicans more directly, in particular when Germany and Italy, above all, were openly intervening on the side of General Franco. The Spanish Civil War was an important moment in the confrontation between democracies and dictatorships in Europe, with a third power – the Soviet Union – giving more and more massive aid to the Republicans and no doubt hoping that any future conflict would be confined to the Western part of Europe.

When Germany annexed Austria in March 1938, neither France nor Britain reacted – France because it once more had a weak transitional government and because Austria was not one of its Central European allies; Britain because appeasement was then its deliberate policy and because it did not wish to be involved in Central and Eastern Europe, where it had always avoided any commitments or alliances.

But it was the Czechoslovak crisis that really tested the power of the Entente to resist Hitler's demands. In 1938, the German chancellor called more and more insistently for the Sudeten Germans to be attached to the Third Reich. This would seriously weaken Czechoslovakia, then France's only reliable ally in Central Europe. The crisis grew throughout most of 1938 and although former British ministers such as Winston Churchill and Anthony Eden urged the government to stand firm, their words had no effect. Chamberlain was then the driving force within the Entente, and despite French reservations he would not be deflected from his strategy of appeasing Hitler to prevent war. On the French side, in any case, there was no firm determination to defend Czechoslovakia by force of arms. The leaders were divided. Foreign Minister Georges Bonnet was reluctant to see France go to war in Central Europe and did his best to dilute French pledges, despite the clearest warning from the Quai d'Orsay. At the Munich conference at the end of September 1938, Hitler secured British and French agreement to annexe the Sudetenland, promising that this would be his last territorial demand. On his return from Munich, Chamberlain was satisfied that he had prevented war, and the public in both Britain and France breathed a sigh of relief. But French Prime Minister Édouard Daladier, although he had been unable to resist Hitler backed by Mussolini, not to mention the tactics of Chamberlain, saw matters more clearly. He knew very well that Hitler would not stop there, and he was not very proud of himself.

Between 1936 and 1938 the French took a line that could be roughly summarised as: follow Britain's tactics and leave it the initiative in dealing with Hitler; act as the junior partner in the Entente, in part because of admitted weakness; partially withdraw from Central Europe, but promote French rearmament and gradually coax the British into a stronger alliance and an acceptance that Britain and France would again have to make war, together, against Germany. During these years both France and Britain practised appeasement, but even within each country the leaders were not always agreed on what appeasement meant. Chamberlain's version stemmed from an explicit political decision no longer to be drawn into a policy of alliances that might replicate the situation before 1914. At the same time, he and other British devotees of appeasement had not perhaps taken the measure of Hitler's ambitions: the British prime minister took a long time to realise that Hitler was 'not a gentleman'. And while certain British diplomatists and politicians called for firmness, they could not effectively block Chamberlain's policy.

The French policy of appeasement was not the same. Some political leaders thought France might rely on its empire and interests in the Western Mediterranean, leaving Germany the predominant role in Eastern Europe. Lack of support from Britain could then be used as a pretext for inaction there. Others knew that Hitler dreamed of dominating the whole of Europe, but they also knew that France was not ready to wage war and must gain time to rearm and to strengthen its links with Britain and perhaps with the Soviet Union. And Daladier, although he had few illusions about Hitler's aims, had not abandoned the idea of a direct understanding between France and Germany.

So the classic image of France's 'British governess' at the end of the 1930s needs to be modified, because by following the British line the French were nevertheless pursuing interests of their own. In certain cases, indeed, they diverged from the British line. In 1937–38, for example, they refused rapprochement with Italy, which they found more and more aggressive towards them, whereas Anglo-Italian reconciliation was one of Chamberlain's great objectives.

After Munich, there were direct Anglo-German and Franco-German talks. For some time, Chamberlain went on pursuing appeasement. But Franco-British relations soon evolved more and more clearly towards a true alliance. Above all, when Germany annexed the rest of Bohemia and Italy attacked Albania (March–April 1939), French and British leaders became convinced that conflict was inevitable and appeasement no longer made sense. France and Britain actively rearmed, strengthened their military cooperation and gave guarantees to countries under threat from Germany. On the other hand, they failed in their talks with Moscow to establish a Franco-British-Soviet alliance – as was shown when the Soviet Union signed its non-aggression pact with Germany on 23 August 1939. When World War II broke out, Franco-British relations had wholly recovered from their low point in 1935–36. The Entente had become an alliance. The two nations had at last realised that Hitler's ambitions meant enslavement for all of continental Europe and a threat to the interests – and the very existence – of Britain, despite the protection of the Channel. Franco-British military cooperation was not flawless, and those in charge did not always agree on every strategic option, but much was put in place more rapidly than in World War I. In 1939–40, until Franco-British relations were broken off by the fall of France, they were much stronger than they had ever been since the Treaty of Versailles.

Raphaële Ulrich-Pier

V
World War II, 1939–45

The fall of France in 1940 was itself a source of Franco-British friction. The military evacuation from Dunkirk rescued 140,000 French troops as well as 200,000 British, but Churchill refused to throw into the Battle of France the aircraft he was saving for the Battle of Britain; and the legend grew, nurtured by Vichy propaganda, that the British had abandoned the French. Robert Merle's novel *Weekend à Zuydcoote* and Ian McEwan's *Atonement* give significantly different pictures of Dunkirk.

A month after Dunkirk, the French naval commander at Mers el-Kebir in the Gulf of Oran, Algeria, refused the British ultimatum that his fleet should resist, be neutralised, or be scuttled in port. The Vichy government had in fact vowed not to let the Axis powers use it. But the British attacked, putting out of action three French capital ships and killing 1,300 French seamen. Churchill later called this 'a hateful decision, the most unnatural and painful in which I have ever been involved'. One British historian, Alan Palmer, even believed that it 'marked the end of the Entente Cordiale'. It did not – any more than the British and Free French attack on Dakar that September, which met unexpected Vichy resistance and, on Churchill's orders, had to be called off.

Other crises marked relations between Britain and Free France during World War II. That they were surmounted was much to the credit of two proud, stubborn, far-sighted nationalists: Charles de Gaulle and Winston Churchill. Before the war ended, each had to come to terms with the United States.

France and Britain 1940–43

Relations between the British and the Free French, from 1940 to 1943, have a very special place in the history of France and Britain during World War II.

Before – and above all after – General de Gaulle's appeal on 18 June 1940, a key question arose: what was to be done about the thousands of French soldiers and sailors who were then in Britain? They included a Light Alpine Division withdrawn from Norway, wounded servicemen rescued from Dunkirk, the crews of ships driven from their home ports by the German advance, and individual volunteers who were daily arriving from France.

Once the Vichy government had signed the Armistice on 22 June, the British government offered a choice to all these French nationals: to join General de Gaulle or to be repatriated to France. If any pressure was used, it was certainly not in favour of the Free French – as witness a speech made to veterans of the Norwegian campaign by two colonels sent to Trentham Park by the War Office: 'You are completely free to serve under General de Gaulle. But we have to tell you, man to man, that if you decide to do so, you will be rebels against your own government.'

That said, once the choice had been made, the Free French were welcomed with exemplary generosity and simplicity. The same was true, overseas, for the civilian and military personnel of the colonies who in July and August 1940 chose to continue the war in Oceania, Equatorial Africa and Cameroon, at a time when the British Empire stood alone against Nazi Germany.

In the fighting units of the three services, combat alongside our allies rapidly formed real fraternity between the French and the British; this feeling was so solid and natural that it was unaffected by the often difficult relationship between Churchill and de Gaulle.

In this connection, consideration of Bir Hakeim is revealing. We know what powerful resonance the British media gave to this battle in June 1942: military communiqués published in the press and on the radio, wide publicity for the admiring messages sent from all over the world, leaflets dropped over occupied France. And the First Free French Division, which had been badly mauled, was fully re-equipped in less than three months. Yet, meanwhile, de Gaulle and Churchill were openly at odds over Madagascar.

A year later, the British Eighth Army, which had linked up in Tunisia with the Americans who had landed in North Africa six months before, included in its ranks two famous Free French units – the First DFL and Leclerc Column. Free French relations with General Giraud's troops were cool, to say the least. But the British high command never let the Free French feel its government's pressure on de Gaulle to come to terms with Giraud. Out of respect for their comrades in arms, as well as out of discretion, the British military authorities preferred to keep well out of a Franco-French problem.

Understandably, the special relationship between the British and the Free French survived the war. In 1958, after General de Gaulle had returned to power, he made Winston Churchill the last of the *Compagnons de la Libération*.

Pierre Messmer

Churchill and France

In the course of Churchill's 90-year span my calculations show that he spent an ascertainable 1,447 days, or just under four years, in France. And this is probably a mild underestimate, with a few lesser visits slipping through my net. It was a formidable total for anyone who was never domiciled or who never owned a residence there. (It contrasts with a total of under 400 days, despite his several extended lecture tours and frequent wartime visits to Roosevelt, spent in the United States.)

The French periods were reasonably spread over much of his life, although with a strong element of 'back-end loading'. When World War II broke out his score was 668 days. During the five and a half years of hostilities he added only another 30, with an obvious gap between the fall of France in June 1940 and the opening of the Second Front four years later. During the six years between Churchill's lost election of July 1945 and the end of his second government nearly ten years later his French score was 140 days. And then in the subsiding last decade of his life it soared to 609 days.

The strength of Churchill's Francophilia, however, rests on many factors other than the statistics of his visits. It was not exactly a love affair based on linguistic affinity. Churchill's extraordinary French was notorious. There is room for doubt about whether he actually said to de Gaulle: 'Si vous m'obstaclerez, je vous liquiderai', but the threat, even if legendary, illustrates a corner of the truth. There is also the testimony of Sir Eric Phipps, British ambassador to Paris in 1938, who, after Churchill had descended on the embassy for a couple of days of intensive discussions with French politicians of nearly all shades, wrote to the foreign secretary (Halifax): 'His French is most strange and at times incomprehensible . . .

You will get a most eloquent first-hand account of this hectic and electric week-end from its brilliant animator . . .'

Yet Churchill's French was not quite as bad as these two references suggest. There is considerable evidence that he could mostly say what he wanted to with a forceful idiosyncrasy. And, sensibly, as he could not achieve a smooth command of either grammar or idiom, he exaggerated the idiosyncrasy in order to give his strangled phrases more force. Furthermore, he rather enjoyed launching into his own version of French, and certainly did not belong to that category of Englishmen who believe in the duty of all foreigners to accommodate themselves to Anglo-Saxon monolingualism. He did not, however, extend this tolerance more widely. French was the only foreign language he ever attempted to embrace.

Most of his time in France was spent in the pursuit of pleasure rather than of politics. And this self-indulgence mostly took place in Anglo-American houses where the culture (or the language) was hardly Gallic. Nevertheless, Churchill's attitude to France was never that of those British 1920s and 1930s *aficionados* of the Riviera who regarded it purely as a place of sojourn and took little more notice of its natives than did Churchill himself of those of Morocco in his later long visits to Marrakesh. The faith that the British governing class reposed in the highly uncertain winter climate of the Côte d'Azur during those decades was quite remarkable. Even such naturally insular figures as Bonar Law were frequently there, while those who saw themselves as more cosmopolitan, such as Lloyd George, F. E. Smith, Rothermere and Beaverbrook, crowded into the grand hotels of Monte Carlo, Nice and Cannes. It was nearly all done in December, January and February, largely I suppose because the more reliably sunny and warmer winter resorts of North Africa and the West Indies were then too difficult to get to. Churchill was a semi-detached part of this migratory tribe. He liked Riviera life, but not until, in his ninth decade, he subsided into a sybaritic cocoon did he like it to be too Anglocentric. Most of his fellow countrymen, when they stepped sedately out of the *wagon-lits* of the *Train Bleu* at Cannes or Nice, never spoke to a Frenchman who was not a servant or a waiter. Churchill, on the contrary, maintained a lively contact with French politicians, generals and even painters. He liked the corridors of power in Paris as much as he did the sun and the casinos of the Côte.

In September 1935, for example, he made a complicated journey in order to spend twenty-four hours at the house of Pierre-Etienne Flandin in his constituency of the Yonne. He got out of his north-bound sleeping car in Dijon at 7.30 on a Sunday morning and was driven sixty miles into the Burgundy countryside. The conversation did not prove satisfactory, but then Flandin was not a satisfactory man. Churchill for a time reposed an excessive faith in him, and when he was placed on trial as an alleged collaborationist after the war, Churchill supplied a written testimony in his favour and his son Randolph attended the trial to give oral evidence. Flandin was acquitted.

A more satisfactory occasion was at the beginning of April 1940, when Churchill went to Paris as First Lord of the Admiralty, and in an interval between talks with Reynaud, who had just taken over from Daladier as prime minister, had General Alphonse Georges, a major figure in the French army, to luncheon at Laperóuse, the then highly regarded restaurant on the Quai Grands-Augustins. General Louis Spears, a British general but strongly Francophile and francophone, was of the party. 'That lunch *à trois*', he subsequently wrote, 'remains in my mind as one of the few pleasant occasions I experienced during the war. We were three friends enjoying each other's company and remarkable food and wine. Georges was tranquil, gay and confident.'

These diversions stemmed from Churchill's view, for at least the greater part of his life, of the centrality of France. From the time that he attended the French army's early autumn manoeuvres in Champagne in 1907 (even though he had been to the German ones in Silesia in 1906) he was imbued with an almost mystical view, which might be described as a mixture of Péguy and the Napoleonic, of the qualities of that force. It showed itself during his relatively brief (November 1915 to April 1916) experience in the trenches of World War I, when one of his favourite pieces of accoutrement was a *bleuâtre* French poilu's helmet, partly because he so disliked the glengarry which, when out of the trenches, he should have worn as a lieutenant-colonel commanding a battalion of the Royal Scots Fusiliers. Still more dramatically did this sentiment display itself when, in March 1933, with disarmament very much *à la mode*, he shocked the House of Commons by suddenly proclaiming: 'Thank God for the French army.' This faith was to be sadly shattered in the devastating first five weeks of his premiership. Early on the morning of 15 May 1940, Churchill was telephoned by a deeply agitated Prime Minister Reynaud (one of the French ministers whom he most respected) and told in effect that France was defeated. The record of this conversation reads: 'the road to Paris was open and the battle was lost. He [Reynaud] even talked about giving up the struggle.'

This brought to an abrupt end the weekend honeymoon Churchill had enjoyed after at last reaching (at the age of 65) his long sought-after goal of 10 Downing Street. It opened up for him two appalling dilemmas, which were to dominate the next two months. The first was whether he was to throw every possible resource into keeping France in the war and not thinking beyond to the consequences if that effort failed. And the second, when France had fallen, was how ruthless he was to be in neutralising the considerable French naval strength rather than run the risk of it falling into the arms of the Germans and gravely weakening Britain's position at sea.

These dilemmas were made much worse for Churchill by his having a greater emotional investment in the alliance with France and a great initial faith in the French army than almost any other British politician. Although Churchill is often thought of as the last Victorian imperialist in British politics, with his outlook permanently influenced by his years as a cavalry subaltern in India around the time of the Queen's Diamond Jubilee, this simplicity contains more falsehood than truth. In the first place he was, and remained, much more of an Edwardian than a Victorian. But second, and more important, he was far more Eurocentric than was either Neville Chamberlain, his immediate predecessor as prime minister, or Edward Halifax, who could have had the prime minister's job had he wished for it, and was still a powerfully placed foreign secretary. These two had in common an instinctive insularity somewhat balanced by different experiences and concepts of empire: Chamberlain by early attempts to grow sisal on a West Indian island, and Halifax by five years as Viceroy of India. Churchill's holiday habits, fortified by the five years he had spent writing his four-volume life of his great ancestor, John, first Duke of Marlborough, as well as his natural tastes and thought patterns, made continental Europe, and above all France, stand, together with Britain, at the centre of the world for him. This was a crucial fault line in the excoriating dispute with Halifax and to some extent with Chamberlain (the only two Conservatives other than himself in his small War Cabinet) that spread over five concentrated meetings of that body at the end of May. Halifax, an honourable but pessimistic Christian gentleman, wanted to explore the possibilities of a peace that, while it would mean Nazi dominance in Europe, might leave Britain to live quietly beyond the Channel rather as Spain was left to do beyond the Pyrenees.

To Churchill such a view was utterly repugnant. He saw no prospect of peace or security for Britain with a Nazi-dominated Europe. But that did not ease his dilemma of whether to denude Britain of the fighter squadrons that were to secure the vital draw in the Battle of Britain in the probably vain hope of saving France. This issue dominated his six visits to the French government (to ever more westerly rendezvous) between 16 May and 13 June. He resolved it not by throwing everything in, but by trying to give just enough to keep up French spirits. It is not difficult to see how differently things must have looked to French eyes. The British had only ten divisions deployed against the Germans. The French had 103, yet we were constantly urging them to show more fighting spirit while hoarding air resources that might have partially compensated for the imbalance on the ground.

With hindsight Churchill must be judged right, even though it was not obvious at the time. From that Reynaud telephone call onwards he envisaged the possibility, even the probability, of the worst in France, and was determined that Britain should fight on alone. His worst-case scenario was that it was better that we should 'each of us die choking in his own blood' than surrender. His best-case scenario was not that Britain could win on its own, but that we could hold out until 'in God's good time the new world, with all its power and might, steps forward to the rescue and liberation of the old'.

The second dilemma, after the Armistice of 18 June was what to do about the French fleet. This led to the notorious action at Oran on 3 July and a separate air attack on the *Richelieu* at Dakar a few days later. At Oran 1,299 French sailors were killed and another 350 wounded, with a legacy of understandable and lasting resentment in France. It cannot be said that the problem was brilliantly handled. At the other end of the Mediterranean Admiral Cunningham, later to be the key British naval figure of the war, managed things better. He secured the surrender of one battleship and four cruisers, three of them modern, without firing a shot. At Oran, on the other hand, not only were too many shots fired but the 'victory' was very partial. One French battleship was blown up and another ran aground, but the third, although damaged, made the safety (from the British) of Toulon, accompanied by three cruisers. As a result there was a hobbling rather than a secure neutralisation of the French navy. But there were huge paradoxes in the outcome. No ship of the French navy was ever used against the British, even when, in 1942, the Germans occupied the whole of France, including Toulon. So, in a sense, the whole operation, quite apart from its damaging impact upon French opinion, was otiose. Yet it had two external benefits for Churchill. When he announced the operation to the House of Commons on 4 July he was better received on the hitherto sullen pro-Chamberlain Conservative benches than he had ever been previously. And the Americans, including Roosevelt, were apparently convinced for the first time that Britain really did intend to fight on.

Interlaced with these events was the first phase of Churchill's tangled relations with de Gaulle. He first encountered him on 9 June when de Gaulle, having just become under-secretary for defence, came to London as an envoy of Reynaud. General de Gaulle was only a two-star general but the military title quickly became almost as much a part of his name as it did of his contemporary but not often enthusiastic ally in Washington, General Marshall. They next met at Briare, which had become the temporary French military and political headquarters, on 11 June. De Gaulle made a strongly favourable impression upon Churchill. He stood out for confident defiance, in contrast not only with Marshal Pétain, but also with several other faltering French ministers. He appeared as a lofty island of calm resolution sticking up out of a sea of defeatist confusion.

There was a third occasion in London five days after Briare, when de Gaulle was engaged in putting together, in association with Halifax and Vansittart from the British Foreign Office and, on the French side, Corbin, René Pleven (the very experienced ambassador in London twice to be prime minister in the early 1950s) and Jean Monnet, the founding father of the European Community, the amazing confection of an Anglo-French union. For Charles de Gaulle, who was subsequently, in both war and peace, to be seen as the symbol and sword of unnegotiable French sovereignty, it was an extraordinary venture with which to be involved. It was a sign of desperation on both sides of the Channel. In retrospect it is difficult to decide which was the more preposterous: the presumption that the disparate and complex mechanisms of the British and French states could be successfully put together in a document of barely 300 words, or the utterly heterogeneous nature of the group of men who put it together. (Or for that matter why it was not shot down in the British War Cabinet by Attlee or Chamberlain, who were both normally good at pricking hot-air balloons.) And to complete the improbability of the exercise it was de Gaulle who conveyed the offer by telephone to the French government in Bordeaux. There it badly misfired. Most ministers saw it as an attempt to turn France into an appendage of the British Empire – a more contiguous New Zealand.

Whether Churchill ever had his heart in, as opposed to giving his acquiescence to, this half-baked proposal cannot be ascertained. What is certain, however, is that when de Gaulle decisively left France and arrived in England on 17 June, just catching the departing aeroplane of General Spears, he landed on a considerable store of Churchillian goodwill. Churchill was insistent, against the caution of Halifax, that the general be allowed immediately to broadcast to France; within ten days he both recognised him and gave him a generous subsidy, and he had him to a mixture of Downing Street luncheons and to Chequers weekends during the remainder of that summer. Churchill–de Gaulle relations were soon to plunge heavily downhill, beginning with the failed Dakar invasion in late

September, for which failure endemically bad security among the Free French was given much of the blame, and they reached very low points between 1941 and 1944.

Nevertheless, one of the general's persistent underlying strengths in Churchill's often sentimental eyes (except when either irritation or high policy dictated the reverse) was that de Gaulle held in his mind a small corner of the sacred myth of that 1940 summer, at once desperate and magical. It was also, for the moment, underpinned by de Gaulle's taking almost as supportive a view about the aggression of Oran as Churchill did about the failure of Dakar.

There were two other longer-term features at work. With every subsequent wartime year that went by the almost unknown and presumptuous two-star general of 1940 became the national leader of 1942, 1943 and 1944. In the second half of the war de Gaulle could not have been jettisoned without the most appalling consequences for the French internal resistance movement. Also, maybe, Churchill increasingly came to apprehend, reluctantly, that for all de Gaulle's tiresome pirouetting on a slender power base, he was genuinely a great man, the greatest statesman in Western Europe apart from himself.

There were considerable countervailing forces. De Gaulle could not get on with Roosevelt and was anathema to his secretary of state, Cordell Hull. And Churchill never hesitated to make it clear, as I suppose sense if not tact dictated, that in the second half of the war Roosevelt was at least ten times as important to him as was de Gaulle. Even given this basic reality he did not handle de Gaulle as well as he might have done. His summoning of the general on 4 June 1944 to come a thousand miles from Algiers to London and then another eighty to join Churchill (and Eden and Ernest Bevin) in his railway train behind Portsmouth, and there to be given forty hours' notice of the Anglo-American invasion of his country, was not a notable act of assuagement. (In fact, because of a postponement dictated by the weather, he was lucky that it was forty and not sixteen.) Both Eden and Bevin were shocked by Churchill's treatment of de Gaulle on that occasion, and it was indeed the case that one of Eden's wisest and most courageous policies as foreign secretary was to resist in the latter stages of the war the persistent anti-de Gaulle bias that came from Washington, and even from 10 Downing Street.

In November 1944, Churchill fulfilled a 1940 commitment to de Gaulle that 'one day we'll go down the Champs Élysées together'. On the twenty-sixth anniversary of the 1918 Armistice Day parade he and de Gaulle did precisely that. It was a curious occasion, out of which neither came especially well. De Gaulle strode down in his familiar general's informal uniform – no polished top boots, no 'scrambled eggs' peak to his *képi* of the sort that was much favoured by most French generals of the defeat – but he nevertheless physically upstaged Churchill, who ambled along in the heavy overcoat of an RAF air commodore, which he most curiously favoured at the time (it did not suit him, and Clementine a couple of years later justifiably pointed out that she thought that 'air-force uniform except when worn by the air crews is rather bogus'). As a result de Gaulle won the *concours d'élégance*, but Churchill won the character prize. He looked benign. De Gaulle looked sour, which stemmed from his not liking to share occasions.

As the war came to an end Churchill fought hard and successfully to secure for France (which at the time meant de Gaulle) both an occupation zone in Germany and a permanent seat on the United Nations Security Council. At least part of his motive was fear that, with American forces gone home, there would be no countervailing power between Russia and the English Channel. De Gaulle in his brief period of early peacetime office had no opportunity, and perhaps no wish, to revenge himself upon Churchill for the insults he felt he had received during the war. If he did exact any revenge it was in his second period of power and upon Churchill's successors, Macmillan and Wilson, by vetoing, first in 1963 and then in 1967, their applications for Britain to join the Six. Between the two vetoes de Gaulle dutifully came to London for Churchill's funeral.

In the nearly ten years between his final retirement from the premiership and his death Churchill visited France more intensively than ever before. In most years he clocked up between two and three months there. Even when he had ceased to paint he loved the strong light of Provence and the indulgent meals. Even when just sitting and dozing he preferred to do it on the Côte d'Azur than almost anywhere else in the world. But he had become only a sybaritic visitor. During this decade, he saw neither de Gaulle nor any other French politician to speak of. He even effectively gave up talking his extraordinary French. He was just an old, rich, famous Englishman abroad.

Roy Jenkins

Franco-British Union

For Britain, 1940 was the year the 'phoney war' ended and the real war began. For some Frenchmen (including the young François Truffaut), it was the year the war seemed to end. But it was also the year when two visceral nationalists – Winston Churchill and Charles de Gaulle – espoused 'real, complete, immediate and enduring unity' between France and Britain.

The words, like so many innovations, came from the fertile, practical imagination of Jean Monnet, then head of the London-based Anglo-French Co-ordinating Committee and later to be the main founding father of the European Union. In one sense, his idea was far from new. Various similar notions had been floated since the beginning of the war.

In September 1939, Arnold Toynbee of the Royal Institute of International Affairs (Chatham House) had suggested Franco-British union to his French counterparts. Some of them had responded, notably in March and April 1940, when a number of papers and articles had appeared in newspapers ranging from *La Dépêche de Toulouse* and *Le Petit Parisien* to *L'Ordre* and *L'Époque*. Meanwhile, Chatham House, after discussions with officials from the Political Intelligence Department of the Foreign Office, had produced a draft 'Act of Perpetual Association', envisaging the joint conduct of foreign relations, the joint control of economic resources for defence, further association between military forces, further economic cooperation, and some measure of reciprocal citizenship. The British government had actually set up a committee under Lord Hankey to study post-war cooperation with France, and Foreign Secretary Lord Halifax had put to it a draft prepared on 22 April by the outspoken federalist Lionel Curtis. This had proposed a single Franco-British Parliament controlling a Joint Executive responsible for defence and foreign policy, with its own financial resources levied from the national incomes of Britain and France.

It would be tempting to see Monnet's 1940 proposal as stemming from these ideas. They no doubt contributed to making it seem feasible. But it sprang in fact from his own frustrating experience of trying to coordinate the French and British economic war efforts. In February 1940 he had declared in a private memorandum: 'Not only are the two countries "integrated" because their actions can only be pursued together, but their decisions can only usefully be taken as joint decisions.' In Britain he had several times lobbied Prime Minister Neville Chamberlain; in general terms, wrote Monnet later, 'he was receptive'. In France, one echo was a proposal by Pierre Cot, the air minister, for an Inter-allied Economic General Staff. And on 28 March the Allied Supreme War Council, on which Paul Reynaud had just succeeded Édouard Daladier as French prime minister, undertook that neither country would make a separate peace and that both would maintain 'a community of action in all spheres' of postwar reconstruction. But at that time, everyone – including Monnet himself – was still thinking only of 'joint action'.

The Nazi invasion of Belgium and the Netherlands on 10 May 1940, outflanking the Maginot Line, changed all that. As the Panzer divisions roared through France, as 338,226 troops (a third of them French) were rescued from Dunkirk, and as the threat of a separate peace loomed larger, 'joint action' began to mean for Monnet what he proposed to Churchill on 6 June: a merger of French and British air power, in effect throwing the RAF into the Battle of France.

Churchill ignored Monnet's advice – and Paul Reynaud's pleas for more air support. 'Twenty-five fighter squadrons', said Churchill, 'must be maintained at all costs for the defence of Britain, and nothing would make us give them up.' Hindsight makes the decision seem wise. The French air force, it turned out later, was not using all its aircraft; and with morale and organisation both defective, the fall of France was not to be long delayed.

But at the time the issue was less clear-cut. With battle raging in France, Britain's attitude seemed unduly cool. In the first week of June, there was still no certainty that France would make a separate peace. If it did, many doubted, especially in France, whether Britain could survive alone.

So, as Monnet wrote in his *Memoirs* a generation later, 'we were led to raise our sights and try to recover on the political level the control of events that was escaping us in the field'. With help from his colleagues Arthur Salter and René Pleven, from Chamberlain and his private secretary Horace Wilson, from the prime minister's security adviser Desmond Morton, from the PUS at the Foreign Office Sir Robert Vansittart, and from a none the less sceptical General de Gaulle, he persuaded Churchill to put the idea to the War Cabinet – which approved it.

That the approval came too late, that it clashed with Britain's earlier permission for Reynaud to make a separate peace, and that Monnet's last-minute mission to Bordeaux failed to prevent the French armistice are all matters of regretful record. What remains extraordinary is that *in extremis* both de Gaulle and Churchill were willing to propose that 'France and Great Britain shall no longer be two nations, but one Franco-British Union', and that 'every citizen of France will enjoy immediately citizenship of Great Britain' and 'every British subject will become a citizen of France.' They were not idealists like Arnold Toynbee or Lionel Curtis. They were not long-term visionaries like Monnet. They were practical men in an overwhelming crisis. To keep France in the war with its fleet and its empire, they were prepared to think what even now, to many, seems unthinkable: a merger of sovereignty far more radical than the European Union has ever proposed.

Richard Mayne

Franco-British Union: A Personal View

Ententes between peoples are based on meetings between people who understand each other. The tandem of Winston Churchill and Charles de Gaulle, the most unusual and also the most symbolic in all World War II, began with a meeting, then an instant attraction, followed by a passionate engagement, a hasty wedding and a stormy marriage, to end in an old couple forever linked by history. Everyone knows the facts. Let us recall the dates.

On 10 May 1940, when that morning Hitler's armies had invaded Holland and Belgium, King George VI summoned Churchill and entrusted him with the government of the United Kingdom. Churchill was an old hand at politics, whose career had had its ups and downs: he was known for his eloquence, his energy and his unruly, jovial, moody character. It was the first time he had been prime minister, a post he had coveted all his life. In a very few days, he would find that the weight of the world had fallen on his shoulders.

On 6 June, when the French armies were being pushed back on all fronts and the enemy was advancing on Paris, French Prime Minister Paul Reynaud appointed Charles de Gaulle secretary of state for war. A recently promoted brigadier-general, de Gaulle had virtually imposed himself on Reynaud. He was not yet fifty. An officer of recognised quality, but curt and haughty, he had proved his strategic abilities in battle. Although few had read his writings, and the French High Command had rejected his theories of mechanised warfare, their value had been shown by the use that the German High Command had made of them. He had practically no political experience. He had quarrelled with Marshal Pétain, with whom he had once served, and his relations with General Maxime Weygand, Foch's former second-in-command, were no better: Weygand thought he was a greenhorn.

On 9 June, de Gaulle went to London. He wanted to make direct contact with the British government and General Staff. Churchill received him in the afternoon, in the Cabinet Room at 10 Downing Street. Those present were struck by the contrast between the two men. Churchill was restless, striding up and down on one side of the table; de Gaulle sat on the other, stiff and motionless. Their conversation, with Churchill speaking his own very personal brand of

French, was cordial, but nothing of capital importance was said. De Gaulle assured Churchill that 'the French government was determined to continue the struggle by every means in its power', which was a little optimistic. Churchill confirmed that some British divisions could be sent to France towards the end of the month, before a larger number were ready by the beginning of 1941. But at present he could not agree to extra air support, and he gave a curious arithmetical demonstration to show that, far from its bases, the RAF lost as many aircraft as the enemy planes it destroyed, whereas at Dunkirk, closer to home, it shot down four for every loss and, above British soil, six.

The instant attraction took place on 11 June at the Château du Muguet near Briare on the Loire, where the French government had taken refuge amid the *débâcle*. It was the fourth time that Churchill had come to France at that time, in great danger, at first without air escort, then protected by a few Spitfires, while the *Luftwaffe* roamed French skies.

The atmosphere at this Supreme War Council was sombre. While Churchill tried with pathetic eloquence to revive energy and hope, the faces around him showed every variety of confusion, despondency and resignation. Weygand spoke only of leaving Paris as an open city, and Pétain already envisaged an armistice. Only the tall young general showed real determination to continue the fight, and a certain scorn for the spiritual collapse around him. At lunch, Churchill asked him to sit next to him. He had recognised in him a man of his own character, with the same obstinate passion. Different as they might be, there was natural affinity between them. They had hit it off, so to speak, and their destinies were henceforth to be linked.

Their engagement was celebrated, not without haste, in London on 16 June. In the days before that, the French government, the assemblies and the civil service had installed themselves in Bordeaux, the capital city of defeat. It was crowded with refugees seeking board and lodging. In place of authority there was nothing but panic, abandonment, gossip and plots.

De Gaulle was disgusted. Thank heavens Mandel had persuaded him not to resign! He decided to go back and see Churchill to tell him about the latest plans being mooted: resistance in the Brittany 'redoubt', or shipping the government to North Africa. Above all he wanted Churchill to press Paul Reynaud to resist the partisans of an immediate armistice.

Setting out on 15 June, he drove north through France via Rennes and Brest, where he embarked in an anti-torpedo boat that took him to Plymouth, from where he reached London on the morning of 16 June. He saw French Ambassador Charles Corbin and Jean Monnet, head of the Coordinating Committee. They, and especially Monnet, called for a major initiative that would impress public opinion and revive people's courage. A plan had been ready for several days: it would proclaim total union between Britain and France.

Jean Monnet was an imaginative originator but, although he embraced the plan, he was not the first to think of it. Who was? A few months earlier, in March, Jean Giraudoux had talked with the historian Arnold Toynbee about 'an Act of Perpetual Association'. Several people had been involved, including no doubt Corbin and René Pleven, and above all Sir Robert Vansittart of the Foreign Office.

At all events, Monnet had the note in his pocket. De Gaulle did not reject it. As things were, he was ready to grasp at any resource. And it was he alone, Monnet assured him, who could convince Churchill.

It was over lunch with Churchill at the Carlton Club that de Gaulle proposed what Eric Roussel has called 'one of the most Utopian texts in history'. What was extraordinary was that Churchill accepted it, and that these two exacting patriots, both deep-rooted nationalists, agreed on a plan that would totally merge their two countries.

De Gaulle, whose motherland had been invaded, really had only one idea: to continue the struggle no matter where, no matter how. Churchill, whose country was to be besieged, was obsessed, come what may, by the need to prevent Germany from seizing the French fleet. So they embraced each other. It was the strangest day of the Entente Cordiale.

De Gaulle at once telephoned Paul Reynaud to tell him about the plan. Reynaud approved it, and was deeply moved. But speed was essential: the French government was to meet at the end of the afternoon, and he feared that the defeatists might win.

Churchill had summoned the War Cabinet to meet at 3.00 p.m. It sat for two hours. The paper was handed round. Amendments were called for, and communicated to General de Gaulle in an adjoining room. He came into the Cabinet Room to discuss them. Churchill pleaded ardently, since this was the only way of keeping France in the war. As he walked up and down, he practised the speech in which he would announce the union. The British ministers, with Churchill at their head, came to tell de Gaulle that they had agreed, and the prime minister promised him that he would be commander-in-chief. Together, they again telephoned Paul Reynaud and read him the text. 'It's very important,' he said. 'I'll use it at the Cabinet meeting in a moment.' Churchill took the telephone to say: 'De Gaulle is right. Our proposal can have great results. We must hold on. Till tomorrow, at Concarneau.' De Gaulle, taking the telephone again, apparently added: 'Do realise, Monsieur le Président, that one day you could become president of the Franco-British War Cabinet.' Hearing this, Churchill smiled and gestured, as if to say: 'Not so fast.'

The two men separated, but sharing an immense hope. Churchill put at de Gaulle's disposal an aircraft to take him direct to Bordeaux, where he arrived at 11.30 p.m. But disappointment awaited him. The French Cabinet had rejected the British offer. Some ministers had been indignant, claiming: 'Britain wants to make France a dominion.' Others had ridiculed the plan, quoting General Weygand's remark: 'By September, Britain will have her neck wrung like a chicken.'

The majority of the French Cabinet called for an end to the war. Paul Reynaud tendered his resignation to poor President Lebrun, who, instead of asking him to form a new government with the ministers who were willing to carry on, appealed in the night to Marshal Pétain, who had his request for an armistice already prepared.

Next day, de Gaulle took his plane back to London. Failing Franco-British union, the Churchill–de Gaulle marriage was celebrated in haste, as happens with wartime unions. The ceremony took place at the BBC, in the form of the 18 June Appeal. A few months later came the first marital disputes.

The British proposal of 16 June was little known in France. Those who used defeat as a stepping-stone, heaving themselves into power the better to accept servitude, simply used the plan as propaganda to denounce British perfidy.

I had no knowledge of the text until I reached London in the early days of 1943. I was astonished.

> In this most fateful moment in the history of the modern world
> ... the Governments of the United Kingdom and the French
> Republic make this declaration of indissoluble and unfailing
> resolve in their common defence of justice and liberty, against
> subjection to a regime that would reduce humanity to a life of
> robots and slaves.

People readily smile at the French taste for grandiloquence, but on
the rare occasions when the British turn lyrical they do so in full
measure.

The declaration continued:

> France and Great Britain will no longer be two nations, but a
> single Franco-British Union. The constitution will ensure the
> working of common institutions for defence, foreign affairs, eco-
> nomic and financial policy. Every French citizen will immediately
> enjoy British citizenship, and every British subject will become a
> citizen of France.

I remember the intense feeling of both enthusiasm and nostalgia that
gripped me when I read those words. I was not yet 25 years old. I
was a young exile, filled with anger and with dreams. And I had just
discovered, with admiration, the formidable courage – humdrum,
quiet and obstinate – of this people that had welcomed me, and from
which nothing distinguished me except the word FRANCE stitched
on my uniform.

> Then came the immediate and essential: 'So long as hostilities
> last there will be a single War Cabinet... It will govern from
> where best it can. The two Parliaments will be formally associ-
> ated.'

These were not vain words. There was a response in British hearts
that truly shared France's grief. Thus Raymond Mortimer – who
lives still in our memories – wrote: 'Since June 1940 France has
become for a time as distant and impenetrable as Tibet. This loss has
made us feel that half of Britain has been engulfed by the sea.'

The plan for Franco-British Union impressed me so much that I
devoted a chapter to it in my first book, *Letters from a European*,

which I wrote in snatches that very year in Britain: it was published in Algiers in 1944.

Today I still wonder what would have happened if those in Bordeaux, instead of submitting, had answered Yes.

To begin with, the French government would have been shipped to North Africa, and the majority of France's remaining troops would have followed. Their officers, certainly those on the active list, would quickly have obeyed orders. I knew their state of mind: I was among them. They wished only to recover after the humiliation of retreat. It was respect for the person of Marshal Pétain that paralysed them and made them lay down their arms.

Where would the common War Cabinet have been based? The formula 'It will govern from where best it can' did not exclude the possibility that Britain too might be invaded – which would have happened if the RAF, whose hangars had only seven reserve aircraft, had not won its crucial, heroic battle in September 1940.

The drama of Mers el-Kebir would not have happened. France's fleets would not have remained in port, one in Alexandria when Egypt was under siege, the other in Toulon, reduced to scuttling itself in the harbour in 1942. France would have been spared the sad affair of Dakar and the dramas of the Levant, where Frenchmen fought against each other. Would Hitler have dared to enter Spain, despite Franco's lukewarm support, to attack the French in Morocco or Algeria? At all events, the battle of Africa would have taken a very different course.

At home, would the French have suffered more? The racial laws would have been no worse than those applied by Vichy to please the occupying power; nor would many more people have been deported or hostages shot. The pillage of France's food supplies could hardly have been greater than it was. 'Collaboration' would have found neither excuse nor forgiveness. The Resistance, more spontaneous and more widespread, would not have taken so many months to arise, to be recognised, and to organise. And the French would not have experienced the internal conflicts between Pétainists, Gaullists and Giraudists whose repercussions are still detectable 60 years later.

It may be supposed that the war might have been shorter. France would have found itself alongside Britain, with Britain, at Tehran and Yalta, speaking with a single voice and carrying twice the weight.

The division of Europe would have been different. No one ever writes the history of catastrophes avoided.

The political difficulty of making the union work would have appeared after victory in World War II. In a fine gesture, the 16 June document postponed to later days the 'modalities' of its application: the word 'constitution' was mentioned, but only the word.

How would a monarchy and a republic have been fused together, the one based from time immemorial on the common law, the other on a written constitution? Of necessity, during the war, common institutions would certainly have been established, and common habits acquired. Would that have led to a single government? I am willing to wager that the principle of double nationality would have survived, along with a common organisation of defence, as well as forms of association in various essential fields.

Above all, I believe that around the Franco-British couple, whatever its links, there would have coalesced, of its own accord, the united Europe that Churchill and de Gaulle had promised in 1943, without having to await, after hesitant beginnings, an impulse from the surprising Franco-German couple.

One always has the right to dream, even about the past. The strangest day of the Entente Cordiale was also that when the greatest opportunity was lost.

Maurice Druon

De Gaulle and Britain

On 29 May 1943, when General de Gaulle was leaving London for Algiers, he remarked to British Foreign Secretary Anthony Eden: 'No one is more likeable than your people. I do not always think the same of your policy.' Basically, those few words tell the story of his feelings about the UK: admiration for the British, criticism of British policy. But they are too simple to represent so complex a history, involving as it does that of the century as a whole.

Charles de Gaulle was born at a time when young people in France could imagine on the horizon only one conceivable war: that against Germany. His precocious early writings envisaged no other, and his choice of a military career reflected his conviction that it would not be long delayed. Nor can it be doubted that he also wished for an alliance with Britain, which all those responsible in France thought almost as essential as alliance with Russia. Indeed, the French longed for confirmation of the *entente* between the two countries, which they saw as a vital defence against the threat of Pan-Germanism. Hence the tumultuous welcome Paris gave to King Edward VII, the architect of *entente*, whose popularity never dimmed. For de Gaulle, the *entente* was self-evident: so was fighting a joint war. In a world marked by the rising power of Germany and its drive for hegemony, France and Britain had a shared destiny. Basically, this was not to change until after World War II, and the new course that history then took made no essential difference. No Franco-British dispute could ever again become a conflict.

This was de Gaulle's life-long experience. The inter-war years gave him the chance to observe and analyse any divergences between London and Paris, and to see how differently national interests could be seen on either side of the Channel. His pessimistic view of history led him to believe that the First World War was only the first round, and he certainly disapproved of British diplomacy when it so deliberately fostered Germany recovery. He was not then convinced that the time had come for Franco-German reconciliation, which French policy under Aristide Briand tirelessly pursued for more than eight years. After Hitler came to power, de Gaulle could well condemn the last British attempts to appease Hitlerite Germany: the Anglo-German naval agreement, drawn up without French agreement and against treaty obligations, and – still more – the British government's advice to do nothing throughout the crisis caused by the remilitarisation of the Rhineland.

This makes it all the more significant that de Gaulle, more than any other, unhesitatingly backed joint action with the British in the decisive hours of June 1940. His decision was based on a double wager: that Britain would continue the war against Nazi Germany, and that in the end it would win. For him, this was more than a gamble. He was indignant when people saw in it a moral reflex, an instinctive and more or less irrational revulsion. On the contrary, he saw it as a reasoned choice, based on the real strength of Britain and the British Empire, an assessment of how other powers – America and Russia – would behave, and the resultant weighting of world scales. But in any case this choice reflected a political principle that he never renounced, even in the most difficult moments, when relations between Britain and Free France seemed seriously compromised. The best evidence is the speech he made just after the drama of Mers el-Kebir. Although expressing the sorrow that it was natural for any Frenchman to feel at that moment, he also stated with incomparable force, vigour, and clarity his determination to pursue the war alongside the British. It was on that occasion that Winston Churchill felt for de Gaulle the genuine admiration that seems never quite to have faded, even during their most bitter disputes.

Colonel Passy, the head of the Free French intelligence services, wrote in his memoirs that on the evening of 7 December 1942 – the day Japan attacked Pearl Harbor – de Gaulle said to him: 'The war is definitively won.' But the next day he told Commandant Pierre Billotte, his assistant chief of General Staff: 'From now on the British will do nothing without Roosevelt's agreement.' This was the root of all the crises that later scarred relations between Fighting France – the joint title of Free France and the Resistance – and its Anglo-American allies. The events of June 1940 had convinced Roosevelt that France would not count as a power or a state until the end of the war. As events unfolded, therefore, his policy was to seek practical agreements with the leaders of Vichy. For them he had no regard – but he was equally insouciant about the independence and the interests of France. This meant that nothing was likely to prevent clashes between America's policy and the actions of General de Gaulle. With hindsight, one can see the true scale of Franco-British disagreements about the Middle East. Churchill was keen to keep on the Allied side as many as possible of the Near Eastern Arab states, who still felt the weight of British colonialism, so he had the best of reasons to proclaim that Syria and Lebanon should no longer be subject to the mandate regime that France had maintained there since the end of World War I. De Gaulle chose a fairer policy, proclaiming immediately after the defeat of Vichy troops that both countries should have 'full and entire' independence. It was also a very bold policy because, although de Gaulle claimed to incarnate the sole legitimacy of France and its Empire, he had no authority to decide the fate of the two mandates. Churchill was wrong to allow his representatives or his agents to criticise French attitudes and systematically encourage Syrian and Lebanese nationalists. But if de Gaulle's strategy was well chosen, his tactics were not. To escape British pressure, his only recourse was to make direct agreements with nationalist leaders in Lebanon and Syria. I remarked on this in my first biography of de Gaulle, and in conversation with him at that time. He did not contradict me.

On the other hand, American attacks on Fighting France and on de Gaulle himself, some of which Churchill echoed, are explicable decades later. The dominant power America already possessed gave it little inclination to bear with de Gaulle's desire for independence, which he championed all the more fiercely because he was trying to rescue France from the abyss. Several episodes confirm this. On 13 May 1943, when the Conseil national de la Résistance unanimously backed de Gaulle, and he was about to leave for Algiers to form a single authority with General Henri Giraud, Roosevelt gave Churchill a dossier describing de Gaulle both as a would-be dictator and as a tool of Soviet policy, and perhaps also reflecting his own intention to redraw the map of Europe, attaching north-eastern France to some new Lotharingia. Churchill made some objections, but then seemed to yield to the US president's views. From Washington he sent a telegram to the British War Cabinet: 'It is urgent to study whether de Gaulle should not be eliminated as a political force, and the [French] National Committee be told that we shall maintain no further relations with it, and give it no more subsidy, so long as it is linked to de Gaulle.' In a second telegram the same day, he proposed replacing de Gaulle with a committee comprising Giraud, the former secretary-general at the Quai d'Orsay Alexis Léger (whose very name was largely forgotten save for his fame as a poet under the pseudonym Saint-John Perse), General Joseph Georges (commander-in-chief in the north-west in 1940, and hence one of those chiefly responsible for France's defeat), and Édouard Herriot, who had just expressed his categorical support for de Gaulle. The British War Cabinet met on 23 May and firmly opposed Churchill's idea. Clement Attlee and Anthony Eden returned to it in a number of telegrams, recalling the commitments made in 1940, Bir Hakeim, Free France's military victories, and the 'disastrous reaction there would be in the whole of the Resistance movements' if the Allies sought to eliminate de Gaulle. Anticipating the future Cold War, they even pointed out that in this case Resistance fighters would believe that the Anglo-Americans had betrayed their leader and that a new impulse towards Russia would become inevitable, given that the Resistance movements were already strongly left-inclined and that the communists played a major role in them.

So Roosevelt's attack failed. It was resumed just before the Allied landings in France, when the American administration proposed to set up in France an Anglo-American military government (AMGOT, or Allied Military Government of Occupied Territory) as it had in Italy, Germany's former ally. The US State Department had even drafted for General Eisenhower the text of a message making no reference to de Gaulle or to the Algiers provisional government. This led to a real trial of strength during the night of 5–6 June 1944, when at 1 a.m. – in the teeth of categorical opposition from Anthony Eden – Churchill even accused de Gaulle of 'treason in battle', threatened to denounce him publicly in the House of Commons, and wrote him a letter ordering him back to Algiers. Brendan Bracken intervened to destroy this before it was sent. Not until 4 a.m. did de Gaulle secure agreement that, independently of Eisenhower's message and speeches by the other heads of governments in exile, he could deliver his own address to the French people, without revealing it to anyone in advance. After the Normandy landings, the matter was settled on the spot by the attitude of the Resistance and the whole population, as well as by the establishment of de Gaulle's own authorities, the Commissaires de la République. The whole episode gave point to the remarks de Gaulle had made the previous evening, when at the end of a dinner which the British prime minister also attended, he had raised his glass in Churchill's honour: 'To Britain, to victory, to Europe!' It was already a hint that what was at stake for the future was the existence of Europe – that is, implicitly but clearly, its independence from the United States.

De Gaulle's severest clashes with Britain during the war years in no way prevented British policy from being basically in favour of restoring

French power. The British government already saw that after the war France would have to be rehabilitated as much as possible so as to minimise the effects of Germany's predictable collapse and the inevitable advance of the Soviet Union.

The proof of this was Winston Churchill's first visit to France after the Liberation. From then on it was agreed that France would have an occupation zone in Germany and would be part of the 'Consultative Commission', alongside the United States, Britain and Russia, dealing with German affairs as a whole. Then, at Yalta, from which France was excluded, it was Churchill who insisted that France have a permanent seat on the UN Security Council and a veto equal to that of America, the United Kingdom, the USSR and China. All this contributed to France's re-establishment on the world scene in a way that no one could have dared hope after the catastrophe of June 1940.

But the essential and basic question was how to organise future relations between France, Britain and the United States. Significantly, the first texts on the occupation of Germany drawn up in Algiers, on 12 August 1944, provided – not unrealistically – that the Soviet zone should extend to the east of the country, that the American army should be in charge of German territory, but that the western part of Germany should be jointly occupied by France, Belgium, the Netherlands and Britain. This – which prefigured a certain vision of the Europe that was to come – would have been a 'European' zone, not a purely French one, in which Britain would have taken part. In this respect the idea was unrealistic. Britain, it was clear, wanted to maintain its own standing among the victorious powers: in 1942 and 1943, when Belgian, Norwegian and Dutch ministers had asked the British government whether it wished to form links with other countries in Western Europe, they had received no reply. In September 1943, de Gaulle had asked René Mayer to study the pros and cons of an economic and political organisation of Western Europe, and he had set his commissioner on foreign affairs, René Massigli, to draft a plan to unite the Ruhr and the Rhineland in 'a strategic federation of four Western States (the Netherlands, Belgium, Italy and France), to which Britain might be attached'. On 18 March 1944, de Gaulle went further. He suggested to the Provisional Consultative Assembly a western grouping that would be 'extended to Africa, in close relations with the East and notably the Arab States, and whose arteries would be the Channel, the Rhine, and the Mediterranean'. If this idea is taken literally, Britain would have been part of the 'grouping', because the Channel would have been one of its 'arteries'. But de Gaulle could not then be definite, because the British position was unknown; and unless Britain took part, the Dutch and

Belgians would do nothing. So de Gaulle remained cautious. He also sometimes spoke of a European ensemble 'linking the three poles – Moscow, London, and Paris'.

It was after his return to power in 1958 that de Gaulle was able to begin implementing his conception of Europe. At that time, people remembered how he had strongly criticised the European Coal and Steel Community, which in its own domain set up a highly integrated power structure, and fiercely opposed the European Defence Community project, which on this vital subject would have threatened French independence. Now, he eroded and circumscribed the European Atomic Energy Community, Euratom. But he applied the Rome Treaty establishing the European Economic Community (EEC), and even accelerated its implementation. Convinced of the need to expose the French economy to international competition, he saw the EEC as an important step in this direction, in that it involved free trade, a common external tariff and common policies. At the same time, however, he was determined to prevent the Community from drifting towards a supranational or federal system in which major decisions could be imposed on states even if they disagreed. The same preoccupation guided him in the effort to establish a European Political Union, in which the states would preserve their independence but coordinate their actions as closely as possible on matters including the key issues of diplomacy and defence. But his German, Italian, Dutch, Belgian and Luxembourg partners blocked his proposal by facing him with a dilemma: accept Britain in the European Community (and thereby delay political union) or at once adopt a federal or supranational system for the EEC. Their position was clearly self–contradictory, since Britain, whose membership of the Community they said they sought, was notoriously hostile to federalism and supranationalism. For the time being, anyway, the debate focused on Britain's role in Europe.

As we have seen, de Gaulle had several times envisaged a Europe in which Britain would have its place. He knew that the British shared his own desire to preserve in Europe the independence of its nations. But he doubted whether the British would relax their links with the Commonwealth countries, and above all he feared that they were still bound by their special relationship with the United States, and would always seek to align European decisions with American policy.

Even so, when in August 1961 British Prime Minister Harold Macmillan officially applied to join the Community, French reactions at first seemed positive – so much so that on 5 September, while recognising 'the complexity of the problem', de Gaulle believed that 'there was every hope of solving it', and said that he could 'only be glad'. Almost a year later, in

June 1962, after de Gaulle and Macmillan met at the Château de Champs, it seemed as if an agreement was in sight and that, even on defence and nuclear weapons, Franco-British cooperation was possible – although the British minutes of the meeting made no express mention of the fact. At all events, several British leaders, including Conservative Party Chairman Ian MacLeod, proposed signing at once an agreement short-circuiting the remaining difficulties. It was then, perhaps, that Britain lost the chance of joining the Community at that time.

The Franco-British 'summit' at Rambouillet on 15 and 16 December was marked by renewed pessimism. No progress had been made on the subjects still in suspense, the British government seemed to be playing a waiting game, and the Labour opposition was still opposed. A few days later, Macmillan met President J. F. Kennedy in Nassau and agreed that British nuclear submarines should be equipped with American Polaris missiles and then be put at the disposal of NATO, while the other NATO states should set up a 'multilateral' force, the MLF, of mixed-manned naval units also dependent on NATO. After Rambouillet, the hope that France would back Britain's application to join the Common Market was already very dim. After Nassau it was extinguished.

If nothing changed thereafter until de Gaulle's retirement, it was because the facts of the problem remained the same. De Gaulle did not want a supranational or federal Europe, and on this point British membership would have suited him very well. But he also did not want a Europe constantly prepared to fall in line with the United States, and on this point British membership would be dangerous or threatening. The talks he had with British Ambassador Christopher Soames at the beginning of 1969, deliberately leaked to the other European governments to prevent their leading anywhere, are in hindsight interesting for only one reason. They revealed that de Gaulle hoped to use Britain's accession to Europe as an opportunity both to reform the EEC by excluding all prospect of supranationality, and to establish a political union respecting the independence of its member states. Looking back, however, one can see better than ever that the fundamental question for any organisation of Europe is that of its independence *vis-à-vis* the United States, whose dominance of the world scene is the essential feature of our time.

Paul-Marie de La Gorce

Churchill and de Gaulle

'Since 1907,' wrote Winston Churchill, 'on bad days as well as good, I have been a sincere friend of France.'[1] Indeed, this eminent Francophile had distant French origins; his maternal grandfather, Leonard Jerome, came from a Huguenot family that emigrated to America at the beginning of the eighteenth century; and his mother Jennie long remembered her years in France during the dazzling period of the Second Empire. As a schoolboy, Winston was sent to France to improve his French – with mediocre results – but his passion for history and his romantic spirit gave him boundless admiration for the great heroes of France's past, beginning with Joan of Arc and Napoleon. By the time he was thirty, Winston Churchill had barely improved his knowledge of French, which remained somewhat idiosyncratic, but as a young minister of the Crown he crossed the Channel to watch French army manoeuvres, and he sided firmly with France during the Agadir crisis. As First Lord of the Admiralty, he was the main architect of the Franco-British naval agreement in February 1913. Nor was this only a matter of personal feelings; since 1911, Churchill had been convinced that war with Germany was inevitable and that, to face the Kaiser, Great Britain must forge a solid alliance with France.

From the very beginning to the very end of World War I, Churchill was constant in his support of France. As First Lord of the Admiralty, he was among the first 'interventionists' – those who believed that both self-interest and honour obliged London to back France and Belgium. Once hostilities were declared, he took personal charge of the air and land

---

1   C. de Gaulle, *Mémoires de Guerre – l'Unité*, Plon, Paris, 1956, p. 647.

defence of Dunkirk, and went several times to Paris to talk with members of the French government. After he left the government as a result of the Dardanelles débâcle, he disembarked at Boulogne to take part in the war of the trenches as a reserve officer. He fought there for six months, and French and British alike were struck by his courage, his determination, his energy, his luck ... and his drinking capacity. He in turn would always be impressed by the gallantry and tenacity of the French soldier. But it was from the summer of 1917 onwards, when Churchill became armaments minister, that his closest links with France were forged. He went there many times to inspect the front, supervise joint arms production, and talk with leading civil and military figures. Two of them left an unforgettable impression on him: General Foch, the commander-in-chief of the Allied armies, and Clemenceau, the Tiger, whom he described as follows:

> As much as any single human being, miraculously magnified, can ever be a nation, he was France. Fancy paints nations in symbolic animals – the British Lion, the American Eagle, the Russian double-headed ditto, the Gallic Cock. But the Old Tiger, with his quaint stylish cap, his white moustache and burning eye, would make a truer mascot for France than any barnyard fowl. He was an apparition of the French Revolution at its sublime moment...[2]

After World War I, France found in Churchill a champion who was as vigorous as he was eloquent. To all those who would listen, he declared that France, 'impoverished, wounded, and weakened', had every right to the security for which it had sacrificed nearly two million of its sons. Yet Great Britain and America had abandoned it after the Treaty of Versailles, and Churchill believed that only a pact pledging Britain to defend France in case of aggression would be enough to quell French fears and guarantee stability in Europe. Throughout the period between the wars, in government as in opposition, in the House of Commons as in Conservative clubs, in public speeches as in private conversation, Churchill tirelessly sought to strengthen the ties between his country and France. Until 1931, he pleaded for reconciliation between France, Germany and Britain: he saw in it the only true guarantee against a further war. But, as Hitler moved towards power in Germany and the British Labour Party persisted in disarmament at France's expense, Churchill returned to his original policy. 'It is not in the immediate interest of European peace that the French army should be

---

2   W. S. Churchill, *Great Contemporaries*, Odhams, London, 1948, p. 236.

seriously weakened. It is certainly not in British interests to antagonize France...'[3]

Once Hitler had come to power, Churchill never ceased repeating this thesis. He had no problem reconciling his attachment to France with his very lively patriotism, because he realised – as he had before World War I – that a strong France was vital to the safety of Britain. Thus, on 24 March 1939, after the signing of a Franco-British agreement on military cooperation, the 'opposition Conservative' Winston Churchill told the House of Commons: 'Some people talk sometimes as if it is very fine and generous of us to go to the help of France. But I can assure you that in the pass to which things have come, we stand at least as much in need of the aid of France as the French do of the aid of Britain.'[4] True, Churchill believed implicitly in the strength of France's army – that of Foch and Clemenceau – led now by his old friend General Gamelin. And there was the famous Maginot Line, which seemed invincible. What is more, Churchill was always prone to wishful thinking: if Britain's safety depended on the strength of France's army, that army absolutely must be supreme – and so it obviously was!

Throughout the inter-war period, in his capacity as minister of war, air minister or colonial secretary, whether as a simple citizen, chancellor of the Exchequer or opposition MP, Winston Churchill never missed an opportunity to enjoy the sun on the Côte d'Azur. The painter in him was attracted by the glowing landscape, the *bon vivant* by his compatriots' luxurious villas, the inveterate gambler by the casinos of Cannes and Monaco. As a statesman, he stopped in Paris to meet the French leaders with whom he had close relations, such as Herriot, Reynaud, Flandin, Paul-Boncour, Daladier, Blum and Mandel. In private talks and over wine and dinner, he urged them to agree on more coherent defence and a firmer foreign policy *vis-à-vis* Nazi Germany.

Once war was declared, and Churchill had again become First Lord of the Admiralty, he made it his business to cooperate as closely as possible with his French colleagues, but in vain. They would neither agree among themselves nor attain the indispensable minimum of coordination between French and British strategy overseas. Daladier and Reynaud – who detested each other – wanted to do far too much, while Chamberlain and Halifax wanted to do nothing at all. This explained the lamentable shilly-shallying at meetings of the Supreme Council, and the humiliating defeat

---

3 W. S. Churchill, *Complete Speeches*, Vol. V, 1928–1935, Chelsea House, London, 1974, p. 5058.
4 Ibid., Vol. VI, 1935–1942, p. 6125.

in Norway in the spring of 1940. Nevertheless, it was this very defeat that led to Neville Chamberlain's resignation and Churchill's accession to power. From then on he could have much more influence on Franco-British relations.

In France, during the dramatic weeks of May and June 1940, while the Allied armies were staggering before the onslaught of the invaders, Churchill had a key role to play. Five times he went to France in order to urge Paul Reynaud's government to continue the struggle. At the same time he faced a cruel dilemma: whether to aid the French with all the resources of the RAF, thereby stripping the defences of the British Isles and risking invasion, or to hold enough of his air strength in reserve to stem Germany's final assault, thus incurring the reproach of having abandoned France. The final decision, dictated largely by circumstances, was very difficult to reach for that old Francophile, who obstinately pursued his efforts to revive the fighting spirit of a French government increasingly beset by defeatism. All the same, he found an ally: General Charles de Gaulle, under-secretary of state for war, who wanted to continue the struggle – in France if possible, abroad if necessary. These two powerful personalities recognised each other at once, and they tried every means of dissuading the French government from giving in. One of these means was the plan for Franco-British Union: it was the boldest, if not the most realistic. De Gaulle, who did not believe in it, induced Churchill to adopt it; Churchill, who did not believe in it either, got his government to endorse it; and both persuaded Paul Reynaud to submit it to his ministers. The project came to naught, but Churchill and de Gaulle had worked closely together on it, and by the evening of 16 June the general knew that he had in Churchill an ally as loyal as he was influential. Clearly, that weighed heavily in his decision to return to Britain the very next day.

In June 1940, when Winston Churchill held out to de Gaulle a strong and willing hand, it was not simply because of his Francophile feelings. A propagandist of genius, he realised what a shock France's capitulation would be to British public opinion: France had been the last continental bastion in World War I; once it crumbled, might not the British, too, succumb to defeatism? By presenting to them a Frenchman with stature, willpower, a name, a reputation, a policy and a voice, he was promoting a fiction: that France had not fallen, since it was continuing the struggle in the person of General de Gaulle. Moreover, immediately after the Dunkirk evacuation, Churchill had planned offensive operations against the Germany army, but it was obviously impossible, at this juncture, to land in force on the continent of Europe. Thus North and West Africa appeared as an immediate step in the process, and these territories belonged to France. By giving solid support to General de Gaulle, by allowing him to recruit soldiers from among the victors of Narvik and the vanquished of Dunkirk, Churchill was preparing the ground for his future plans. At the outset, the two great men cooperated admirably, despite very serious setbacks such as Mers el-Kebir or Dakar. In fact, de Gaulle's public endorsement of Britain's naval action against the French fleet, and Churchill's unconditional support of de Gaulle after Dakar, both strengthened their mutual confidence and esteem.

But the prime minister, far from falling victim to the myth he had created, could not bring himself to regard General de Gaulle as the sole incarnation of France. So he discreetly pursued his own policy towards Vichy, French North Africa, the Levant and Madagascar; he tried out personal approaches to Marshal Pétain and Generals Weygand, Georges and Giraud; and he even made his own direct radio broadcasts to France. Once the United States had entered the war, Churchill meekly accepted the rabid anti-Gaullism of Roosevelt and his entourage. American aid and cooperation were essential to Britain's survival, so feelings – and the interests of France – had to take second place. The state, we know, is the coldest of cold monsters; and a state fighting for its life is colder still than all the others. Unfortunately, the policy of President Roosevelt *vis-à-vis* France, notably as regards Darlan and Giraud, was as unrealistic as it was deeply amoral; Churchill, by endorsing it, faced incomprehension on the part of his Cabinet colleagues, Parliament, the press, public opinion and the governments in exile – not to mention the devastating fury of General de Gaulle. In the process, the prime minister even risked cutting himself off from the French Resistance – an inconceivable outcome for a veteran Francophile who had always cherished in his heart the prospect of a revived French army. As it turned out, the liberation of France, and his own triumphal visit to Paris in November 1944, brought to a happy conclusion the very troubled episode of his wartime relationship with the Free French.

For Churchill, liberated France became once again a favourite resort. He visited the country many times, to meet old friends, to receive the Croix de Guerre and honorary doctorates, and to take his place in the Académie des Sciences morales et politiques. He went more often still to paint and write on the Côte d'Azur, in the luxurious villas of Lord Beaverbrook and of his literary agent Emery Reeves, or in the Hôtel de Paris, in the hospitable principality of Monaco. But behind the masks of the statesman, the artist, the dilettante and the *bon vivant*, Winston Churchill remained more coldly realistic than sentimentally Francophile. Long before the end of the war, partly under the influence of Foreign Secretary

Anthony Eden, he had realised the crucial importance of France as a barrier to Soviet expansionism. Hence his energetic pleas at Yalta for a French zone in occupied Germany, and a French seat on the Control Commission. After the war, he gradually returned to the views he had espoused in the 1920s: the security of Europe must be built on a rapprochement between the new Germany and France restored to its role as Britain's first bastion on the continent.

But whether in opposition, in power or in retirement, Churchill saw with regret that France, so much loved and so much needed, was still a prey to its old demons. The chronic instability of the Fourth Republic was a terrible weakness that led him to long for the return to power of his difficult wartime ally. He thus resumed with General de Gaulle the cordial relations they had enjoyed in the summer of 1940. The two men corresponded, and they met again in Paris in November 1958, when Prime Minister Charles de Gaulle solemnly decorated the august pensioner Winston Churchill with the Croix de la Libération. They met twice more in 1960, in London in April and in Nice in October. After that, Churchill wrote several times to the general, encouraging him with good wishes during the long ordeal of the Algerian War. By this time, the old lion had become as much a Gaullophile as a Francophile, and he remained so until 24 January 1965...

On the first anniversary of Churchill's death, his widow Clementine received the following note, handwritten by General de Gaulle:

> Let me say that, in casting my thoughts to the memory of Sir Winston Churchill's greatness, I feel again, more than ever, the scope of his life's work, and the quality of the bonds that linked me to him and, through us, also united Britain and France.[5]

François Kersaudy

---

5   M. Soames, *Clementine Churchill*, Penguin, London, 1981, p. 732.

Britain and the French Resistance

Even before the projected Franco–British Union and de Gaulle's *Appel* of 18 June 1940, an anthology of texts on Britain and France was being edited. Its aim was to anchor the war against Germany in centuries of Anglo–French literary and historical understanding. 'When France fell,' said the editor William G. Corp, 'it seemed that the project might have to be abandoned.' It looked even less likely to be published after the French capitulation leading to the Armistice, and the British attack on the French fleet at Mers el-Kebir on 3 July, when over 1,200 French sailors were killed. The editor feared that these events might be 'portents of a violent change in the relations between the two peoples'. As it was, he continued, 'those of us who love France and admire the French found no change of temper in England'. He persevered and the anthology of essays and poems, together with de Gaulle's *Appel*, was published in 1941 as *Free France and Britain*. At the time nobody could be sure that these writers had their place in history, but they were, in discourse terms, 'writing' France. 'Comme un Michelet passionné,' said Emmanuel d'Astier of de Gaulle.

Opening the anthology was a piece by André Labarthe called 'The True France'. It set the tone and direction not only of this particular publication but of *La France Libre*, the journal Labarthe founded in London, and of numerous books, essays and memoirs by Francophiles and Anglophiles promoting the relationship of Britain and French Resistance. Titles such as *This is Not The End of France* (Gustav Winter), *France Still Lives* ('Michael'), *One Enemy Only – the Invader* (Paul Simon) and *France Is a Democracy* (Louis Lévy), expressed a determination that was also a rediscovery of two cultures. Labarthe's own piece concluded: 'France will remain faithful to her historic ideal.'

Of all the hostages to fortune this was as bold as any, but the readiness to define a 'true' France as against any other version was neither new to French writers nor unexpected by British Francophiles who had studied French history and culture across the centuries. It was little more than a cliché to observe that France had been deeply divided over its identity since the Revolution of 1789. Now, in the stark realities of 1940, there was a new dichotomy created by the different responses to the traumatic events: on the one hand Free France as constituted by de Gaulle in London and on the other the France of Pétain, the Armistice and Vichy. 'My detestation for the men of Vichy', wrote C. F. Melville in *Guilty Frenchmen*, '...is the measure of my love for the real France they have betrayed.'

It is not difficult to see that this new polarisation was anything but an equal balance at the start. Free France was a very speculative affair of a few thousand, some would say a mere handful of, French exiles, in contrast to the millions of French who made Pétain into a cult figure of religious proportions. In the opinions of many, articulated by Gustave Hervé's panegyric *C'est Pétain qu'il nous faut* of 1936, he was already visualised as a *deus ex machina* who would save France from internal political conflict. Only a few hundred out of over eleven thousand registered French residents in Britain rallied to de Gaulle, and the rest behaved no differently from the majority of the mainland French, or indeed those in North Africa, the only part of France overseas to which a retreat of the government and army had been considered before Pétain's call for a cease-fire. The army commander there, General Noguès, was extremely alarmed at the prospect of an Armistice, but he remained loyal to Pétain and refused to rally to the breakaway French in London.

De Gaulle's urgent need was therefore one of legitimacy. The predicament of early resisters inside France was similar but different. They also needed legitimacy, but simply by being in France they were immune from the charge of being rebels in exile, with all the negative memories of émigré counter-revolutionaries in Koblenz 150 years before. In 1940 they were isolated individuals or very small groups, unknown to each other, with few resources beyond their own skills and initiative, and surrounded by the multiple and debilitating effects of defeat and occupation. Their own quest for recognition involved the same need to persuade others that there was a viable alternative, but there was no question in 1940 of creating a single institutional authority in France in open opposition to Vichy.

Resistance inside France was not a military or political decision from above: it grew unevenly but richly from below. It was always a minority. It started as dissent and refusal. Its pluralism certainly involved military plans and ambitions, but also a myriad of clandestine tracts and newspapers fighting German and Vichy propaganda, a revolt against submission, a constellation of hiding places and forged passports for those on the run, a defence of persecuted sections of society, a cultural, literary and psychological assertion of individual freedom. It was heavily influenced by the different zones into which France was divided. Initially it was extremely hard to counter the popular illusion that Pétain, celebrated as 'the victor of Verdun' in 1916, was secretly outwitting the Germans, and a few leading resisters, such as Henri Frenay of COMBAT, remained hopeful of Pétain until 1942. The Free French could not afford to entertain even a hint of that illusion. They set out to create an institutional and charismatic existence of their own.

On 7 August 1940 de Gaulle's initial search for legitimacy was rewarded by British recognition. Churchill followed his impromptu assent to de Gaulle's broadcasts by acknowledging the general as 'chef de tous les Français libres, où qu'ils soient, qui se rallient à vous pour défendre la cause alliée'. De Gaulle was now relatively free, within overall British strategy, to set up his own intelligence services in London and plan operations in France through a complex web of clandestine networks, coordinated by the 29-year-old officer from the Norwegian campaign, Captain André Dewavrin, known to resistance history as Colonel Passy. From this point it has often been argued that what linked resisters in France indissolubly with the Free French in London was material and military dependence on Britain, and this is how the relationship of Britain and the French Resistance is frequently presented. Clearly this is not inaccurate but it is also not the whole picture, and for a few pages it is more the duality of the struggle that I wish to emphasise.

Embryonic resistance within France had an immediate sense of something tangible to offer the British, in terms of escape routes for British servicemen and intelligence gathering. The Germans earmarked Brittany as a key to the control of the Atlantic. The British needed regular and reliable information on the Breton ports and others on the Atlantic coast of France. It was soon available. As early as the summer of 1940 Marcel Hévin created the core of an information network in Nantes. In the Côtes-d'Armor Claude Robinet-Rivière infiltrated the semaphore station of Bilfot, close to Paimpol, from which he stole a detailed plan of coastal defences, transmitting it to London before arriving there himself in January 1942. Small groups with access to information did not immediately know how to convince London of their value. The picaresque Dordogne notable and farmer, Louis de la Bardonnie, was not entirely untypical in his frustration that London did not seem to take seriously his early reconnaissance of the German fleet in Bordeaux. They thought his material too good to be true. When I interviewed him in 1972 he was still smarting at the failure of the film *Sink the Bismarck* to credit his section of the network Confrérie Notre-Dame with what he claimed was the vital information that enabled the *Bismarck* to be located.

In Lyon the engineer Alban Vistel, a leader of resistance in the southeast, said that he formed the first nucleus in his factory by pretending that he had contact with London. Getting through to Britain was a gauge of serious intent. It was the link that was all-important, not the dependency. In the north of France making such links was the first thought for resisters in the Nord and Pas-de-Calais region, cut off from the rest of France and subject to direct rule by the German army in Brussels. A popular sympathy for the British had been consolidated in the area during World War I, and recruitment for the escape network 'Pat O'Leary', which began in 1942 to serve the British secret services, was impressive. Between the summer of 1941 and the end of 1943 a rapidly expanding network secured the escape of hundreds of airmen across the various zones and into Spain.

A rare photograph in the local history of the region shows three British airmen with the family of Maître Havet, who hid them at Lumbres in the Pas-de-Calais before their successful escape back to Britain. They are posing assertively against a poster headed 'Recherches des aviateurs anglais'. The notary and his daughter both died in deportation.[1] In rural areas and towns throughout France, men and women helped over 3,000 Allied airmen to escape. 'We took risks for them,' wrote André Rougeyron, who survived deportation to Buchenwald, 'because of sympathy . . . and belief in the same ideals, without hope of any gain.'[2] Donald Caskie, minister of the Scots Kirk in the rue Bayard in Paris, met Pat O'Leary, *nom de guerre* of the Belgian army doctor Albert Guérisse, in Marseille. Caskie had joined the *exode* of June 1940, which led him first to Bayonne and then to Marseille. There, as a displaced person himself, he reopened the Seamen's Mission in the rue Forbin in the Vieux Port to help other similar British refugees. Escape networks were created to Toulouse and on to Spain. Caskie survived arrest and imprisonment and later entitled his memoirs *The Tartan Pimpernel* – not necessarily a historical reference acceptable to all political strands of the resistance.

---

1 Etienne Dejonghe and Yves Maner, *Le Nord-Pas-de-Calais dans la main allemande, 1940–1944*, La Voix du Nord, Lille, 1999, p. 311.

2 André Rougeyron, *Agents for Escape. Inside the French Resistance 1939–1945*, Louisiana State University Press, Baton Rouge, 1996, Preface. Translated by Marie-Antoinette McConnell.

Even Caskie's largely forgotten corner of activity in south-eastern France demonstrated that there were two-way needs of Britain and internal French resistance in the early years, and this was before any talk of sabotage and derailments, let alone armed combat or insurrection. The British Intelligence Services were never in any doubt that information was needed from France, and the nascent French groups in Brittany and else-where were soon structured into *réseaux de renseignements* working for the British as well as for Passy. Stressing interdependence beyond the gathering of information nevertheless remains controversial. Historians who do so, however guarded their approach, are often seen by their military colleagues as exaggerating what resistance in France had to offer to Britain and the wider war effort. This cannot have been a problem for Churchill, otherwise there would have been no history of the Special Operations Executive (SOE).

On 16 July 1940 Churchill entrusted Hugh Dalton, minister for economic warfare, with responsibility for subversion behind enemy lines; the SOE was created shortly afterwards. Dalton had written some days earlier of the need for 'a new organisation to co-ordinate, inspire, control and assist the nationals of oppressed countries who must themselves be the direct participants. We need absolute secrecy, a certain fanatical enthusiasm, willingness to work with people of different nationalities, complete political reliability.'[3]

This was more or less the brief for the SOE inside occupied Europe. Of the two sections that sent agents into France, one (RF) worked closely with de Gaulle, and the other (F) recruited and operated independently, to de Gaulle's permanent vexation. From 1941 F section, under Major Maurice Buckmaster (from December 1941), set up over a hundred circuits in France in which hand-picked agents, smuggled or dropped into the country, built up clusters of French resisters for military tasks decided in theory by London but in fact determined by local circumstances. About a quarter of the main body of agents were killed or died in deportation. They were not technically spies and resented the implication that they were, but the Germans, finding them often in civilian clothes, were less meticulous in making the distinction. They were, however, an irregular form of warfare, as indeed was all resistance within France: they were special forces, from whom creative thinking, leadership and exceptional courage were expected. Again, the same applied to French resisters them-

---

3 Quoted in M. R. D. Foot, *SOE in France*, HMSO, London, 1966, p. 8. This outstanding, detailed history remains a landmark in the historiography of Britain and French Resistance.

selves, the main difference being that SOE agents were specially recruited by a military organisation. Most French resisters arrived at resistance by their own decisions or by various indeterminate routes: they were not specifically trained, although some *maquis* units in 1943–44 did set up rough and brief equivalents of training camps. Until the start of military action by the *maquis* in the hills and the *groupes francs* in the towns, the vast majority of resisters in France were never in a position to handle a gun or throw a grenade, although much sabotage involved the use of explosives. It cannot be emphasised too often that the real innovation in French resistance was the labyrinthine spread of civilian subversion by ordinary men and women, without which no British agent would have been able to operate.

Given this predominantly civilian origin of resistance, the agents of F section were important for bringing military skills and technology. But so too were RF agents and many of those in Passy's organisation, the Bureau Central de Renseignement et d'Action (BCRA). Inevitably, the question arises as to why F section was necessary. On the surface it looks like a calculated insult to the Free French, a lack of trust in the almost ethereal Entente Cordiale, which was given increasingly iconic status in literary circles in London. Was it such an affront? As an institution it was certainly created in a context of British alarm at the rumours, suspicions and careless talk that weakened de Gaulle's entourage and threatened to fracture his movement, especially after the failed expedition to Dakar. No less than the French military hierarchy, the British Chiefs of Staff were acutely conscious of de Gaulle's junior status, although his own probity was never in doubt. F section was a way of setting conditions to the untried mechanisms of subversive warfare in France: at least, argued the conventional strategists, there will be British officers in charge on the ground. In this light it was set up less as an official attack on the Entente Cordiale than as a *sine qua non* of its survival. Its autonomy was, however, non-negotiable, and it was this that continued to irritate de Gaulle right through to the Liberation, when he made a point of telling F agents in no uncertain terms to leave the country.

Anyone dwelling on the hostility of General de Gaulle towards F section of the SOE, or indeed on some of the SOE policies that reveal British arrogance, will miss the intricate history of partnership between the British agents and their French contacts and recruits. If the centenary and future of the Entente Cordiale is not just to be at governmental level it is precisely individual and collective experience at the grassroots that needs to be carefully researched. Few experiences were as close to the ground as resistance. A whole gamut of attitudes, personalities, situations and outcomes is thrown into sharp relief by the accounts of the SOE, from both British and French participants. It has been exaggerated from the British side, and downplayed from the French. It has been the stuff of colourful documentaries that stress failure as often as success, betrayals alongside martyrdom, political intrigue and personal love affairs. F section is no longer an inviolate secret of state. It is time that it ceased to be a pawn in national historiography on either side of the Channel.

If there was arrogance it was not one of language: the agents were mostly bilingual and had grown up, or lived and worked for long periods, in France. Radio operators such as Yvonne Cormeau, working in the south-west, were often the ones who were closest to understanding the motivation of those who risked everything to provide cover and shelter: she said that she was never refused a meal or a bed. Pearl Witherington made SOE history when she took over a circuit in the Indre after the arrest of Maurice Southgate, a leadership role for which the SOE would train only men. No single agent can speak for the whole, although Harry Rée's account of organising the sabotage of the Peugeot factory at Montbéliard has become almost the epitome of SOE action, alongside the deep and lasting relationships through which Francis Cammaerts constructed his effective circuit (codenamed Jockey) from Marseille to the Vercors.[4] Both had been conscientious objectors at the outset of war: resistance was a form of warfare that placed a premium on achieving its aims with the minimum loss of life.

The technical brilliance of a Hugh Verity in landing Lysanders and Hudsons in small fields by night, or of a Brooks Richards navigating in and out of Brittany harbours without lights, was awesome. The agents they transported between Britain and France provided British people with memories of 'working for the French Resistance' in the Cornish creeks of Helford Passage, and 'French Resistance in Sussex', the title of Barbara Bertram's memoir of Bignor as a first stop-over for some two hundred of the French men and women resisters in transit through Britain. The local pride in these British memories echoes that of regions everywhere in France that have their own specific histories of resistance, whether coastal communities in Brittany from which volunteers in small fishing craft sailed to join the Free French in the earliest days, or the mainly Protestant community of le Chambon-sur-Lignon in the Haute-Loire, including the young English teacher, Gladys Maber, which saved the lives of hundreds of Jewish children in 1942–44.

Many of the first tracts dropped by the RAF over occupied France were headed 'Français! L'Angleterre vous parle.' As Tom Harrisson has shown

4 See the documentary film *No Ordinary People* shown on BBC2, 28 November 1995, directed by Mike Fox for Foxy Films and Elizabeth O'Hara Boyce.

in his Mass-Observation classic, *Living through the Blitz*, the format of 'us' speaking to 'you' was common practice in the first days of wartime information in Britain. Its alienating properties were eventually realised by the Ministry of Information and a more inclusive form was adopted. The BBC's evening French broadcasts from 1 July were inclusive from the start, and within a fortnight Maurice Schumann had become the voice of de Gaulle and the Free French in the programme 'Honneur et Patrie', speaking over a thousand times during the Occupation, while a longer broadcast, entitled 'Ici la France' was entrusted to a French team under the creative talent of Michel Saint-Denis, known for his experimental theatre in both Paris and London. Adopting the name of Jacques Duchesne, he turned 'Ici la France' into the almost mystical lifeline to France, 'Les Français parlent aux Français'. Duchesne worked in close harmony with the BBC's head of French broadcasts, Darsie Gillie, the *Manchester Guardian* correspondent in Paris before and after the war, and although British censorship was maintained, it was in the hands of Francis Williams, whose democratic views chimed with the popular demand to be kept informed: the 'right to know'.

The BBC had to build up absolute trust in France, argued Buckmaster, so that it could be used to convey instructions to the French people when necessary. This trust was achieved. The BBC was at the centre of shared ideals and resistance experience: it was often the instigator of action. Instructions to French people to cover walls with V for Victory signs, to stay at home for an hour or fill the streets at a given time, forged pacts between London and the French public. Widely valued as expressions of hope and defiance, they carried an open message no less dramatic than the secret codes (*messages personnels*) directed at specific resistance groups, which Jean Cocteau used after the war as evocative poetry in his stylised film *Orphée*. It was not a misuse. Repeated codes, slogans and signature tunes created a distinctive cultural genre of reassuring familiarity spiced with mystery, to which was added the excitement and danger of tuning in, once it became an offence and thus a gesture of defiance.

The BBC did not broadcast to a void. Voices coming in the other direction, either by letter or in person, were scrutinised and interrogated by a Frenchman, Émile Delavenay, who moved from the London branch of the news agency Havas to be Assistant Director of European Intelligence at the BBC.[5] Enough letters from France arrived, surprisingly by the normal

---

5 Martyn Cornick, 'The BBC and the Propaganda War against Occupied France: The Work of Émile Delavenay and the European Intelligence Department', *French History*, Vol. 8, No. 3, 1994, pp. 316–54.

postal service, for Jacques Duchesne to read a selection on 7 October 1940. The first one was clearly chosen for its historical reference to French sacrifices at Verdun, which might have led to pro-Pétain sentiments, but instead inspired the statement that 'notre patrie, c'est maintenant l'Angleterre'. Authenticity was suggested by the detail that the woman writer had used violet ink and Duchesne stressed the reciprocal relationship of programme and listeners by ending with the hope that the letter writers themselves would be listening 'ce soir'. Delavenay made this reciprocity the hub of his task of analysing the letters and interviewing volunteers and known resisters who arrived in Britain. As a sounding of public opinion in France it could hardly match the *Contrôle technique* of Vichy, which opened thousands of letters in every *département* on a regular, secret basis, but among those received in London the handful that had clearly been opened by Vichy censors and yet still arrived indicated the vulnerability of the *Contrôle* to pro-resistance sympathies.

The voices of hope and defiance became the voices of combat in 1943. An increasingly wide range of resisters were brought to London, including the communist representative Fernand Grenier, and were given access to the BBC. Grenier objected that he was not allowed to use the word 'partisan', permitted to describe resistance fighters in Yugoslavia but not in France. It was just a single knot in the tangle of resistance politics and Allied strategy in which the BBC was caught, not least by the debilitating, often purely personal, disagreements between de Gaulle, Churchill and Roosevelt. This is a complex story for which other essays are needed, but from the listeners' point of view the BBC broadcasts effectively met the challenge of reflecting the shift of internal resistance into armed struggle. Maurice Schumann on 18 March 1943 may have anticipated the *maquis* uprisings in the Alps by a whole year, but his tribute to the *Légion des montagnes* was the first explicit BBC reference to young men escaping forced labour in Germany (STO) and forming bands in the hills. He was rebuked, but the connection had been made.

Civilians into combatants was the agonised issue of Britain and French Resistance from the moment that the *maquis* potential was realised through to the Liberation of 1944. The suspicions and accusations that fuelled it made for quite a different kind of joint experience. It was again two-way. It did not eclipse the overwhelming sense of a successful partnership, but it left its resentments within Franco-British relationships, at institutional and grassroots level. Mixing the two levels we must note both the incomprehension of internal resisters that their dedication and capabilities were not fully integrated into Allied military strategy, and at the same time the belief of Allied commanders that the resistance was too fractious and unreliable to take into their confidence. The human anguish caused by the Allied bombing of the Breton ports of Lorient and Saint-Nazaire in February 1943, which destroyed the towns and killed civilians, but missed the target of the submarine bases, was replicated many times across France. Bombs too often conspicuously failed to do what sabotage or local armed action might have been entrusted to achieve.

What is astonishing is the resilience of pro-British sentiments even in the areas heavily scarred. Marcel Baudot in his paper on 'France and Britain' at the first major British conference on comparative resistance in 1962, stressed that it was paradoxical that the Vichy Prefects should consistently report the degree of popular support for 'Gaullisme' and the British, and yet this did not seem to register as a military potential in Allied thinking. Even after Churchill had decided to arm the Resistance in March 1944, Buckmaster found it difficult to persuade Arthur Harris of British Bomber Command (a quite other BBC) to make sufficient planes available. Buckmaster admitted that there was always a certain arbitrariness in when and where arms were dropped, and said that he could only trust to the reliability of the agent on the ground. This was not the same as a coherent strategic plan.[6]

There was a plan integrating the local resistance into vital support for the Normandy landings. It worked far better than Allied Commanders expected, and their appreciation of the resistance grew exponentially. The *maquis* in the Vercors, by contrast, did not know whether they had simply been used as a decoy and then abandoned. Their appreciation of Allied strategy, in which they included de Gaulle in Algiers, collapsed in equal measure. But de Gaulle was not fully integrated either, and the military complexities of the internal resistance, de Gaulle and the Allies in the critical stages that led to the Liberation are a further history of their own.

As far as Britain and French Resistance can be evaluated overall, the controversy over policies that did not converge in 1943–44 was more than outweighed by the impact of those that did. The strength of resistance was its ability to concentrate on local objectives. Not all of these were of major, or even minor, significance in the global strategy of the war. They involved acts to release fellow resisters from Vichy prisons; raids to secure arms, food and clothes for the *maquis*; revenge against collaborators; and ambushes of German movements by rail and road, all a powerful declaration that resistance existed. The ontological importance of this *action directe* was easy to ignore from the point of view of Allied Command, which placed a premium on training resisters for Jour-J (D-Day). But the

---

6 Author's interview with Maurice Buckmaster, 4 November 1990.

prolific acts of internal resistance in the period of armed combat continued to reflect the plurality of motivation and defiance of the early years.

In this sense the raid on the prison of Nîmes on 4 February 1944 to liberate 20 resisters was as subversive of Vichy authority, and of German occupation, as Labarthe's essay on 'The True France' or the arrival of a small boat of Breton fishermen to join the Free French. At the same time it was the guerrilla tactics of *maquis* and *franc-tireur* units as well as the actions of SOE-led groups that finalised the multiple contribution of the internal resistance to the liberation of France by Allied invasions.

'Sometimes,' wrote Labarthe in another of his essays, 'we can see France shining like a mirage at the end of a London street.' Britain and French Resistance were interlocked, mostly creatively, at times uncomfortably, throughout the whole of the Occupation period. Beyond, and within, historical controversy, it is the *entente* between groups and individuals of the two nations that still continues to be celebrated as a remarkable shared history.

H. Roderick Kedward

Liberating France

The diplomatic relationship between the British and the French during the Liberation period (1944) has often been characterised as one of ill-concealed enmity, epitomised by the stormy relationship of the two principal actors, Churchill and de Gaulle. For Churchill, the continued frustrations included bearing the hardest cross of all, the Cross of Lorraine. For de Gaulle, there was a long catalogue of slights and insults, culminating on the very eve of D-Day with the proposed distribution by foreign countries of so-called 'French' currency.

What is less well documented is the ambivalent Franco-British relationship in those turbulent early months after the liberation of Paris. As de Gaulle strove to impose the rule of his central government over the patchwork of Liberation experiences throughout France, the Allies began to develop a policy of 'controlled interference' designed to support the Gaullist drive for law and order against what was perceived as an incipient descent into disorder.

From the vantage point of Paris, the British observed post-Liberation France to be violent and potentially revolutionary. The position of de Gaulle's provisional government seemed by no means secure. The food situation in late 1944/early 1945 was so appalling that the parliamentary secretary at the Ministry of Food commented that London would 'be in uproar long before it had reached the condition of scarcity which Paris has ... endured quietly'. The British Embassy counselled caution in the face of existing lawlessness in France, with the ambassador, Duff Cooper, arguing that: 'Such excesses as may have been committed by young armed guerrilla bands constitute little more than a natural phenomenon after an abnormal period of foreign intervention.'

Nevertheless, fears about the possibility of major disorder in France in the rear of the Allied armies were so acute that, in early 1945, a directive was drafted outlining how and why the Allies might feel obliged to intervene directly in French internal affairs. This time however, plans were predicated not on the spurious and despised AMGOT (Allied Military Government of Occupied Territory), but on the need to involve and support a possibly faltering Gaullist regime. At the end of January 1945, the directive was ready. It posited a situation where:

economic and political factors may induce a feeling of unrest in France which may, in turn, result in internal disorder and strife. Such disorders may require military force to restore order ... the sole concern of the military authorities is to ensure that the Allied war effort is not impeded by internal disorders in France. We have no desire to intervene in French internal affairs, but it is our duty adequately to secure our installations and lines of communication.

Allied intervention was deemed possible under two separate headings: first, where the French government itself requested assistance, and second, in instances such as riots, strikes and picketing, where direct military intervention was necessary to protect life and property.

It was clear that such intervention in the affairs of Liberated France would be a highly sensitive and delicate matter. The military drew up detailed charts of the channels by which the French government itself might seek such direct help, if for example it proved unable to control a particular situation using French police. In any case it was vital that any intervention came with irrefutable evidence of the desire of the French provisional government for such active military support, given that the 'political repercussions of Allied intervention tend to be so violent'.

Underlying these preparations to support the new Gaullist government was a clear sense that France was in a revolutionary situation and that the French were temperamentally likely to fall into a civil war. As one senior officer expressed it:

I do not think that we are proposing to issue this directive because we are 'windy'. France has been quiet since its Liberation and there is nothing to indicate at the moment that it will not remain quiet. The French, however, have a great name for internal strife and it cannot be doubted that the economic situation and political development in the country provide a potential for trouble. I believe it would be better to get this directive out while all is quiet and let our doctrine of controlled interference filter down to the lower levels.

By April 1945, however, with the political parties concentrating on the elections, the law and order position in France seemed a lot calmer, and 'controlled interference' moved down the policy agenda. The French Ministry of the Interior explained that 'the political situation is well in hand and is not likely to necessitate . . . intervention'. It was agreed therefore not to publish the plans for Allied military intervention.

From D-Day, it had taken the British government five months to recognise the provisional government of France officially. It took another six months for them to shelve the policy of 'controlled interference' and recognise, with their American allies, that 'the French may . . . take offence at an inference of their inability to cope with internal disturbances'.

Hilary Footitt

A Francophile

By any definition of the word, Anthony Eden, arguably the single most important figure in the making of British foreign policy between the mid-1930s and the mid-1950s, was a committed Francophile. The origins of what was probably more of an emotional than an intellectual reaction to things French are not easy to trace with any precision. Eden's experience of allied warfare on the Western Front may have been a factor. At all events, from an early age Eden derived a large part of his cultural milieu from across the Channel. A natural linguist – he secured a first in oriental languages from Christ Church, Oxford – Eden spoke French fluently and, as a young man, perfected his skills with several study trips to La Rochelle. Eden would use this expertise to advantage over his long diplomatic career to converse privately with foreign statesmen, although he avoided negotiating in the language in case an unnoticed nuance should lead to a diplomatic misunderstanding. Eden's considerable collection of fine art included works by such French painters as Corot, Monet, Degas, Braque and Cézanne and, as an undergraduate, he spoke learnedly about the last-named to a meeting of the Uffizi Society, which he had helped to found. His literary tastes embraced the writings of Balzac, Flaubert, Stendhal and Zola, as well as more recent French authors and philosophers.

These enthusiasms no doubt predisposed Eden, the British politician and diplomat, to a sympathetic but not uncritical approach towards France. The international positions of the two countries changed dramatically over the course of Eden's lifetime but, at both the beginning and the end of his career, France appeared to be Britain's one, indispensable ally, whether the challenge came from Hitler's Germany or the Egypt of Colonel Nasser. Eden was at the forefront of British attempts to reach a settlement with the Nazis but, fortunately for his later reputation, resigned from the government in February 1938 before the policy of appeasement began to blacken the names of its proponents. His resignation has usually been seen in terms of differences with the government over the way to handle Britain's potential enemies. But differing perceptions of the country's potential allies were also a factor in the equation. Eden took a conspicuously more optimistic view of Britain's overall predicament than did many of his colleagues, Neville Chamberlain in particular, largely because of the faith he placed in countries such as France. As the international scene grew ever more threatening, so Eden became increasingly concerned to maintain close and supportive relations with the French government. He took comfort from the fact that the French navy was stronger than it had been in 1914 and, relative to the German navy, considerably stronger. He also believed, perhaps misguidedly, that the French army was absolutely sound.

By the time Eden resumed direct responsibility for British diplomacy in December 1940, when he began his second spell as foreign secretary, France had been confined to the sidelines of the military struggle against Nazi Germany, an eventuality that even the most pessimistic of British planners of the 1930s had scarcely dared envisage as they pondered their country's prospects in the face of Hitlerian aggression. But France quickly re-emerged as a political and diplomatic issue of the greatest importance. Indeed, Eden in his retirement described the triangular relationship between Britain, the USA and France as the 'principal problem of the war'. The foreign secretary's role was to uphold French interests even when Churchill's determination to give priority to his relationship with the USA and the almost wilful determination of General de Gaulle, the leader of the Free French, to alienate and outrage the British prime minister made this an almost impossible task. Eden had reacted to the fall of France in June with dismay. The country had incurred such shame that he doubted, whatever the overall outcome of the war, whether it could ever reclaim its position among the world's great powers. But Eden quickly adopted the Foreign Office view that the revival of a strong France should be a central goal of Britain's wartime diplomacy. The United Kingdom's future security, particularly in the event of American withdrawal from the continent once the war was over, would depend upon the creation of a Western European bloc to act as a barrier both to German revival and to the possibility of a westward Soviet expansion. Eden and the Foreign Office also accepted that the revival of France could not be separated from the person of General de Gaulle, intolerable though he so often was. Thereafter Eden worked tirelessly and with great skill to persuade both Churchill and Roosevelt that an accommodation with de Gaulle's Free French was a diplomatic and political necessity. The position France again enjoyed by the end of the war, with the trappings of Great Power status, including a permanent seat on the

United Nations Security Council and a zone of occupation in defeated Germany, probably owed more to Eden than to any other single individual. For him the Cross of Lorraine, though heavy to bear, was never entirely insupportable.

In the post-war era Eden's enthusiasm for France cooled somewhat, or at least he was wary of the European project in which her leaders became engaged as leading players. Nevertheless, it was Eden, in his third spell as foreign secretary, who offered the French an escape route from the collapse of their project for a European army and whose negotiating skills at the Geneva Conference of 1954 navigated a way out for France from the colonial and military imbroglio of Indo-China. Against this background it was a supreme irony that it should have been in the field of Anglo-French relations that Eden, as prime minister in 1956, committed the most serious misjudgement of his whole career. It was in response to a seductive but fatally flawed French plan following the nationalisation of the Suez Canal Company that Eden agreed to encourage an Israeli attack on Egypt, designed to give Britain and France spurious justification for military intervention in Egypt to separate the combatants, but in reality to recover the canal and topple Colonel Nasser. The pretence could not be sustained. Illness forced Eden to resign, although the charge of collusion might in any case have been enough to drive him from office. The French could never understand why the British took this issue so seriously, but they did resent being left in the lurch when Eden gave in to American pressure and abandoned the invasion before its task was completed. By this date Britain and France were moving in different directions and Suez probably had little impact in determining this. But it was at least symbolic that, only weeks after Eden's final resignation, France signed the Treaty of Rome, setting up the European Economic Community, from which Britain stood aloof.

David Dutton

VI
The End of Empire, 1945–97

The end of World War II found France and Britain in a divided Europe facing the US and Soviet superpowers. Paris and London were no longer the pivots of international destiny. That role had been displaced to Washington and Moscow – and, potentially, Peking. Washington overtly disapproved of Empire: Moscow covertly backed its opponents. Decolonisation became inevitable for both France and Britain. Each approached it in a characteristic way.

Two Colonial Powers

The French colonial empire was smaller, much less wealthy and – except in the West Indies and Réunion – younger than the British Empire 'on which the sun never sets'. But they died together, in less than fifteen years, in the mid-twentieth century, as victims of two world wars. In appearance, World War I had strengthened them by destroying the German and Turkish Empires of which, in Africa and the Near East, they shared the remains.

In reality, many things had weakened them. The mother countries had lost men, money and prestige. Self-determination in Europe, urged by the United States, had destroyed the old Austro-Hungarian Empire. Soviet propaganda had preached world revolution. In the colonies, all this had encouraged nationalist movements, some of which, in World War II, joined the enemies of their colonial masters.

World War II sounded the death-knell of all the old colonial empires. Europe was exhausted, cut down to size by the two victorious superpowers, the USA and the USSR. Wartime calls for freedom and independence, aimed originally at German Nazism, Italian Fascism and Japanese military dictatorship, were powerfully echoed in all the colonies by nationalist movements, which now emerged in broad daylight and no longer had scruples over taking up arms.

The two biggest colonial empires, the French and the British, were the first to be attacked. They had no prospect of survival. They perished together, but in different ways. Save for Quebec, the people of the dominions – Canada, Australia and New Zealand – were akin to those of the mother country, and retained links with it.

The huge population of the Indian sub-continent – some 500 million at the time of independence – made any trial of strength unthinkable. In these circumstances, a flexible Commonwealth was compatible with independence.

The demographic picture in the French Empire was more complex – for example, in the Maghreb and especially Algeria – and the local population less numerous, even in the Far East. French colonial administrators relied on direct rule and, often, assimilation. Hence the strong temptation to curb by force the struggle for independence: two wars, in Indochina and Algeria, made the attempt in vain.

Nor did the 'French Community', established on paper as a counterpart to the Commonwealth, survive for very long. All that remains of it, in sub-Saharan Africa, is 'Francophonia' and a monetary zone, the African Financial Community, with its CFA franc.

Although the causes and consequences were the same, resulting in independence for former colonies (with the exception of France's overseas territories), France and Britain themselves reacted very differently to decolonisation.

Britain suffered from an economic and monetary crisis. Traditional industries lost much of their markets, and sterling gradually ceased to be a major world currency. But the country suffered no political, constitutional, or even governmental crisis.

In France, the reaction was the exact opposite. During the so-called 'Glorious Thirty Years' from 1945 to 1974, the French enjoyed unprecedented economic growth: in real terms, their income doubled every ten years.

Their crisis – and it was very serious – was political. The Fourth Republic, born on the morrow of World War II, could not survive the two colonial wars into which it had plunged the country. And for four years General de Gaulle's Algerian policy aroused vehement opposition from blind and hate-filled minorities.

For both France and Britain, decolonisation was a crisis. Now that crisis is past. It would be interesting to compare their present policies *vis-à-vis* their former colonies.

But that, in the words of Kipling, an expert on colonial affairs, 'is another story'.

Pierre Messmer

Entrance to Court of Honour,
Franco-British Exhibition, London, 1908

Plate 1 White City, the current site of the BBC, was so-called owing to the brilliant 'fibrous plaster' applied to the pavilions and halls which formed the Franco-British Exhibition of Science, Arts and Industries, held on a 140-acre site at Shepherd's Bush in west London. This shows the entrance to the Court of Honour and the 'Flip-Flap' (Chapter I).

Flip-Flap,
Franco-British Exhibition, London, 1908

Plate 1 cont.

Plate 2 A French soldier and a British sergeant toasting each other in French ration wine, Boesinghe, 18 August 1917. Photograph Q2742, courtesy of the Imperial War Museum, London (Chapter III)

Plate 3 British soldiers on the boat taking them to France, World War II. Photograph B5207, courtesy of the Imperial War Museum, London (Chapter V)

Plate 4 General de Gaulle speaking to the people, 1945. Photograph courtesy of the Imperial War Museum, London (Chapter V)

Plate 5 Saint Michael's Abbey in Sussex – for many decades an oasis of French prayer and of French living (Chapter IX)

Plate 6 Sir Christopher Mallaby walks into the Channel Tunnel in 1993 to become British Ambassador in France (Chapter X). Photocredit: Stockwave/COI

Plate 7 For British football fans, French players and managers have become true
heroes and role models. Their integration into British society is illustrated
by the award of OBEs in 2003 to managers Gérard Houllier and Arsène
Wenger. Here we see one of the top French players, Thierry Henry,
playing for Arsenal Football Club (Chapter X). Photocredit: PA Photos

Plate 8 Prime Minister Tony Blair of Great Britain and President Jacques Chirac of France in lively debate in St Malo in 1998. The St Malo summit agreement committed the two leading military powers in Europe to building capabilities and institutional structures for a common defence (Chapter X). Photocredit: PA Photos

France and Britain Decolonise

By themselves, dates can be surprising. That of 1945 is fairly obvious, but 1997 may look curious, at least to a French reader. It seems to have no connection with decolonisation, which by that time was surely a thing of the past. But it has meaning for the British. In 1997, the return to China of Hong Kong, the last bastion of the Union flag, was for them the real end of the imperial dream, the final dissolution of the Empire established in the nineteenth century.[1] Here was a first paradox. The United Kingdom, which had long seemed the pioneer in decolonisation, was now the last to complete it. And even on the continent of Africa, where Britain began the process, it was soon largely caught up by France.

This leads to a second paradox. France was often accused of being slow to grasp that anti-colonial forces were irresistible, while Britain – held to be more pragmatic and adroit – was thought to have been astute enough to withdraw from places where it could no longer play the leading role, thereby serving as an example to the French. Instead of getting bogged down in shameful, hopeless wars, Britain was believed to know how to 'negotiate in good time'. Yet closer study reveals that it was barely more successful in avoiding armed conflict. For more than ten years, from 1965 to 1979, Britain had trouble disengaging from the hornets' nest of Rhodesia. For nearly ten years, after the uprising of 1952, it had to impose a severely repressive state of emergency in Kenya. While France was embroiled in Indochina, Britain had to face a revolutionary war in Malaysia. (The obvious difference is that in this case it won.)

Furthermore, the French have always generally believed that 'imperial

---

1 'End of Empire' was the headline in *The Times* on 1 July 1997.

awareness' was much more widespread in Britain. Certainly, very many of the British had personal or family links with other countries in the empire. But, if one includes North Africa, were they more numerous than their counterparts in France? And does 'awareness' imply 'understanding'? As regards decolonisation, were there not as many ambiguities on each side?

It was equally believed, by both parties, that France and Britain acted as rivals in decolonisation, as they had in colonisation itself. From the 'Syrian affair' to the Algerian War and later, relations between the two powers were marked by suspicions, apparently more so in France than in Britain. But these suspicions need to be tested against historical reality. Even if they existed, as they certainly did, is it not the case that political convergence and connivance overcame them?

It is alleged, then, that Britain knew how to 'depart in good time'; that the British left behind, without too much trouble, their model of democracy; and that the French remained wedded to an archaic idea of colonisation. If this had been so, the comparison would undoubtedly favour the British, and relations between the two powers would have been marked by a long history of rivalry rather than *entente*. It is time to look at the facts.

Let us first look backwards. To begin with, at the end of World War II, France and Britain had more mutual grievances than points in common as regards their colonies, especially from the French point of view. The Entente Cordiale had not done away with the Fashoda syndrome, while Mers el-Kebir in 1940 and the Syrian affair in 1945 had even revived ancient rancour against 'perfidious Albion', which was accused of backing France's Arab enemies. For de Gaulle, this dispute reflected nothing but an alliance between 'the frenzy of Arab nationalists and the desire of the British . . . to dominate the Orient'.[2]

So the situation was not propitious for a rapprochement between the British and the French. Yet there were at least three areas of future agreement that I should like to emphasise here: the desire for a joint attitude to the youthful United Nations Organisation; the working out of a common development policy for Africa in the coming decade; and a concerted riposte to Nasser's provocation in 1956. It may be easy to stress the failures, of which the most spectacular was of course the Suez affair. But it would be wrong to ignore these points of agreement.

The first involved a sort of Franco-British common front in 1945–46 against criticisms and initiatives from the United Nations that were deemed unacceptable. Vague attempts to internationalise colonial questions were blocked by this Franco-British *entente*. The French and the

---

2 Charles de Gaulle, *Mémoires de Guerre, Le Salut*, Plon, Paris, 1959, pp. 184–5.

British successfully insisted that UN supervision be imposed only on former 'mandated territories' and on lands freed from enemy control. These latter came under the aegis of a council comprising representatives of 'administrant' and 'non-administrant' states. It had greater power than the former League of Nations Mandates Commission; the change was not merely semantic. The 'administrant' powers had to accept closer supervision, in the form of official visits and the right of petition for the subjects of their dependencies. So the Commission was more than the defunct Mandates Commission. The 'administrant' powers worked to reduce its role, at least by controlling its membership – to the point that an expert as authoritative as Henri Laurentie could describe it in 1948 as 'a tribunal of retired governors-general'.[3] At least on this matter, the French and the British – with also the Belgians – presented a united front.

As regards what were euphemistically called at San Francisco the 'non-autonomous' territories – that is, colonies proper – France's and Britain's positions were even closer. Churchill had declared that he had not become His Majesty's prime minister 'to liquidate the British Empire', and de Gaulle had made the restoration of the French Empire a condition of France's recovery of its world rank. True, Churchill left office in 1945, and de Gaulle in 1946. But their successors' attitude to UN 'interference' remained the same: the colonial powers' only obligations should be to inform the UN and fulfil their 'sacred' duty of leading their peoples to 'the capacity to administer their own affairs'.

The second great point of agreement was a joint attempt to develop sub-tropical Africa. This was a geographical area where the two powers could implement their declarations in favour of the 'native' populations – North Africa and Southeast Asia both being excluded from this prospect, though for very different reasons. In Africa, it was a question not just of bringing up to date the old theme of 'development and reclamation', but of enriching it with 'progressive' content and giving a new sense to the idea of 'Eurafrica'. And on the part of both the French and the British there was evident goodwill. This was shown by the concrete (and comparable) steps the governments took to help their dependencies. They included the Colonial and Welfare Act, passed by the House of Commons in 1939 but interrupted by the war, and the Economic and Social Development Fund, established by the French in 1946. Pursuing this new 'colonial spirit', French and British leaders who had come to prominence during the war

---

3 Henri Laurentie, a colonial administrator in 1940 who then went to London, had been the organiser of the Brazzaville Conference; director of Political Affairs in the Ministry for Overseas France, he became assistant French representative at the UN.

now tried to achieve real inter-colonial cooperation.[4] It resulted in the establishment of the Commission pour la Coopération technique sud du Sahara (CCTA), which was finally incorporated in the Organisation for African Unity in 1963. If it did not have the impact and the success its promoters had hoped, this was not at all because of some Franco-British misunderstanding. In fact, the CCTA was at first run by a sort of tripartite directorate of France, Britain and Belgium. It aimed to include all the colonial powers in its Africa development programme, but it fell into disrepute when it was discredited by the participation of Portugal and South Africa.

The third point of Franco-British agreement was 1956. Whatever retrospective verdict may be passed on the Suez venture and on Israel's part in it, this was when Franco-British cooperation reached its climax – and pause. Never had cooperation between the two governments and the convergence of their views on Nasser better represented the Entente Cordiale. Presented as a dictator similar to Hitler and a friend of the Soviets, accused of helping the Algerian rebels and all the anti-colonial agitators, Nasser was also suspected of pan-African ambitions. To yield to his provocation seemed to risk opening the flood-gates to waves of anti-French and anti-British hostility in Africa and the Third World.

For the French, moreover, the Franco-British operation of 1956 made some amends for the unilateral British occupation of Suez in 1882, which had ended the Franco-British dual role there. It was also an undoubted military success. But Suez in 1956, far more than Bandung in 1955, put an end to the two powers' illusions and made them soft-pedal too strident a colonial cooperation. After de Gaulle's return to power in 1958, divergences increased – not that colonial problems were really the reasons for this.

Altogether, it would be a mistake to see Franco-British relations during the dismantlement of their respective empires solely in terms of rivalry and antagonism, or reciprocal dirty tricks. On the contrary, there are many more instances of agreement than those already mentioned. In 1945, for example, General Leclerc's French expeditionary force sailed to Indochina in British ships, and it was the United Kingdom that acted as moderator in the crisis of Sakiet Sidi Youssef in 1958.

Even so, disagreements seem to have outnumbered agreements, and for several reasons. The first is that France's and Britain's ideas about colonialism were always incompatible.

The French had long been perplexed by the complexity of the British

---

4 See on this subject John Kent, *The Internationalisation of Colonialism: Britain, France and Black Africa, 1939–1956*, Clarendon Press, Oxford, 1997.

Empire. What did its countries have in common? They included colonies, overseas territories, more or less informal protectorates, mandates and dominions. The definition of 'Empire' itself seemed curiously vague to 'Cartesian' minds when in 1926 it was transformed at least in part into the Commonwealth, defined as follows:

> Autonomous communities within the British Empire, equal in status, in no way subordinate one to another in any aspect of their internal or external affairs, although bound by common allegiance to the Crown, and freely associated as members of the British *Commonwealth* of nations.

It was obvious, however, that such a definition could not apply to the subjects of His Majesty who lived in the *Dependent Empire*, for instance in black Africa. Nor could it cover 'semi-colonies' such as Egypt, which in principle became a sovereign nation, admitted to the League of Nations in 1936 – although in reality it remained a state 'under influence'. Nor did the definition fit 'British India' (and likewise Burma and Ceylon). In other words, the British Empire had always seemed to the French an irregular and barely comprehensible collection of states, a fearsome but loose-knit *Imperium*.

France, on the contrary, seemed to have built a much more coherent and centralised system: great federations governed from imperial capitals, as well as protectorates and mandates. Yet in reality the French Empire was little more coherent than the British. The members of the Constituent Assembly in 1945 certainly had in mind a great integrating structure: the French Union. Lame, and in reality very limited, this offered its colonial peoples only 'a fictitious association' which was 'neither federation nor self-government nor emancipation'.[5] It included neither the protectorates nor Algeria (which was France's only real settlement colony and, as everyone knows, comprised three *départements* of France). After 1946 it no longer included the 'old colonies' that had recently been made into *départements*: the Antilles, Guyana and Réunion. Ancient Indochina, transformed into associated states, was already torn by a Vietnam war that was sapping the very foundations of the French Union.

To go further, the fundamental differences between the two imperial systems lay less in their architecture than in their 'projects' – in so far as such a term is apt. This became clear just after World War II. While

---

5   Jean-Pierre Roux, *La France de la Quatrième République, I. L'ardeur et la nécessité, 1944–1952*, Le Seuil, Points Histoire, Paris, 1980, p. 128.

Britain seemed to adapt to the new situation and agree to 'go home' from Palestine, India, Ceylon and so on, France seemed to cling on everywhere, and be willing to oppose decolonisation against the wishes of the colonised and against world opinion itself. The two contrasting attitudes represented deeply conflicting views. Among the British, there was a kind of general line described as the 'Official Mind', summarised very well in 1938 by the Colonial Secretary Malcolm MacDonald: 'The supreme goal of the British Empire is the progressive expansion of freedom among all His Majesty's subjects, wherever in the world they live.'[6]

Clearly, the achievement of this 'goal' depended on the view held by the Crown. It 'could take generations, or centuries, before the people in certain parts of the colonial Empire could attain self-government,' the minister added. Even so, he laid down the principle of *gradualism* leading to emancipation, and implied the famous pragmatism in the face of 'the force of events' with which the United Kingdom was credited in later years. Nothing of this kind was expressed in France. The Brazzaville Conference had affirmed:

> The aims of the civilising mission accomplished by France in the colonies exclude any idea of autonomy and any possibility of evolving outside the French Empire; even the possible long-term establishment of self-government in the colonies is to be avoided.

It could not have been more clearly stated: for France, the British model was out. As a result, it had to give way to force, and not by consent.

On the other hand, the French were convinced that they were offering an authentic model of emancipation not by recognising independence for the colonies, but by integrating them into the same community. This idea, in its various forms, went on being pursued until de Gaulle's return to power. It was based on a premise very well defined in 1949, in a remarkable report from an observer of mark, the British ambassador in France. Recalling the saying that 'the British educate the natives to govern themselves, while the French educate them to govern France', he explained:

> So long as the policy of the French Union, politically as well as culturally, continues to be based on the assimilation of native populations into metropolitan France, French education will retain the same cohe-

---

6 Malcolm MacDonald, Speech in the House of Commons, 7 December 1938, quoted in Marc Michel, *Décolonisations et émergence du tiers-monde*, Hachette Supérieur, coll. Carré-Histoire, Paris, 1993, p. 24.

sive force. Frenchmen of all parties share profound faith in the power of cultural proselytism among the colonial peoples and the Arabs.[7]

That, it seems to me, is the heart of the problem. One might add that this proselytism involved something which had perverse results: the desire to make oneself loved. So the phrase 'selling off the colonies' meant not only selling one's interests short, but deserting, giving up influence, breaking trust. It would be a mistake to neglect the role of feelings, especially in Algeria, where there was also a sizeable French population. Was this not also true of the British? Obviously not: they were very keen to hand over to 'gentlemen' who were sure the British political system was excellent and certain they should stay in the Commonwealth. At the same time, however, the cultural factor seems to have weighed less heavily in the British case – partly, perhaps, because the English language was so predominant. To paraphrase the great Nigerian writer Wole Soyinka: does the tiger need to demonstrate its 'tigritude'?

There was, however, one feeling that the French and the British – or their general opinion-formers – tended to share. This was their relative indifference to colonial problems. Unless they greatly disturbed the life of the nation, these were thought of as questions for experts. The experts themselves were aware of this. They knew that public opinion was largely indifferent to what went on in the colonies, even if it involved trouble. It was this indifference, rather than governmental news blackouts, that explained why reactions were so muted for so long. The war in Indochina, despite repeated efforts by the communists – and perhaps because of their ideology – scarcely stirred the crowds. This is why Dien Bien Phû came as such a surprise. The 'disturbances' in Algeria became a serious national preoccupation only after young conscripts were sent there in 1956. And what can be said of the revolt in Madagascar in 1947, unrest in the Ivory Coast in 1949, and the Cameroon insurrection in 1955? Were matters very different on the British side? Did Kwame Nkrumah's 'Positive Action' on the Gold Coast greatly arouse public opinion in Britain? It would appear not, even though Mau Mau violence in Kenya and the Rhodesian affair in 1965 seem to have caused greater concern.

Why was British and French public opinion so quiescent? There are many reasons, not least the fact that these distant events only marginally affected life in the 'mother countries'. There was also incredible ignorance about overseas dependencies. In 1948 and 1949, opinion polls requested by

7 Public Record Office, FO 371/79165, Sir Oliver Harvey to Clement Attlee, 13 September 1949, 'French colonial policy and the organisation of the French Union'.

the British Colonial Office and the Assembly of the French Union make comparisons possible, and somewhat scotch the notion that a real imperial spirit was entrenched in France and Britain after the war.[8] The results show that such a spirit existed, but that it was extremely vague. Seventy per cent of those British people questioned could not describe the difference between a dominion and a colony; fewer than half could correctly name a 'Crown colony'; nearly two-thirds admitted that they had no direct or indirect link with any part of the Commonwealth, including the Dominions. In France, more than a fifth of those questioned said they might accept a job in the United States, but only 4 per cent in Africa (3 per cent in North Africa). In the list of 'colonies' where France was thought to have been most successful, Algeria came top with a third of the positive answers, while Indochina (because of the news) came bottom, with 55 per cent of negative views. The news of the day also seemed to dominate British public opinion, because more than two-thirds of respondents mentioned the 'Ground-nut Scheme', a large-scale agricultural project in East Africa, as a recent colonial project – because, it was said, the post-war British house-wife would gain from it. But exactly the same proportion of those asked were unable to name any foodstuff that came from the colonies. There is no evidence, either, that this degree of ignorance later diminished. In both countries, in fact, the only dominant feeling seems for a long time to have been the vague sentiment that empire meant power.

In the 1950s things gradually changed. Once again, 1956 seems to have been a turning-point. Public opinion then began to come round to the idea of lowering the flag, except in very special places such as Britain's 'fortress colonies' or French Algeria. Anti-colonialist pressure seemed more and more irresistible in the countries concerned; defeat followed defeat; and the defence of the colonies turned ever more plainly into a rearguard action. Behind this gradual renunciation one can detect the pressure of something new: 'international opinion'. So far, the best definition of this nebulous entity seems to me to have been given by a Belgian historian:

> International opinion is essentially an amorphous notion. It is an amalgam of tendencies that are often mutually contradictory and in any case very different in their nuances. It is born of the convergence of new principles, resolutions voted by international bodies, popular

---

8   Assembly of the French Union, 1949, Appendix to the Report on the Session of July 8, Report made in the name of the Committee on Cultural Affairs; 1. 'Results of polls conducted in France since 1945 on questions concerning the French Union'; 2. 'Results of a poll conducted at the request of the Colonial Office from May 17 to June 3, 1948'.

demonstrations, the formation of diverse associations, academic works published in the four corners of the world, and editorials in leading dailies or periodicals. Hard as it is to grasp in its consensus and concrete reality, international opinion will weigh heavily on the attitude of certain colonial powers.[9]

After 1948, however, a curious reversal of positions took place. Until then, Britain had been ahead in the race to decolonise. After leaving Palestine and then India – which, as malicious Frenchmen observed, led to catastrophes – and before leaving Malaysia, the British Crown had been the first to grant independence to an African country, the Gold Coast, which on 6 March 1957, became Nkrumah's Ghana. France seemed to be lagging behind. In Africa, only Morocco and Tunisia preceded the other countries in the forced march that was beginning. At the same time, the famous 'Defferre framework law' of 1956 was conceived not as a step towards independence, but on the contrary as the last chance for the French Union and a nostrum against any possible contagion from the war that was raging in Algeria. When General de Gaulle returned to power, the pace dizzily quickened. Guinea gave the signal in startling fashion in 1958. The hope of building a community, and then an enlarged community, vanished in some twenty months. In 1959 Madagascar and the Mali Federation (Senegal and Sudan) began the process that would lead thirteen new French-speaking black African countries to join the UN together. In 1962, the process ended tragically in Algeria. Essentially, French decolonisation was coming to an end. There remained the Somali Coast, which did not achieve independence until 1977, and a few scatterings of empire such as Oceania and New Caledonia.

It was Britain that now seemed to be lagging behind, but it soon gave signs of wanting to catch up. Prime Minister Harold Macmillan's great tour of Africa in 1960 set things in motion when he made his famous (and, for South Africa, provocative) speech at the Cape in February. Addressing his South African audience, he recognised that 'the winds of change' were blowing so strongly that it was no longer possible, or wise, to resist them.

But was there so much difference between the attitudes of Macmillan and de Gaulle? Both, in fact, would seem to have followed the same policy of *Realpolitik* in the face of situations that, although different, were equally dramatic for both France and Britain – for France in Algeria, for Britain in eastern and southern Africa. So if, since 1956, the two countries were no

9   Jacques Vanderlinden, *La Crise congolaise, 1959–1960*, La Mémoire du siècle, Editions Complexe, Brussels, 1985, p. 17.

longer 'hand in hand', they were nevertheless marching in parallel, taking turns to lead the way to the freedom of their former colonies. As for public opinion, it seemed as ready to abandon lost causes as to shed increasingly unbearable burdens.

Yet what the British prime minister said at the Cape had wider repercussions. A new era, he declared, was at hand. It would involve 'a battle for the conquest of souls'. One should not forget that in 1960 the Cold War was still a basic fact of international relations, and that it had spread to developing countries since they had emerged on to the world scene. The former colonial powers had to give way to the superpowers. The end of decolonisation, from the Congo crisis to the fall of the Portuguese empire in 1975, saw the irruption of the superpowers into the competition for influence in Africa. But by the beginning of the 1960s, time was up for France and Britain: the white man would have to go. In this situation the Rhodesian affair was no more than an aftershock, a last stand by one of the few white minorities left in ex-colonial Africa.

That said, the former colonial powers maintained their presence in other ways, at the risk of being implicated every two years in the attack on neo-colonialism and also being accused of having prepared the way for anarchy or dictatorship in the newly independent countries. It was alleged that the legacy of both powers had been the same: under-development, artificial frontiers, predatory bureaucracies, tribalism, and finally civil wars. This is not the place to pick over the charges. They aroused controversy and animosity between the French and the British soon after independence. 'And now Lord Lugard' was the title of an accusing article by Hubert Deschamps, a former colonial senior official who became the first professor of African history at the Sorbonne. His aim was to stress 'before the tribunal of history' the responsibility of Britain's colonial policy of 'indirect rule', which he accused of dividing the élites from the masses and exacerbating 'tribalism', the germ of future conflicts.[10] With hindsight, and in view of contemporary conflicts in so-called 'francophone' Africa, the accusation looks very unjust, and the plaintiffs and the defendants look rather alike. Yet the old quarrels between the French and the British in Africa have not been completely forgotten. As late as 1997, a respectable periodical showed this in an article about Rwanda.[11] The French, it declared, suspected 'an Anglo-Saxon plot' to expel them from their 'chosen acre' and were ready to take their revenge for Fashoda. The

10 Hubert Deschamps, 'And now Lord Lugard', *Africa*, XXXIII, 40, October 1963.
11 'Fashoda revisited', *The Economist*, 8 February 1997.

article concluded: ' "*Allons enfants*", by the dawn's early light.' Today such polemics seem totally obsolete: local and international circumstances are fundamentally changed. And does it make sense today to go on talking about Franco-British rivalry when, even in Africa, the British have handed over to the Americans?

Marc Michel

Suez

International crises nurture national stereotypes. Over Suez British hypocrisy encountered French collusion; together, they gave birth to the Protocol of Sèvres, that ultra-secret pact between Britain, France and Israel, which provided for an Israeli attack on Egypt to be followed by the pretence of an impartial Anglo-French intervention between two warring states, Egypt and Israel. Until now the Middle East had been the region in which Britain and France had been most at odds, but Egyptian ruler Gamal Abdul Nasser had forced them temporarily together in mid-1956. Yet the year had begun with the publication between governments by the Quai d'Orsay, supposedly by mistake, of an internal memorandum sharply critical of a British policy as reliant on Iraq continuing to be a friendly state. Its main instrument, the Baghdad Pact between Britain, Iraq, Pakistan and Turkey, was portrayed as being less of a barrier to the Soviet Union, more of a provocation to intervene.

The British retained the conviction that deep down in the Middle East they were loved and when not loved respected; the French, they were sure, were hated. 'The French are so powerless in the Middle East now that any fingerhold has to be exploited,' wrote a Whitehall official with some complacency; and in December 1955 the British Embassy in Paris recorded that:

> We would not contest the argument that to achieve concerted action with the French on major issues in the Middle East will probably be either impossible or unduly hampering ... There is also the major difficulty which always crops up sooner or later, that on the most secret matters the French are too bad on security.

Once the Suez crisis had started it was indeed the security factor that was mainly responsible for the frustrating delay between the three dates of 29 July 1956, when the French first conveyed their readiness to act over Suez under British command, 9 August, when their staff officers were at last able to come over to Whitehall to concert plans, and 16 August, when they were fully taken into confidence in the claustrophobic atmosphere of the Montagu House annexe. For a week the British officers had been told to withhold from their French colleagues the rather essential fact that the main landing was to take place not in congested Port Said but using the ample facilities of Alexandria. This was a procedure that was held by General Sir Hugh Stockwell, the designated Allied land force commander, to be 'both distasteful and foreign to British principles'. (In the end, of course, the landing did take place at Port Said.) And, as an additional overture to a close alliance, Sir Gladwyn Jebb, the British Ambassador in Paris, was instructed to hold political discussions with the French about, among other things, Algeria, since 'France is at present the most unpopular country in the Arab world. We must try to minimise the additional burden of French unpopularity to the greatest possible extent.'

When the French had swallowed the tight British stipulations about secrecy the collaboration was, according to those who took part, warm and close. This was despite French discomfiture with the collegiate practice of British staffs for developing military plans, which the French found too slow and ponderous. Certainly the British planners, such as Group Captain (later Air Chief Marshal) Denis Smallwood, always spoke most highly of their colleagues. 'It is true to say that all of us', Smallwood has said, 'formed a very high opinion of our French counterparts and of the performance of their squadrons [that] in many respects ... outshone the performance of some of the RAF squadrons.' Nor did Colonel Maurice Perdrizet's British Service colleagues think the worse of him when he suddenly disappeared from the Montagu House basement telling people no more than that he had been ordered to leave immediately, before later turning up as the commander of the air detachment that the French, as part of their separate 'collusion', had promised to Israel.

The two prime ministers in office in 1956, Anthony Eden and Guy Mollet, were both temperamentally attracted to a revival of the Entente Cordiale. As foreign secretary in Winston Churchill's wartime government, Anthony Eden had been noted for pressing the case for France to be treated as one of the principal victorious powers, while Mollet was a former English-language teacher (on which subject he had published a book), with a Protestant father who counted Huguenot exiles in England among his ancestors. Moreover, the very fact that his government was in the process of negotiating the Treaty of Rome, which set up the European Economic Community, made him particularly sensitive to the danger of this creating a breach with Britain. On 10 September in the midst of the Suez crisis, the handling of which Mollet saw as a pilot operation for a permanently close working relationship between the two countries, he suddenly, without any preliminary staff work, proposed to revive Churchill's 1940 offer of a Franco-British Union with one common citizenship. Eden, taken aback but not allowing the notion to throw him, referred it to key government departments. These, each in due course, produced comments disparaging to the French.

With the ease of a fluent French-speaker Eden clearly enjoyed his conferences with the French, unlike his foreign secretary, Selwyn Lloyd, who felt rather left out. More than once Eden expressed his personal admiration for the youthful members of Mollet's Cabinet, mainly Resistance heroes whom he held to be bringing about 'a renaissance of France'. He used the argument in Cabinet whenever some colleagues were lagging in enthusiasm for his plans that they must not disappoint the French. Reciprocally, Mollet, whenever he was urged that France should not be bound by Britain's faltering footsteps, threw his weight on to the side of maintaining the British connection.

The system of the British exercising the top commands with Frenchmen as deputies, which the French, preoccupied by the Algerian rebellion, had themselves proposed in the hope of strengthening British commitment to regime change in Cairo, led to some odd couplings. The French land force commander, General André Beaufre, was a perfect English-speaker who combined an English stiff upper lip with a Gallic resort to logic, while his British counterpart, General Stockwell, was said to be emotional 'in the continental way', with alternate peaks and troughs. 'Stockwell, stubborn as a mule,' writes the French historian Paul Gaujac, 'would consistently reject any decisions taken by Beaufre, however impeccably well presented they were.' Nevertheless many of the French, especially the paratroopers, preferred Stockwell to their own countryman.

The air commanders worked well together, with the top commander, a New Zealander, isolated in a command ship with poor communications and his French deputy effectively controlling operations from Cyprus. But with the navies it was different. The French had selected Rear-Admiral Lancelot, whose career had previously involved successful liaison with the British but who found his British superior, Vice-Admiral Robin Durnford-Slater, to be 'a sailor of the old school . . . of Lord Nelson', appearing to believe that 'there was no naval truth outside the Royal Navy'. Lancelot afterwards described the attitude of his British counterparts as one of 'sympathetic condescension and light but unmistakable mistrust'.

Because of British leadership of the integrated command – and also because General Beaufre was not, in the express opinion of some of his compatriots, the type of French officer to press on down the Suez Canal at the head of his men regardless of orders – the operation was aborted overnight on 6–7 November. The proximate reason was that the British Cabinet put the health of the British currency, threatened by US displeasure, ahead of Britain's understanding with France. By the time, a few weeks later, that the young Valéry Giscard d'Estaing appeared before the UN General Assembly as a special envoy brimming over with evidence that Nasser had launched a major cultural offensive against French influence in his country, Britain was unwilling to provide more than formal support. Following Suez Britain's first priority was to restore the fractured relationship with the United States.

Suez seemed to confirm to the French that when the chips were down the Anglo-Saxon countries would always prefer their own unity to solidarity with a European partner. West German Chancellor Konrad Adenauer said to Mollet on 6 November when Eden had telephoned his agreement with the American President to declare a ceasefire, 'Europe will be your revenge.' General de Gaulle's subsequent repudiation of NATO's integrated command system and his veto of British membership of the European Economic Community on the ground of Britain's extra-European allegiances followed from the Suez experience, as did the decision, prior even to de Gaulle's return to power, that France needed to possess the nuclear weapon.

Keith Kyle

VII
France, Britain and Europe

Western Europe's response to past internal strife and present international weakness was to seek unity as a source of peace and strength. Jean Monnet, the founding father of the European Union, tried in 1949 to persuade Britain and France to pursue joint economic planning. When he failed, he turned to the reconciliation of France and Germany and in 1950 proposed the European Coal and Steel Community, joined also by Italy, the Netherlands, Belgium and Luxembourg. Monnet tried hard to persuade Britain to be a founder-member, but there too he failed. A further failure was the attempt to build a European Defence Community, but after its collapse in 1954 the six Community countries met in Messina in 1955 to begin what came to be called the 're-launching' of Europe through the European Economic Community and Euratom.

Franco-British Father of Europe: Jean Monnet

What was Jean Monnet's job? For years, the Larousse dictionary described him as an 'economist'. It was an understandable misnomer. After World War II, he had invented and headed France's Commissariat au Plan, bringing together employers, unions and civil servants to boost the French economy. But a far better description is that offered by his biographer François Duchêne: 'an entrepreneur in the public interest'.

He remains best known as the 'Father of Europe'. In 1950 he instigated the Schuman Plan for a European Coal and Steel Community and the abortive Pleven Plan for European defence. In 1955 he helped launch Euratom and the 'Common Market'. In 1976, three years before his death at the age of 90, the European Council proclaimed him an 'Honorary Citizen of Europe'.

But he began his public career in 1914 as a Franco-British official coordinating wartime supplies – a task he resumed in 1939. Straddling two nations, he was misunderstood by both sides.

'Oh, Monnet? He's just an *adventurer*.' So, in private in the 1950s, said Sir James Marjoribanks. In 1940 another British official, Oliver Harvey, wrote: 'Monnet seemed a mixture of gangster and conspirator . . . I don't care for him and I don't trust him.'

What was it that so troubled them? Not, obviously, Monnet's being French. He spoke English well, having learned it as a teenager in a London wine merchant's. He retained a French accent – usually charming to British ears. But his dry, husky voice also echoed North America, where he had spent eight years selling brandy for his family's firm in Cognac. Did the transatlantic tang make Oliver Harvey think of gangsters? In English Monnet tended to grin and chuckle: in French, his face was often impassive. He was good at keeping secrets. Did the switch from joviality to discretion make him seem 'conspiratorial'?

What made him seem 'an adventurer' was certainly his unconventional career. He had left school at 16, and never attended a university or a *grande école*. He had become an Allied official in 1914 at his own behest, having warned French Prime Minister René Viviani that Britain and France were competing for scarce supplies. Viviani appointed him to sort things out in London: the battle with bureaucracy took him two years. His lack of civil service conditioning may have helped. After World War I, when at 31 he was made deputy secretary-general of the League of Nations, he seldom kept office hours. He piled dossiers on his desk unread, preferring to quiz their authors. But he solved thorny problems, notably in Upper Silesia and Austria. He failed, however, to persuade Raymond Poincaré to moderate demands for German reparations, and left Geneva to rescue the family firm.

After two years back in Cognac he changed profession again, becoming an investment banker. He made (and lost) a fortune, stabilised the Romanian economy, helped wind up the Kreuger match empire, and found new ways to finance the Chinese railways. Yet he remained unique. Montagu Norman, governor of the Bank of England, said he was 'not so much a banker as a conjuror' – an equivocal tribute.

If some Britons mistrusted Monnet, so did some French. In 1917 Georges Clémenceau's minister of armaments, Louis Loucheur, complained that 'those people in London, and particularly Monsieur Monnet, are completely incompetent'. Loucheur resented Monnet's allocating resources among the Allies according to need. The minister added: 'He must be recalled. He has never been to the Front.' The accusation was misguided: Monnet had been rejected as medically unfit. But Clémenceau summoned him to Paris and, as Monnet said later, 'received me very coldly, very icily ... He said to me, I remember very well: "It is time you went to the Front."' When Monnet explained his work, Clémenceau changed his mind – and made Loucheur do the same.

During and after World War II, Monnet aroused further resentment in France. In part, again, it was because he was *sui generis.* Charles de Gaulle called him a 'petty financier', and later, scornfully, '*l'inspirateur*' of European integrationist dreams. Others accused him of undue allegiance to Britain and/or the United States. What really disconcerted them was his openness to the wider world. This stemmed from his inter-war experience as a banker and his World War II role in the States on the British Supply Council, in contact with countless Americans who later gave him such influence as an *éminence grise.*

But it also sprang from his upbringing. In those distant days, Cognac was less provincial than Paris. 'From the days of my childhood,' Monnet wrote in his *Memoirs*, 'it was natural for me to expect to meet people who spoke other languages and had different customs... But it did not make us feel different, or dependent. In Cognac, one was on equal terms with the British: in Paris, one was somewhat under their influence. So we avoided ... proud or defensive nationalistic reactions... I have never had to fight against reflexes that I have never acquired.' A rare advantage, even today.

Richard Mayne

Britain into Europe

The Messina Conference met in 1955, and the Treaty of Rome was signed in 1958. The period between these events and the beginning of 1973, when the United Kingdom joined the European Community, is relatively short by comparison with the century-long Entente Cordiale whose permanence this book intends to mark.

It has to be admitted that the decade-and-a-half in question lacked both *entente* and cordiality. During the 'hesitation waltz' that preceded the signature of the Treaty of Brussels in January 1972, much rancour and bitterness arose between the two countries, threatening in the long term to form insurmountable obstacles.

In historical terms, the period was brief – little more than fifteen years or, strictly speaking, less than ten years between the beginning of the first British membership negotiations, in 1961, and the end of those among the Nine in the last months of 1971. The political success of these talks had been broadly expected. As early as the dawn of 23 June 1971, the foreign ministers of the original Six and of the UK, Denmark, Ireland and Norway[1] had judged the negotiations far enough advanced to drink – a final test – the Luxembourg champagne that they had been generously offered.

In this process, what had been at stake was fundamental. To say this is not to exaggerate. The decision concerned the very essence of the United Kingdom, and it was to determine the internal development of the European Union, notably making inevitable its further enlargement. It accelerated – and not by chance – a change in the Community's title. Great Britain had applied to join what was then generally known as 'the Common

---

1 Norway finally failed to ratify its accession treaty.

Market' (in reality the European Economic Community, Euratom and the ECSC). But at their first summit meeting, in Paris in October 1972, the nine heads of state and government decided to adopt the name 'European Union', stressing thereby that its aim was more than purely economic. This nomenclature, incidentally, was only much later formally adopted in print.

The preceding period of debate, marked at first by hostility, then by British reservations, and then by two French refusals to let the Community conclude or begin talks on British entry, spurred the Six – by a very 'Hegelian' process of thesis, antithesis and synthesis – to mature the nascent Community. The start of the successful negotiations in fact coincided with the end of the transition period laid down by the Treaty of Rome. During this time, attitudes in Britain had evolved in the face of new realities – so much so that by 1967 the three main political parties at Westminster, despite some deep-rooted misgivings, were theoretically agreed that Community membership was in Britain's interest.

It is not paradoxical, I believe, to argue that both General de Gaulle and President Pompidou were right to act as they did – General de Gaulle throwing all his weight into delaying British membership, which in the 1960s would have been premature, and President Pompidou beginning his presidency by dropping France's opposition to what her five continental partners constantly and unanimously wished.

Nevertheless, the shock and humiliation felt by the British when de Gaulle broke off negotiations in January 1963 had a lasting effect on their feelings towards the building of Europe, and crystallised hostile emotions. It could hardly have been otherwise.

The diplomatic activity that led from the Conference in The Hague in December 1969 to the Treaty of Brussels on British, Danish and Irish membership included agreement among the Six on the financial regulation marking the end of the Common Market's transition period and the organisation of various agricultural markets. Thus were settled the main economic and financial problems still unresolved.

On a more political level, when President Pompidou announced in January 1972 that France would hold a referendum on ratifying the Treaty to enlarge the Community, he insisted that:

> This accession is very much more than a simple enlargement. It will change not only Europe's external role, but the internal future of Europe and of Europe's nations and, as a result, the future of Frenchmen.

He added:

> To unite with a people which, perhaps more than any in the world, is

concerned to keep its national identity, is also to choose for Europe a formula that will preserve the personality of its nations.

In the 1950s, Great Britain was rightly esteemed for the unique role it had played in World War II. It could pride itself on its special relationship with the United States, and it stood at the head of a still close-knit Commonwealth.

For all these reasons – historical, military, psychological, economic – it did not feel concerned by the attempt to create a sub-regional continental entity. This attempt, which it had at first encouraged (for instance, in Winston Churchill's Zurich speech of 1946) did not tempt the British government to join its six continental neighbours. In 1950, Britain refused to join the Schuman Plan for a Coal and Steel Community, and then to back the 'relaunching of Europe' by the Messina Conference and the Spaak Committee, which led in 1957 to the Treaty of Rome. At the time the British press poured scorn on 'the Messina brothers' – an allusion to two then celebrated London gangsters of that name.

The diplomatic and practical success of the Treaty of Rome seemed to take the United Kingdom aback. The end of the 1950s saw attempts by the British government to drown this nascent customs union in a broad free trade area including all the member states of the OEEC. Reginald Maudling failed in this project, whose sole opponent was France. The United Kingdom had to content itself, in 1969, with EFTA, the seven-nation European Free Trade Association, alongside the Six. The attempt to envelop the Community in a wider free-trading system without common policies had come to grief.

Meanwhile, one of General de Gaulle's very first acts when he returned to power in 1958 had been – to many people's surprise – the decision that France would fulfil all its obligations under the Treaty of Rome. As Olivier Guichard has remarked, 'The Common Market treaty was signed by politicians who would have been unable to implement it, and implemented by someone who would never have signed it.' A first consideration, no doubt, was General de Gaulle's desire to stand by France's signature. But he may also have been attracted by the chance to break with protectionist traditions and open France to a wider world. (The boldness of his economic and financial reform plan in December 1958 had the same classically liberal roots.) Finally, and perhaps chiefly, de Gaulle could not have failed to realise the political and diplomatic scope that such a 'European space' could offer France. At all events he was clear about the problems that it would cause France's British friends, because he remarked to Georges Pompidou, who was then his *Directeur de cabinet*: 'What bothers me about your Common Market is that it will stir up trouble with the British.'

The EEC began in a climate of economic euphoria that greatly helped its success. The British soon became worried as customs duties and quota restrictions were lowered among the member states, whose mutual trade enjoyed a growth that outsiders only partly shared. The result was that in British government circles, as in business and the City, the conviction grew that membership of this growing community was a perhaps unfortunate necessity.

In July 1961, Prime Minister Harold Macmillan announced to the House of Commons his decision to explore the conditions of his country's accession to the European Communities. To head the talks on the British side he appointed the convinced 'European' Edward Heath, the Lord Privy Seal, a minister without portfolio somewhat on the fringes of government, and certainly atypical. His remit faced considerable difficulties, notably on the future Common Agricultural Policy, on Britain's imports of Commonwealth products, and on the future of its partners in EFTA.

A great deal has been written about the 1962 meetings between de Gaulle and Macmillan, at Champs (rather positive, but so lofty as to encourage misunderstandings), then at Rambouillet, as well as about the concomitance of Britain's request for talks with the Six and its agreement at Nassau with the USA. Nassau, General de Gaulle explained in October 1966, was the reason for his decision to break off negotiations with Britain:

> In 1963, we were obliged to call a halt to the Brussels negotiations on Britain's accession to the organisation. Not by any means that we despaired of one day seeing this great island people truly unite its destiny with that of the Continent. But the fact is that it was not then able to accept the common rules, and it had just shown, at Nassau, that it owed allegiance outside Europe. Had the negotiations continued in vain, they would have prevented the Six from building their Community.

So the negotiations were adjourned. There was a long pause, for at least two reasons. The first was that Mr Heath was bound by instructions that were too restrictive. The second, less obvious, was that in 1962 the British Government thought, it seems to me, that it could block any progress in building the Common Market thanks to the coalition of those countries it thought of as 'the Friendly Five' – that is, France's five continental partners. But at that time the president of the Commission, Walter Hallstein, had doubts about British membership, which he feared might be premature. This was certainly the view in France, because the Common Agricultural Policy was still not fully settled.

Last but not least, the United States government seemed to be exerting only moderate pressure for British membership. So Britain did not hold a full hand of cards. General de Gaulle's press conference on 14 January 1963 put a resounding end to these first talks, and their adjournment was officially confirmed in Brussels on 29 January. Between these two dates, on 22 January, France and Germany signed the Elysée Treaty of Friendship and Cooperation.

Naturally enough, life went on. The Common Market continued to be built, gradually, in spite of crises. In particular, France's interpretation of the January 1966 Luxembourg Compromise (or 'gentlemen's disagreement' on majority voting) gave the United Kingdom reason to hope that its national sovereignty would not be unreasonably endangered by joining the Community. At the same time, the British economy was performing less and less well and, quite logically, opinion in favour of membership – which was always highly volatile – peaked in the 1966 polls. It may be noted that while at the beginning of the 1950s the Commonwealth had taken more than half Britain's exports, by 1967 it was taking less than a third.

In these circumstances, Prime Minister Harold Wilson and Foreign Secretary George Brown in 1966 tried a new approach, studying with the Six whether, if the United Kingdom accepted the Treaty of Rome and joined the EEC, its essential interests and those of the Commonwealth could be safeguarded. This amounted to a real request for membership, which had not been the case in 1961. At the same time, external pressure and support had increased. US President Lyndon Johnson had made it crystal clear to Harold Wilson that he favoured British membership, and the new president of the Commission had said the same. But although the United Kingdom had couched its request in more conciliatory terms than in 1961, the application was very short-lived, partly because of Britain's truly deplorable economic situation and the sterling crisis that accompanied it. As a matter of procedure, France argued that Article 237 of the Rome Treaty, which called for unanimity in the Council on new members, should apply to the opening of negotiations, a point it had not raised in 1961.

No one could claim that General de Gaulle was eager to see the United Kingdom join the Community. But, after consulting many documents, I do not have the impression that he was implacably hostile. As early as 1951, when he was out of office, he had remarked: 'When a solid and resolute system arises on the Continent, the insular tendency that is imputed to Great Britain can and should disappear.' In 1967, as president of the Republic, General de Gaulle clearly thought that the time had not yet come.

Going further, he thought fit to wonder in public about the considerable repercussions that British entry would have on the working of the Community, and especially on the common market in agriculture. He declared: 'It would clearly explode a Community that has been built and that functions according to rules which could not bear so huge an exception.' He denounced in advance 'any artifice, delay or deception that might disguise the building's destruction'.

In Brussels, by contrast, French Foreign Minister Maurice Couve de Murville based his argument essentially on Britain's economic and monetary inability to fulfil the commitments it would have had to make on joining the Community at that time.

After this second veto, British resentment naturally ran deep, although the negotiations as such had been extremely brief. (Edward Heath, then a member of the opposition, gently described them as a 'minor curiosity of European diplomatic history'.) Meanwhile, however, pressure for British membership became more powerful. One example was that Jean Monnet, whom de Gaulle called '*l'Inspirateur*' of the European Community, in 1968 welcomed British members on to the Action Committee for the United States of Europe.

Eventually, after the *événements* that shook France in May 1968, General de Gaulle must have thought it desirable to allow some leeway. The cross-Channel climate had deteriorated so much that at the beginning of 1969 the Wilson Government's resentment had culminated in the so-called 'Soames Affair'.[2] This had involved the rapid, widespread and perhaps ill-intentioned diffusion among France's continental partners of some broad-brush hints and ideas confided by General de Gaulle in a tête-à-tête meeting with the ambassador. After the negative result of the April 1969 referendum on a quite different subject, General de Gaulle left office, bequeathing his successor a still unsolved British problem, although the fact that he had hinted at a change of attitude seemed to indicate that he had not wished to leave France's relations with the United Kingdom too long in so bad a state.[3]

The French presidential election campaign, in May–June 1969, was given very little space in the British press. It knew nothing about Georges

---

2 Christopher Soames later played a very active role. Still ambassador in Paris, he convinced Edward Heath of the positive attitude of President Pompidou, who on 10 October 1969 had told him that he would not exercise a veto. The British Embassy, incidentally, served as the forward base for the prime minister in preparing the May 1971 talks.

3 Maurice Schumann confided to the present translator that when he was foreign minister de Gaulle told him that he could now let the British in.

Pompidou: in 1966, when he had been received by Harold Wilson, the BBC had found no one to brief it on the French prime minister. Likewise, London seemed curiously unaware that Valéry Giscard d'Estaing, president of the Independent Republicans, and Jacques Duhamel, the most important centrist leader, had said that they would support Pompidou for president only if he favoured British entry to the Common Market.

The enlargement of the presidential majority in France very much improved Britain's chances. The formation of Jacques Chaban-Delmas' government confirmed this tendency. The ministers most closely involved (Maurice Schumann at the Ministry of Foreign Affairs and Valéry Giscard d'Estaing at the Treasury) were in favour. And Georges Pompidou, long before he became president, had several times expressed his personal desire to see Britain one day join the Common Market (the memoirs of Guy de Rothschild are quite explicit on this point). Finally, it seems to me that in 1969, given the degree of annoyance with France among its continental partners, the United Kingdom was in a position to paralyse the working of the Common Market from outside. This, incidentally, was one of the reasons that Pompidou gave when seeking ratification of the Accession Treaty: 'To refuse the entry of Great Britain would condemn the Common Market to decline and perish.' He stressed also that 'This accession is very much more than a simple enlargement. It is a new Europe in the making.'

Furthermore, there was no valid reason for refusing to begin talks with the United Kingdom once it had accepted the Treaties and the *acquis communautaire* of subsequent legislation – including the Common Agricultural Policy. The negotiations – a term that does not appear in the Treaty of Rome – would be limited to what was to happen in the transition period.

Georges Pompidou was elected president in June 1969. Less than a month later, at his first press conference on 10 July, he proposed calling a meeting of the heads of state and government of the Six before the beginning of the definitive period of the Common Market on 1 January 1970. This procedure, which now seems commonplace, was then unusual: its solemnity suggested that an important decision was about to be taken on the main subject of the day. At the Conference in The Hague on 1–2 December 1969, France's partners urged it to accept a date for the beginning of talks with those countries wishing to join.

This conference made possible a bargain that was reflected in the final communiqué: it embodied the well-known trio of 'completion, deepening and enlargement'. The Six agreed that the definitive Financial Regulation must be established and that national contributions must be replaced by the Community's 'own resources'.

On accession, the communiqué merely noted political agreement to open negotiations 'in so far as the applicant States accept the Treaties and their political aim, the decisions taken since they came into force, and the negotiations undertaken in the field of [overseas] development'. It mentioned no date officially, but the Six agreed that in response to questions they would state that by the end of the first half of 1970 a joint position should have been reached and that the negotiations proper should begin at once after that.

And so it happened. The negotiations began on 30 June 1970 and took place in Brussels between the Six and each of the applicants in a structure involving the Council and the Commission, as in 1967.

The British and the other applicants had already had to accept the prospect of joining a ready-made club. They had to take on board not only the rules laid down in the Treaties, but also the whole *acquis communautaire*, including matters on which the Six might agree among themselves during the accession negotiations. The adjustments needed by the applicants could take place only within the transition periods, which had to be settled by common accord.

With the framework thus established, the negotiations proper began on 30 June 1970, and continued until the end of 1971. In the second half of 1970, with the German Federal Republic chairing the Community, the main points of difficulty were identified.

The French presidency, which began on 1 January 1971, was much more exacting. It soon became clear that France was not changing its position on Britain's contribution to the Community budget. For France and for the Commission, the starting level for this contribution must be high enough to make the exercise as convincing as possible and to avoid too sharp an increase at the end of the transition period.

In March 1971, moreover, after a detailed study by the Commission presented by Raymond Barre, France asked for a serious debate on the monetary problems of British accession, and in particular on the 'sterling balances'. This increased the tension, because the request for closer scrutiny made some people doubt France's intentions.

On 7 May, however, the announcement that the French president and the British prime minister were to meet showed that a solution was in the offing. If the French and the British were to hold a summit meeting, they no doubt wished and hoped to succeed. With this in prospect, agreements were reached in Brussels on Commonwealth sugar and Community preference.

Edward Heath and Georges Pompidou met in Paris on 20–21 May 1971. Their talks were prepared by two small teams drawn exclusively from the two statesmen's inner circles. Their tête-à-tête took almost eleven hours over less than two days – which must be a record. These two facts show how very personal their meeting was. 'The British', Georges Pompidou sometimes said, 'are very enticing. One has to be on one's guard.' These one-to-one talks shielded France's ministers from temptation.

This is not the place to describe in detail the Heath–Pompidou talks. Let me recall only that the two men agreed in principle on the problem of Britain's budgetary contribution, and that Heath managed to persuade Pompidou that for the British government the sterling balances were not a question of prestige or emotion, but essentially a practical matter.

On monetary problems, at the later meeting of finance ministers Valéry Giscard d'Estaing declared himself fully satisfied by the very general explanations given by the British delegation following a report by the Commission. The debate was then suspended with what seemed deliberate haste. The negotiations on Britain's contribution to the Community budget ended in an agreement whose application later caused long and tumultuous argument. The UK government had taken the precaution of notifying Brussels, in a general statement that Edward Heath repeated in Westminster, that if an intolerable situation were to arise an appropriate solution would have to be sought by common accord. With wholly involuntary symbolism, it was a few hours before the announcement of President Pompidou's death, on 2 April 1974, that the foreign secretary of Harold Wilson's new government asked to renegotiate Britain's contribution to the budget.

Let me return briefly to monetary matters. It would, I think, have been rather difficult, in 1971, to break off negotiations with Britain on a subject whose Community aspect was barely outlined in the Treaty of Rome. Nevertheless, in a world divided by the suspension of dollar convertibility and the *de facto* abandonment of the Bretton Woods agreements, these questions were on an international agenda that the Community could not ignore. The Paris Conference of October 1972 confirmed the solemn pledge by the states of the European Union, including the UK, to move as swiftly as possible to economic and monetary union.

More generally, what is striking when one reads the account of the 1971 Heath–Pompidou talks is the great identity of views between the two statesmen – so much so that several times I had to check which one of them was speaking. Good agreements need mutual understanding. Edward Heath and Georges Pompidou had such reciprocal confidence and esteem. Personal feelings play their part at summits as elsewhere, and it seems to me that historians too often underestimate their importance.

That said, the Heath–Pompidou meeting was intended not to reach decisions, but to clear the ground for a Community agreement. In the words of Edmond Wellenstein, so ably supporting the Brussels commissioner concerned, Jean-François Deniau: 'One of President Pompidou's great achievements was to put the question of Great Britain's accession back on the track of the Community institutions.'

Without any doubt, the enlargement of the Community – more simply, the accession of Great Britain to the Common Market – was the most fateful foreign policy decision taken by President Pompidou during his five years in office. It was a key decision, which he reached as soon as he came to power – or perhaps a long time earlier.

Georges Pompidou wanted to negotiate Britain's accession, which provoked bitter debate among his supporters. He trusted his interlocutor, who was undoubtedly the most European of British statesmen. He judged the result satisfactory enough to submit its ratification to a referendum. He was greatly disappointed to find that the number saying 'Yes' were only just over 40 per cent of those eligible to vote.

For the British, the essential problem was public opinion. In a House of Commons debate on 28 October 1971, Edward Heath won a 112-vote majority, including 60 Labour supporters of Roy Jenkins. From this perspective, the choice of 20–21 May 1971 for the Heath–Pompidou summit was astute: France chaired the Community's Council of Ministers until 30 June, and the Labour, Conservative and Trade Union conferences were due in September. At that time and for several years to come, public opinion favoured the Treaty: people voted yes in the referendum held by Harold Wilson in 1975.[4] Perhaps British citizens felt that, having been twice denied entry to the Community, their own team had finally won the decisive match against the motley team of the Continentals. Even so, mistrust remained powerful, as witness an editorial in the *Guardian*: 'The Europeans have made such a mess with their farm agreements that Britain could not join at this time . . . De Gaulle was one obstacle to membership, but butter at nine shillings a pound is another.'

I am well aware of how arbitrarily I have chosen what to draw from my memories of the last accession negotiations. Since objectivity is impossible, I hope I may be forgiven for ending this chapter with some personal remarks.

First, the success of the Franco-British summit in May 1971 was by no means inevitable. Pure chance plays its part in elections and in democracy;

---

4   In this referendum, which took place on 5 June 1975, votes were cast by 64.5 per cent of those eligible, 67 per cent of them voting 'Yes'.

here its role was decisive. It brought to power two statesmen who realised that they shared 'complete identity of views on the working and development of the Community', and who had the courage to trust each other. Edward Heath, in particular, overcame the bitterness and defiance that were very strongly felt on that side of the Channel after the two French vetoes of 1963 and 1967. True, he had always believed (as he said in a BBC interview on 8 October 1969) that it was good for Great Britain to enter the European Community because its long-term interest was to exert political influence in Europe. Lord Chalfont, responsible for European affairs in a Labour government, had said the same thing in September 1967 in a speech to the Foreign Press Association: 'We wish to exert the influence we can in world affairs from a European basis.'

As regards Georges Pompidou, I am convinced that he was not making a virtue of necessity, or the best of a bad job. On the contrary, he wanted the negotiations to begin and to succeed. He realised the consequences, which he thought were positive, notably for the Community institutions, because he told Edward Heath, rather sadly, that (in this respect) 'our partners think us slightly mad'. Nor is it easy for a Frenchman to understand why Federal Germany, Italy and the three Benelux countries had for so long two mutually contradictory obsessions: on the one hand to build a federal Europe and on the other to recruit into the core of Europe a nation – the UK – which they knew full well would never accept such a development. This consideration leads to another. If France's priority had been to build a Europe confined to the Six, the surest way of deterring the British would have been to espouse a federal future for the Community while Britain was still outside. Our partners preferred to build Europe with the British, even if it meant building Europe on British lines.

Georges Pompidou knew very well, too, that still further enlargement of the Community was inevitable. At a Cabinet meeting in September 1972 he told his ministers (it was not a public statement) that 'Spain, one day, should also join the Community.' At that time the idea was certainly not universally accepted, and it also took a long time to come to fruition. It may likewise be argued that President Pompidou felt that British membership of the Community would enable France to improve the balance within it.

There remains the eternal question of relations between Europe and the United States. This problem – and problem it is – was described as follows by General de Gaulle's highly orthodox minister of foreign affairs, Maurice Couve de Murville:

Beyond Britain, *and also in its absence*, one always comes back to America. Should Europe's policy always be the same as that of the

United States, or should the personality of the old continent affirm itself, not at all against its transatlantic ally but independently of it and under its own responsibility? That is the fundamental problem.[5]

This is also, I think, what Georges Pompidou believed, and it would be a great mistake to suppose that his belief was not deeply held. Nevertheless, one would need the naïve optimism of young countries to believe that all problems can be solved.

Space denies me, unfortunately, the chance to describe even briefly the United Kingdom's actions since 1973 within the European Community, and how they may appear in French eyes.

Since Britain's membership is of historic importance, may I nevertheless try to make good this serious omission by recalling its historical context? Asked by a visitor how he judged the French Revolution of 1789, Chou En Lai is said to have replied: 'It is still a little too early to answer that question.' After all, Britain has been in the European Union for only some thirty years, and this is a short time in historical terms.

Still, one may note that the European Union still exists and that the United Kingdom joined it not to destroy it, but stubbornly to stand up for its national interests, as well as to expound and defend its opinions, which are not, it has to be said, always based on the same experiences as those of its continental friends. One might well ask, moreover, what would have happened if the Franco-British summit of 1971, with all its attendant risks and hazards, had not led to an agreement. At Jericho, the Jews brought down the walls at their seventh attempt. Perhaps because history is accelerating, the British entered the Community at their third. But the city is still standing, because it finally adopted the simple idea of opening its gates.

Jean-René Bernard

---

5 Maurice Couve de Murville, *Une Politique étrangère, 1958–1969*, Plon, Paris, 1971; emphasis added.

Heath and Pompidou

On 13 May 1971, Prime Minister Edward Heath asked me to involve myself in preparing his crucial visit to President Pompidou in Paris, with a view to Britain's joining the European Community. That afternoon he sat under the cherry tree in the garden of No. 10, dunking digestive biscuits in his teacup, while senior officials briefed him on the issues in the negotiations – sugar, butter, sterling, many others. Ducks from the nearby lake waddled across the lawn; workmen noisily erected stands on Horse Guards for the Trooping the Colour parade. The next day Ted was travelling to Aberdeen for the Scottish Party Conference. I went to Chequers in the morning with a packed suitcase, not knowing whether I would unpack in Aberdeen with the prime minister, or in Paris as one of the advance party who were to explore the French position. Ted greatly admired the Foreign Office, but that morning he spoke critically of their anti-French mutterings, recalling in my mind the fierce argument we had had with Foreign Office officials at The Hague Conference in 1968. Probably because the Foreign Office associated me with these criticisms, Christopher Soames, our ambassador in Paris, did not want me to be part of the advance team. Ted overruled the objection, and I flew to Paris that afternoon with his senior private secretary, Robert Armstrong, and an experienced civil servant, Peter Thornton. We dined lightheartedly with Christopher Soames, who from then on treated me as an ally. Sterling, he was sure that evening, would be the Bechers Brook of the negotiation.

We spent the morning of 15 May going through the agenda in the Élysée with Chef de Cabinet Jobert, small, dark and witty. Jobert had not yet developed, or at least did not express, the abrasive Gaullist views for which he later became famous as foreign minister. The French were friendly, cautious and evidently determined that there should be a precise and detailed discussion between the prime minister and the president before the French veto could be lifted. Because our visit was secret, we had to avoid being spotted by the BBC Panorama team, which was interviewing President Pompidou a few yards away in the gardens of the Élysée.

The next few days were spent in further intensive briefings in London. Advice on Europe poured in to the prime minister from many sides. The Italian ambassador in London told me that we must cosset Madame Pompidou because of her influence over the president: 'separate beds but no secrets'. On 19 May the prime minister flew to Paris with an imposing team of senior negotiators. I tagged along, enjoying my small walk-on part. We dined again with Christopher Soames, 'gold and white [dining room] and lobster and windows open to the lighted trees. The Knights in full cry, especially on sterling.' The crucial discussions took place during the next few days. In fact the advisers on both sides had little to do except wait while the prime minister and president tested each other out. The great men strolled and talked in the garden, and talked and strolled again. The news that reached us on the first evening was scant and slightly disturbing: 'It emerges that the great men have got through the agenda in high good humour without settling anything of importance.' As Christopher Soames said, 'This won't do.' After dinner at the Élysée the Jobert/Armstrong group met upstairs among the tapestries; we were dismayed at how little had been finally decided. We mistook the process. The two men both liked detail, and were briefed to the eyebrows. But the outcome depended on trust, which was built gradually through the two days. The answer came as a whole at the end, not piecemeal problem by problem. On 21 May, a grey, wet day, President Pompidou was ready. He bravely chose the Salon des Fêtes, where de Gaulle had pronounced his British veto, in which to tell the world that he had reversed it. Ted took his triumph quietly, as he had taken the election victory a year before. These successes, which he regarded as the logical result of his own hard work and determination, came as no surprise to him. He knew that he had a further struggle ahead to secure the consent of the House of Commons. But the winning round of President Pompidou was probably the greatest personal feat of his premiership.

Douglas Hurd

VIII

The Entente in a Unipolar World

The fall of the Berlin Wall, and the collapse of the Soviet Union and its 'empire' of satellites, fundamentally changed the international scene. The United States was now the only remaining superpower, and deeply entrenched post-war hopes of creating a partnership of equals between it and a uniting Europe began to look less realistic. How would Europe – and the Entente – respond to the challenge?

Mitterrand, Thatcher and the Berlin Wall

The fall of the Berlin Wall most vividly recalls images of people pouring through and over the wall on the evening of 9 November 1989. The celebrations and jubilations around Checkpoint Charlie and the Brandenberg Gate were broadcast live around the world. Nine million East Germans visited the West in the following week. Public opinion polls across the West favoured uniting East and West Germany.

Within two years Germany was peacefully united, was still a member of NATO, and was a key player in the developing European Union. This was the result of an extraordinary and rushed series of high-level bilateral meetings, as well as multilateral meetings of NATO and the European Community. These were to transform both institutions, and ensure unification and a major geo-political change in Europe without bloodshed. The flow of history was towards self-determination, German unification and a transformation of the European continent. Indeed, within months of Germany's unification the Soviet Union itself had collapsed.

However, both François Mitterrand, president of France since 1981, and Margaret Thatcher, prime minister of Britain since 1979, viewed the fall of the wall with apprehension. The wall had snaked its way across Berlin for nearly thirty years, reminding Germans and Europeans alike of the division of their continent. Despite its brooding presence, it had come to represent safety and security for those on the Western side. Its fall was seen as a harbinger of uncontrollable change in the European landscape. Both leaders feared the rise of German power on the European continent – that German history might repeat itself; both leaders also feared diminished roles for themselves in a new Europe. Neither could immediately see a way forward. Both were to see the process of unification led by others: in particular Chancellor Helmut Kohl, President George Bush, and, more reluctantly, Mikhail Gorbachev.

In 1984 Mitterrand and Kohl had stood, hand in hand, on the battlefield at Verdun. The diminutive president and the portly chancellor together represented a symbol of post-war reconciliation between France and West Germany. Now, Mitterrand feared the change in the balance of power between the two countries, and saw a challenge to the elaborate structure of the European Communities that had benefited both of them.

Soon after the fall of the wall, he called a special meeting of European Community heads of state in Paris. Mitterrand was deeply troubled by the prospect of a united Germany, but urged that the European Community must be strengthened through greater integration. Kohl's surprise ten-point plan for German unity embedded in the European process and East–West relations had captured the strategic high ground and isolated the doubters. Mitterrand saw that more Europe, and more integration, was the only way forward.

By December 1989, although he and Thatcher shared deep anxieties about Germany – Mitterrand talked of the Germans as a people in constant movement and flux, and Thatcher even produced from her handbag a map showing the various configurations of Germany in the past – plans for renewed special Anglo-French relations to balance German power came to nothing. Instead, the European Community endorsed Germany's movement towards unification, and determined both to amend its own institutions and to adopt economic and monetary union as part of a package to anchor Germany still more firmly in the club. Thatcher opposed this initiative, but was forced to concede that she had been out-manoeuvred.

So, by 1990, as Thatcher herself later put it, 'there was no force in Europe which could stop reunification happening'. Her resistance to unification was deeper and longer-lasting than that of Mitterrand, and she freely admits to the unambiguous failure of her German policy. This policy had turned upon a deep fear of German power coupled with distaste for the EC. So the EC seemed to be the very worst mechanism for containing Germany, or 'tying down Gulliver', as she put it.

What she preferred was democracy and reform across Eastern Europe, not a unified Germany. The Soviet Union was a partner in this endeavour, and it, too, had clear security interests, for Gorbachev's programme for political reform could be undermined by German unification. She told Bush that NATO, and with it the Warsaw Pact, must be preserved and expectations for unification must be dampened. She hoped that the Western Alliance could prevent political change in Europe. In this she was proved wrong, while her support for NATO still did not turn her into a key player with Kohl, Bush and Gorbachev.

There was a darker side to Thatcher's policy. The depth of the cultural resistance to Germany among some parts of the British establishment was made public with the unauthorised publication of the minutes of the celebrated Chequers meeting that had been called to brief Thatcher on the German question in March 1990. These minutes caused a storm in Britain, not least because they contained an unflattering list of so-called German characteristics.

Thatcher's German and European policies were to be her undoing by November 1990: Mitterrand, although he also found acceptance of the new European realities of 1989 painful, was to survive in office for another four years.

Anne Deighton

Paris, London and Washington

Since World War II, Britain and France have struggled with the problem of how to manoeuvre American power to support their national interests. Their approaches to the problem have differed fundamentally. Britain seeks to influence Washington in its role as a privileged partner of the United States. France, on the other hand, has always used conventional methods to induce the United States to accept its positions. This is not only because the French feel that the intimate Anglo–American arrangements dating to World War II, plus the English language, have created a special relationship probably beyond their reach.

It is a conviction (and instinctive feeling) that the potential pitfalls in the role of *demandeur* or junior partner (as in the case of Britain) – betrayal, disappointment and failure – outweigh the possible gains over the long run. Best to drink from one's own glass, as General Charles de Gaulle observed, while touching glasses all around. A French leader can normally be relied on never to put himself in the position of seeking by other than scrupulously correct and traditional diplomacy to obtain satisfaction for French interests.

Not long before Prime Minister Anthony Eden and his co-conspirators in Paris set in motion their misbegotten Suez campaign in 1956, he dispatched an observer to Brussels, where the Continental Six were laying the foundations for the Treaty of Rome. Eden took a jaundiced view of what seemed to be going on there – and so apparently did his observer, who allegedly commented, 'I leave happy because even if you continue meeting you will not agree; even if you agree, nothing will result; and even if something results, it will be a disaster.'

Eden's observer was reflecting what was then a typically derisive British

184

view of whatever the continentals might be up to. Eden himself was soon to be driven from power by the Suez folly, which had a huge ripple effect. For a start, it did more harm to relations between France and the Anglo-Saxons, especially the Americans, who caused it to be aborted, than any other episode in the post World War II era. France's latent mistrust of both Washington and London came to the surface. Washington was seen to have betrayed its chief allies. France's chattering classes regarded Britain as having lived up to their pejorative, *perfide Albion* reputation, by abandoning France and Israel at the first sign of disapproval in Washington.

Suez, Hugh Thomas has written, destroyed the Entente Cordiale, 'which thus died, as it was born, over Egypt'.[1] Among the lessons drawn by Britain's political class was that Britain should never again permit itself the luxury of a major row with the United States. But the effect of Suez in France was even more profound and pervasive. While the affair divided Britain, it tended to unite France. And far from reaching the same conclusion as Britain's political hierarchy, the French had as their prevailing attitude the belief that France – make that Europe – must develop the means to run its affairs without interference from Washington. America was Europe's ally, not its sovereign. Briefly, the heavy deposit of frustration left by the Suez affair produced much of the energy that led to the creation of the European Common Market, forerunner of the European Union (EU). It also had much to do with animating France's nuclear weapons programme.

Shortly before closing out a long and brilliant run as Britain's foreign secretary in June 1995, Douglas Hurd said that in British interests, in its assets, in its view of Europe, in its hopes and fears for the outside world, there were not two substantial countries as similar as France and Britain.[2] What Hurd didn't say was that Britain and France are the only two members of the European Union with serious traditions of nation-statehood to protect. Most of the others find in the EU a makeweight for their own deficiencies as free-standing entities.

Throughout much of the Cold War period, many diplomats (and some officials) in Paris and London regarded the Anglo-French relationship as potentially nearly as important as the close tie between those old enemies, France and Germany. All sides depended on the special French–German link. None of the parties, including Britain, wanted to see the two countries going their separate ways as in the past. But by building up its

---

1 Hugh Thomas, *Suez*, Harper & Row, New York, 1967, p. 154.
2 Reginald Dale, *Europe's Odd Couple*, France, Summer 1995, p. 4.

relationship with France, Whitehall could see Britain becoming more important to both Paris and Bonn. In some ways, Britain had more in common with both of them than either did with the other. In Europe, only Britain and France deploy large, modern navies and have nuclear weapons. Only they are permanent members of the United Nations Security Council, however anachronistic their presence at the top table seems to much of the world. On trade policy, Britain, the most convinced free trader of the major EU countries, has been closer to Germany than to France. London and Bonn were always closer together on NATO-related issues than either was with France.

It was largely because of these considerations that President de Gaulle kept Britain out of the European Community in the 1960s; he didn't want to share the leadership of Europe, which he sought for France alone, although he disguised his motives with repeated warnings that granting Britain membership would give America a Trojan horse inside the European edifice.

Today Britain continues to be seen by many, if not most, continental Europeans as insular and joined at the hip to America. This isn't caricature, at least not altogether. Granted, Britain played a leadership role in the 1980s on some of the EU's critical issues, including the creation of the single market, and has probably complied with a vast body of EU rules and regulations with at least as much punctilio as any other member. But the charge that Britain has in general failed to play a full-blooded role within the club since joining it is beyond dispute.

EU members like to say that the 'pace of progress' won't be set by the slowest ship in the convoy. British experts feel, however, that when push comes to shove their government will stay whatever course the others agree on. Monetary union is, of course, putting that proposition to the stiffest of tests and the outcome is in serious doubt.

Whitehall and Paris, although they are normally divided on some of the touchy issues, are close together on others, even though they do not as a rule coordinate their positions. Regarding the EU, they have the same architectural preferences. They have both wanted to strengthen the Council of Ministers – the country representatives – but not the European Parliament.

The British and French also sound very much alike when they are talking about the Arab–Israeli quarrel. For years, they have rightly seen it as a major threat that can only broaden and become more acute. Their leaders and civil servants alike have always regarded the conflict as political and social, and their hostility to the government of Ariel Sharon and his political party, the Likkud, has become a constant. A great deal of the anti-Americanism in France and elsewhere in Europe is traceable to Washington's commitment to this extremist political bloc, most notably its settlements policy on the West Bank.

Defence is, of course, the hard-edged issue that divides Paris and London, and the French have often said that it bears out their view of Britain as unwilling to put its role in Europe ahead of a special relationship with Washington. Relations between the three capitals were for several years largely shaped by nuclear issues – by the determination of London and Paris to deploy their own nuclear weapons rather than relying entirely on America's. But each wanted American help; without it, the path to a nuclear deterrent would be longer, much more costly, and laden with uncertainty.

'Contradictory' best describes Washington's attitude towards assisting the British and French nuclear programmes. The Eisenhower administration, like Truman's, initially tended to keep both at arm's length, even though Eisenhower himself fully understood and sympathized with Britain's interests. In 1950, the British began working on their own gaseous diffusion plant but got no help even though the technology had originated with them. In 1952, the British asked Washington if they could test a bomb at one of the American test sites in the Pacific. The Americans were stand-offish and tried to discourage the British, who then got permission from Australia to test their first atom bomb at Monte Bello Island; the date was 3 October 1952.

Washington's ambiguous policy on aiding France's weapons programme marked both the Eisenhower and Kennedy years. Few issues in the period between 1958 and 1963 pre-empted more of the time and thought of high officials, including the two presidents. And perhaps none stimulated so much division, even bitterness, within the American government as the question of whether to put American relations with France on the same footing as those with Britain. Major agencies, including the State Department, were split. Since France was sure to have nuclear weapons one day, the argument was why not help and thereby spare France part of the huge investment in time and resources the task would require; in return, France would presumably play a stronger role in NATO and become more supportive of American policy. Other advocates, mainly in the Defense Department, wanted to offset the heavy pressure on America's balance of payments arising from its NATO commitments. The advocates lost the argument.

One thing that de Gaulle did want from Washington was the help with nuclear weapons that had been denied his predecessors. To have access to Anglo-American expertise in inertial guidance systems, isotope separation and warhead technology would be vastly beneficial to the French programme. But de Gaulle was not willing to trim his principles to gain access to advanced technology. He never told his government not to seek this aid from America or Britain. He merely established that he would never pay a political price for it; that being the case, he told his ministers and generals that they were free to seek the aid but stood little chance of succeeding.

In recent years, Whitehall seems to have assumed that Britain's special tie to the White House, whoever the occupant might be, would sustain and enhance Britain's position in the EU and the world. And that calculation has been largely borne out over the past twenty-five or so years. Still, there have been moments when the so-called special relationship with America, to which there is sometimes less than meets the eye, was threatened by an expanding German role. Britain at such moments seemed to have vanished from Washington's radar screen.

Prime Minister Margaret Thatcher reckoned that the Anglo-American tie and the relationship she forged with Mikhail Gorbachev, the transitional Soviet leader, put her in the privileged role of go-between and *interlocuteur*; and in the years of Ronald Reagan's White House tenure she did play that role, not just with Gorbachev but with the Saudis, among others. But she didn't understand that her importance to the then superpowers would decline as long as Britain seemed to be half in and half out of Europe's great institutional venture. Only with Britain playing its European role to the hilt – becoming Europe's balance wheel, as in the distant past, and influencing what happened in Eastern Europe – would the bigger players have an interest in holding Britain's place at what former Prime Minister Harold Macmillan used to call the top table.

The breach in the Berlin wall in 1989 was expected at the time to produce elections and political reform in East Germany – nothing more. And precisely because unification wasn't supposed to happen, various officials could glibly endorse it, as NATO's leaders did at the end of a summit meeting in May 1989; as French President François Mitterrand did in a newspaper interview that July; as he did again on 3 November, a week before the wall became a target of souvenir hunters.

Then to have him and Mrs Thatcher take – or try to take – steps to prevent unification was interesting but not surprising. Her fierce anti-German phobia lay unconcealed. But France was certain to be the big loser from German unification because it had the most to lose. Paris had been the centre of political gravity in Western Europe since 1963, when de Gaulle and West Germany's Chancellor Konrad Adenauer drew up a treaty celebrating Franco-German reconciliation. Europe west of the Elbe would be a confederation built on a French–German axis. The two eminences – both world-class practitioners of statecraft – tacitly agreed that the political leadership of the structure would be French; Germany's past excluded any alternative, and anyway Adenauer distrusted his fellow Germans nearly as much as de Gaulle did.

De Gaulle's successors kept faith with his vision: French defence foreign policy continued to be independent. As Europe's leader, a nuclear power, and the only one of America's allies that was immune to pressure from Washington, France, unlike Germany, would perform on a world stage. Membership in NATO was an ellipse in de Gaulle's design that he had blurred by withdrawing France from the alliance's integrated military structure and expelling NATO from the country. Still, the entire construct relied upon the division of Europe and upon a West Germany carpeted with American troops and nuclear weapons. With the end of the Cold War and the unification of Germany, the assumptions on which French policy had been based were shattered and most capitals saw the centre of political gravity as shifting to Bonn and, eventually, to Berlin (when it became the German capital).

Setting policy was much easier during the Cold War. Germany had been confined to a small field of manoeuvre by the two superpowers, one of them providing the threat, the other the security. France had been free to shelter within the penumbra of the NATO security system and occasionally put pressure on its German partner by taking some modest initiative *vis-à-vis* Moscow. France was a member of the two best clubs, one of which – the European Community – it dominated. The other one – NATO – was dominated by the Americans. Sooner or later, the dominant member of the all-European club is likely to be Germany, not France, although Germany will take reasonable care not to make too great a point of its growing influence.

Tony Blair's assumption that his special tie to the White House sustains and enhances Britain's influence in Europe and the world has not been borne out. Granted, his role in manoeuvring George W. Bush towards a multilateral approach to Iraq in the autumn of 2002 was pivotal. In the end, however, this expedient changed nothing. Bush had decided to make war with or without international support.

Blair tried unavailingly to persuade Bush to take an even-handed approach to the Palestine question and restart the peace process. If he expected Bush to do that, Blair was deceiving himself, as leadership often does. He is likely to be seen as having been exploited.

Let's suppose that since the end of the Cold War a snapshot of relations among the key members of NATO had been taken annually. Almost certainly, it would show these relationships undergoing change in varying degrees from one year to the next and in the case of some relationships revealing a somewhat dated quality. Moreover, starting in 2001, the snap-shot would have had to include Russia, which, while not technically a member, is carving out its own special relationship with Washington and is expected as well to find a place in Western security arrangements, albeit gradually.

John Newhouse

The 2003 Iraq War divided the Atlantic Alliance, the European Union and the Entente Cordiale. That all three survived very deep disagreement may be a testimony to their leaders' statesmanship: but it also shows that ineluctable circumstances can lastingly overcome temporary disputes. As a French minister once remarked during one of Europe's late-night wrangles, 'We are condemned to succeed.'

Four's a Crowd

That the so-called Entente Cordiale is celebrating its hundredth birthday proves at least that it has a tougher skin than its forerunner in the early years of Queen Victoria. That earlier *entente* owed a great deal to Louis-Philippe. He adored Britain, and dismissed his prime minister, Adolphe Thiers, for his readiness to break with it over Egypt. But many French people found that the price of peace was too high, and the return to the Foreign Office of the unemotional Lord Palmerston soon put an end to an idyll that had included reciprocal visits by the two sovereigns.

It was a miracle that the new Entente of 1904 did not suffer the same fate, in view of the number of crises it has had to face – last but not least over the attack on Iraq in 2003. Although France owed its veto on the UN Security Council to Churchill's insistence at Yalta, President Jacques Chirac did not hesitate to threaten its use to prevent Tony Blair cloaking in what seemed to him vital legitimacy a pre-emptive operation hard to reconcile with the UN Charter. Chirac compounded his offence by joining with only Gerhard Schroeder and the Luxembourg prime minister in a rather absurd Belgian mini-European defence project deliberately omitting the United Kingdom, which had the strongest army in the European Union, and had recently sought to relaunch cooperation with France on armaments and defence.

The British prime minister riposted by rejecting as 'dangerous and destabilising'[1] the idea of a 'multipolar' world as championed by the French president. Whereupon Chirac came to an agreement with Germany, which the removal of the eastern threat had freed from having

---

1   Interview, *Financial Times*, 26–27 April 2003.

to be 'the best pupil in the Atlantic class', and with Russia, whose actions in Chechnya hardly qualified it as a defender of the rights of man. This finally very ephemeral 'Paris–Berlin–Moscow axis', reminiscent of the continental *ententes* that Britain had always opposed, had no precedent except the very different and ephemeral alliance between Napoleon and Czar Alexander.

But there were many precedents for the solid support given by New Labour's Tony Blair to the most conservative and, if not the most imperialist, at least the most imperial president of the United States since William McKinley and Theodore Roosevelt. They, at the beginning of the twentieth century, conquered the Philippines and achieved the 'incomparable advance'[2] in the Pacific celebrated by Admiral Alfred Thayer Mahan. It was then that London decided that henceforth 'nothing should be done to offend the U.S.A.'[3] Winston Churchill thought this principle important enough to mention to General de Gaulle at the time of the Normandy landings. 'You should know', he said, 'that if ever we have to choose between Europe and the open sea, we shall choose the open sea.'[4] There is doubtless no better definition of the often cited 'Special Relationship'. The only real exception to the rule, the lamentable Suez crisis of 1956, in reality confirmed it, since Anthony Eden took only a few moments to give in when President Eisenhower telephoned him, threatening to sell massive amounts of sterling if the expeditionary force was not immediately withdrawn. Guy Mollet, the French prime minister and former teacher of English, found his efforts unrewarded: he had dreamed of reviving on this occasion the bold and wholly unrealistic plan for Franco-British union that Jean Monnet had devised in June 1940 in the débâcle of the fall of France.

Many of Britain's leading families have blood ties and interests in common with the New World. Churchill had a mother of French descent from New York, which led him to introduce himself as 'half American and wholly British'.[5] But, despite divergences that led George Bernard Shaw to say that Britain and America were 'divided by a common language', the strongest link between them remains linguistic, as witness among other things the importance of the press group owned by the Australo-American Rupert Murdoch, and the growing influence of the internet. It was no

---

2 Quoted by Fernand L'huillier, *De la Sainte Alliance au Pacte Atlantique*, la Baconnière, Neuchâtel, 1954, Vol. I, p. 206.

3 Anthony Hartley, *A State of England*, Hutchinson, London, 1963, p. 60.

4 Charles de Gaulle, *Mémoires de Guerre*, Plon, Paris, 1954, Vol. II, p. 224.

5 Quoted by Monique Charlot, *L'Angleterre 1945–1980*. Imprimerie Nationale, Paris, 1981, p. 6.

accident that Churchill, again, devoted part of his declining years to writing a monumental *History of the English-Speaking Peoples*.[6] It was they, and not (as might have been expected) the whole of the 'free world', to whom he appealed in his famous Fulton speech of 5 March 1946 to unite urgently and removal all 'temptation to ambition or adventure'.[7]

It was to President Harry S. Truman that Clement Attlee's government turned in 1947, to ask for help with the growing burden of police action against communist guerrillas in Greece. More recently, London even reached an understanding with the White House on American mediation in Northern Ireland. Could anyone imagine Paris accepting similar intervention in Corsica?

The fact is that the American War of Independence divided the people less than it divided the politicians. The dispute over the tea tax was of course important, but so was the passion for liberty, that fugitive 'hunted round the globe', which Tom Paine, newly arrived in Philadelphia, urged all the countless readers of his *Common Sense* to 'receive', preparing 'in time an asylum for mankind.'[8] Here already was a hint of that 'Messianism' for which Henry Kissinger so reproached Woodrow Wilson, and which in two and a quarter centuries has so often been expressed on the banks of the Potomac, until and including the days of George W. Bush and his fellow servants of the Divine Will.

In 1983, receiving the 'Iron Lady' in the former residence of the British governor of Virginia, President Ronald Reagan offered her a toast: 'Margaret, if some of your predecessors had been a little more intelligent...' 'I know', interrupted the British Prime Minister, who sometimes seemed to see herself as the reincarnation of William Pitt and Churchill, 'I should have been your hostess at Williamsburg.'[9] The *Financial Times* did not hesitate to headline one of her interviews: 'Her head in Europe, her heart in the United States.' That said, Margaret Thatcher never advocated systematic alignment on American positions, and she was furious a few months later when Washington landed troops in Grenada, a Commonwealth country, to counter a pro-Cuban putsch. It was Reagan, at the time of the Falklands War, who supplied intelligence to the Royal Navy, forgetting for once the sacrosanct Monroe Doctrine. Likewise, Mrs Thatcher was at Aspen, Colorado, with George Bush Senior when Saddam Hussein

6 Winston S. Churchill, *History of the English-Speaking Peoples*, 4 vols, 1956–58.
7 Winston S. Churchill, *The Sinews of Peace: Post-war Speeches*, ed. Randolph S. Churchill, Cassell, London, 1948, p. 104.
8 Thomas Paine, *Common Sense*, Everyman's Library, London, 1994, p. 281.
9 Ronald Reagan, 'My heart was with her', *Newsweek*, 3 December 1990.

invaded Kuwait, and she was partly responsible for Washington's prompt decision to use force against Iraqi troops. Yet Reagan's successor pressed hard for German reunification at a time when Mrs Thatcher remained doubtful, fearing to see Europe run by a new *Reich*, which she thought François Mitterrand only mildly opposed.

Franklin Roosevelt told his son Elliott before Yalta that America would help Britain in the war, but would not allow it to go on dominating the colonial peoples.'[10] Although the Americans themselves had succumbed to imperialist temptations from Texas to China, they strongly pressed their British allies to dismantle their immense empire, with scant regard for the 'Special Relationship'. This led a university professor in New York to ask – without finding a satisfactory answer – why the devil London had sacrificed so much since 1945. Harold Wilson, who stubbornly refused to send a symbolic contingent to Vietnam, and the very pro-European Edward Heath were the only British prime ministers – apart from Anthony Eden – who sometimes kept their distance from the White House. Former Secretary of State Dean Acheson remarked that Britain had lost an Empire but not found a role.[11] Anthony Eden's notion of the 'three circles' (Commonwealth, Europe and English-speaking peoples, with Britain at the centre of all three), made no headway. Harold Macmillan dreamed of making the United Kingdom 'the Athens of the new Rome'; but President John F. Kennedy, who would no doubt have liked to oblige him, nevertheless inflicted a real rebuff in 1962, when on grounds of 'reduplication' he halted the manufacture of Skybolt air-to-ground missiles, promised to the RAF in exchange for use of the Holy Loch base in Scotland and to replace another missile, Blue Streak, which was too slow to launch.

It was time to sound out what the Entente Cordiale might mean. The British prime minister set out to see de Gaulle at Rambouillet. The general suggested that France and Britain might build a missile together, but he did so in terms so 'Delphic and cryptic', as Kennedy put it, that Macmillan could not make head or tail of them. At all events, the talks had little chance of success. Determined to pursue his 'grand design' of completing the 1776 Declaration of Independence by 'interdependence' with Europe as the 'second pillar' of an 'Atlantic Partnership', Kennedy had persuaded Macmillan, despite initial hesitation, to apply for membership of the Common Market. But the general, although he admired no country more than Britain, had no intention of welcoming it into the Europe he

---

10 Elliott Roosevelt, *As He Saw It*, Greenwood Press, Westport, CT, 1974 (first published 1946).
11 Niall Ferguson, 'The Special Relationship', *Financial Times*, 16 March 2003.

envisaged until it had drawn further away from the United States. 'I want her naked,' he was reported as saying.

If Kennedy was to be believed, the two 'pillars' were to be completely 'equal'. But how was this to be achieved when the American super-power held 97 per cent of the Alliance's nuclear power; when the watchword at the White House and the Pentagon was to concentrate in American hands the 'three Cs' – the *command* of operations, the *control* of decision-making, and *communication* with the enemy; when Secretary of Defense Robert S. McNamara had some months earlier dismissed 'national nuclear forces' as weak, dangerous, open to obsolescence, and lacking credibility as a deterrent?[12]

This is not the place to dwell on the Nassau agreements, whereby Kennedy and Macmillan sought to solve the inextricable problems of 'nuclear-sharing' within the Alliance. That the solutions were proposed to de Gaulle ready-made, without his involvement in the negotiations, guaranteed that he would reject them. Hence the general's double 'No' – to Britain's application to join the EEC and to the Nassau agreements – at his dramatic press conference of 14 January 1963. Hence his signature, a week later, of the Elysée Treaty with Chancellor Adenauer, completing what he called the 'earthquake'[13] and forcing the hand of those who opposed the kind of Europe he sought.

Like the Americans, the British had at first seen only benefits in Franco-German reconciliation, partly because this was the *sine qua non* of German rearmament, thought essential in view of the Korean War. Churchill, then in opposition, had campaigned in 1946 for the 'United States of Europe' which, long before Victor Hugo, George Washington had seen as inevitable.[14] Some weeks before the Korean War, Churchill had been the first to call for a European army; however, there was no question in his mind of Britain's joining it. He did not for a moment imagine that the United Kingdom could abdicate its seniority, its 'rank' (to use a word that both de Gaulle and, oddly, François Mitterrand were to employ). Some animals are more equal than others, aren't they?

London was no less fearful of the 'dirigiste' leanings of the first builders of Europe, and its first reaction, after de Gaulle's return to politics, had been a sense of relief, believing that the general would soon put paid to the 'Community' dream and work towards a large free trade area. But, after

12 Quoted by William Kaufmann, *The McNamara Strategy*, Harper and Row, New York, 1964, pp. 116–17.
13 Quoted by Alain Peyrefitte, *C'était de Gaulle*, Gallimard, Paris, 2002, p. 819.
14 Quoted by Bernard Voyenne, *Histoire de l'idée européenne*, Payot, Paris, 1964.

having called – without much optimism – for an American–English–French world triumvirate, de Gaulle declared his intention to build a 'European Europe' – that is, independent of the United States.

That Europe will never see the light of day. The German Bundestag ratified the Elysée Treaty only after unanimously adding to it – under pressure from Washington and London, certainly, but also from Ludwig Erhard, the federal vice-chancellor, finance minister and designated successor of Adenauer – a preamble proclaiming Germany's loyalty to European and Atlantic integration, exactly what the general had hoped it would shun.

Everyone remembers the disillusioned remarks he then made about the evanescent nature of treaties, young girls and roses. It was not until 1974, when Valéry Giscard d'Estaing and Helmut Schmidt came to power almost simultaneously, that relations between Paris and Bonn recovered their warmth. During one bilateral summit meeting, President Giscard even made his own a little-known sentence from Heinrich Heine: 'The great task of my life has been to work towards the Franco-German *entente cordiale.*'[15] The new German chancellor, who was an intellectual as well as a man of action, spoke his mind, was easily irritated by the behaviour of the Americans, notably over the neutron bomb affair, where they had seriously misled him, and above all saw in Giscard, as he told me himself, one of the few statesmen who shared his own firm grasp of monetary problems.

Georges Pompidou had been very different. He had mistrusted Germany, whose reunification had seemed to him inevitable, and had sought for counterweights in Washington, in Moscow and at first in London. In this he was following Michel Debré, who had become foreign minister when Maurice Couve de Murville had become prime minister in the summer of 1968. Even General de Gaulle, annoyed at Bonn's refusal to help the franc after the psychodrama of May 1968, had once been persuaded to stretch out a hand to 'perfidious Albion'. The gesture occurred at a memorable luncheon with Christopher Soames, then UK ambassador in Paris, but the Francophobe old guard at the Foreign Office had sabotaged the project. When Pompidou became president, he set out to pick up the pieces, and finally to welcome Britain into the EEC. Edward Heath ably assisted him, but disillusion soon followed, and the French president came to the conclusion that the British prime minister was the only European on that side of the Channel. At all events, Heath lost the general election of 1974, and the

---

15 Quoted by Michèle Weinachter, *Valéry Giscard d'Estaing et l'Allemagne, le double rêve inachevé*, Documents, No. 1, Paris, 2002.

Labour Party seemed unlikely to favour European integration. Still less likely was Margaret Thatcher, elected with a fair majority in 1979.

It was becoming clearer every day that ideas of Europe were not the same on either side of the Channel. London sought as large as possible a free trade area, with a minimum of institutions and a general right of veto: it could not get used to either subsidising the Common Agricultural Policy with little hope of return, or seeing the 'Franco-German partnership' wielding *de facto* leadership of the EEC. Despite François Mitterrand's support for Britain during the Falklands War, his speech in the Bundestag on the Euromissiles, and France's participation in the first Gulf War, the Conservative Margaret Thatcher was not on the same wavelength as the Socialist French president. And, as we have seen, she had hardly welcomed German reunification. But it was at that moment that she was obliged to resign. Had she stayed in power, she might well have put more pressure on George Bush Senior to 'finish the job' in the Gulf – to eliminate Saddam Hussein instead of letting him crush the Shia uprising in Basra, as he would have crushed the Kurds had world opinion not reacted so strongly.

Jacques Chirac's success in the presidential election of 1995 improved French relations with the United Kingdom. It was clear, first of all, that although he and Chancellor Kohl were both on the political right, there was not the same sympathy between them as between Kohl and Mitterrand, de Gaulle and Adenauer, or Giscard d'Estaing and Helmut Schmidt. A pragmatist rather than a visionary, Chirac distanced himself somewhat from the inheritance of General de Gaulle. He reoccupied France's place in the military committee of NATO; he signed the non-proliferation and nuclear test ban treaties; he cooperated with the White House in Bosnia. Yet his joining the single European currency (after having strongly criticised it) and his passionate espousal of the Common Agricultural Policy, plus the BSE crisis, limited Chirac's rapprochement with John Major, who for his part rejected the social aspects of the Maastricht Treaty. John Major also had difficulty asserting his authority over the Conservative Party, which in the parliamentary election of 1 May 1997 won only 30.6 per cent of the votes.

A few weeks later, the dissolution of the National Assembly rashly decreed by Jacques Chirac led to a scarcely less abrupt defeat of the French Right. A year after that it was Helmut Kohl's turn to lose the legislative election and step down for a coalition of the Social Democrats and the Greens. For a time, Spain under Manuel Aznar was the only large member state of the European Union to have a right-wing government, and many people believed that the 'rise of the left' would greatly facilitate Europe's Community enterprise – all the more so because Tony Blair, Britain's prime minister, made no secret of his European convictions, and even promised to join the euro. Very soon, however, it became clear that the new British premier was far from repudiating the Thatcherite heritage, and that his rather vague socialism, with its somewhat confused notion of a 'third way' between the free market and *dirigisme*, was closer to the position of Gerhard Schroeder, or even of Bill Clinton, than to that of the French Socialist Party. The latter, moreover, would not have won the election without the support of the Communist Party and the Greens, and the persistence in the second round of numerous Front National candidates who could not forgive Chirac for having side-stepped their party. Soon, the Italian left was beaten in the parliamentary election, reflecting a general swing whose last manifestation, in 2002, was Lionel Jospin's humiliating defeat in the first round of voting for the French president. The left, fearing a victory by Jean-Marie Le Pen, at once called on its supporters to vote for Chirac, whose score leapt from 19 per cent in the first round to 82 per cent in the second. The parliamentary election that followed gave his party a very large majority, and in foreign policy he now enjoyed greater freedom of movement than he had ever had.

At the time Chirac did not, to put it mildly, quite see eye to eye with Gerhard Schroeder. He seemed to have affinities with Tony Blair, with whom he agreed on the idea of developing military cooperation, which led to the St Malo Treaty. Not without difficulty, the Fifteen reached a settlement with ten of the countries seeking to join the EU in 2004. Meanwhile, however, the election of George W. Bush and the drama of 11 September 2001 had a profound effect on Franco-British relations. To begin with, the new US president – unlike his father – had been barely interested in foreign policy: he had expected to implement the programme worked out by his national security adviser, Condoleeza Rice, at the beginning of the year 2000. Unwilling to recognise anything but the national interest, she took little account of treaties, concentrated on relations with the 'big' (not the 'great') powers, referring only to China and Russia, and demanded decisive action against the threat of 'rogue states'.[16] It was in view of this threat that George W. Bush decided to establish an anti-missile system, updating President Reagan's 'Star Wars' effort to preserve American territory from any surprise attack.

The destruction of the twin towers was a tragic awakening. Assuming his full powers as 'commander in chief', to the plaudits of the vast majority of his compatriots, Bush found it quite natural to extend that role to the whole of the planet, allies included. He explained this in June 2002 when

---

16 Condoleeza Rice, 'Promoting the National Interest', *Foreign Affairs*, January–February 2000.

he told the West Point military academy that: 'America has, and intends to keep, military forces beyond challenge – thereby making the destabilising arms races of other eras pointless, and limiting rivalries to trade and other pursuits of peace.'[17]

In the face of such claims, Tony Blair and Jacques Chirac each reacted as might have been expected. Blair played the role of Uncle Sam's first lieutenant and intermediary with the rest of the troops. Chirac played the Gaullist, if not the Gaul, all the more determined not to take orders in that he knew he had massive backing from public opinion, and not only in France. Did this mean that Blair and Chirac were now committed to disagreeing about everything, and that not only the Entente Cordiale but also the United Nations, NATO and the European Union were too divided for their voices to be heard? In fact, the essential difference between Paris and London is less about aims than about method. Neither side has enough confidence in the wisdom and disinterest of the new Rome not to seek better transatlantic balance, so often mooted over the last fifty years. But one side believes that the best way to achieve it is to work from within, while the other considers that pressure from outside is more effective, because, according to the well-known columnist William Pfaff, 'This American administration does not accept an alliance that is not one of domination and subordination.'[18] Hence the need, proclaimed by Condoleeza Rice, to punish France for disobedience.

Unless, as Hubert Beuve-Méry, the founder of *Le Monde*, once jokingly suggested, Europeans could take part in electing the president of the United States, they could not long be satisfied by such a situation. When Germany was reunited it was feared that the spirit of domination might seize it once again, but its evident decline, notably in the demographic field, has led some to wonder whether the Soviet dissident Alexander Zinoviev was not right when he wrote in 1982 that Germany's 'historic role' was 'over' – 'the great, terrible, tragic role' that it had ceased to play.[19] Neither France nor Britain has reached that stage, and they seem now to understand that they have a better chance of preserving their identities – which at heart are so alike – when they succeed in working towards common goals.

Timothy Garton Ash, in a penetrating article,[20] recalled that the

---

17 Quoted by G. John Ikenberry, 'American Imperial Ambitions', *Foreign Affairs*, September–October 2002.

18 William Pfaff, 'Europe can gently check America', *International Herald Tribune*, 2 May 2003.

19 *Le Figaro*, 30 December 1982.

20 Timothy Garton Ash, 'Entente cordiale', *Le Monde*, 8 May 2003.

Entente Cordiale was not established to confirm an existing agreement but to overcome profound disaccord. He concluded that, since one could wonder whether it still existed, its hundredth anniversary should be used to renew it. A year after the conflict over Iraq, that would at least have its attractions. It might give food for thought to His Majesty the President of the United States.

André Fontaine

IX

The Entente and Mutual Understanding

While France and Britain still differ in international affairs, in cultural matters their common heritage has spawned both diversity and interaction.

THE ENTENTE AND MUTUAL UNDERSTANDING

Franglais and Amerenglish

One of the better jokes of recent years was the remark, ascribed to President Bush, that the trouble with the French is that they don't have a word for entrepreneur.

Two funny things about the joke. One, of course, is that the word entrepreneur *is* French and we laugh because we are pleased with ourselves that we knew that. Two is that we think President Bush could never have made that joke in a million years because we assume that *he* wouldn't have known.

And it's true that the Americans do not, generally, speak French and tend to feel ever so slightly inferior because of it. The American humorist Dave Barry once wrote, at the time of a crisis in Haiti, that in order for Americans to look down on the backward and impoverished natives of Haiti, they always had to forget that every Haitian above the age of twelve can pronounce the French word *fauteuil* better than any American would ever be able to do.

This would never occur to a Briton. Not being able to speak French does not worry the British. And the fact that so many words come into our language from French, from 'gigolo' and 'charlatan' to 'trousseau' and 'maisonette', never unsettles us. Why should it? It hardly occurs to us that they are French imports at all. As with food and drink and cars, we just take as much as we want from abroad and think nothing of it. We call it broad-mindedness. Others call it selfishness.

Americans are different. They have an exaggerated idea of the status of all things French, so they are simultaneously in awe of and scornful of them. That is why they make jokes like the one about the up-market New Yorker who exclaims 'Pretentious? Moi?', a joke that strikes a Briton as too feeble even to make a cartoon in the *New Yorker*. That is why no American would ever dream of seeing a French film, only of getting it turned by Hollywood into another film that has had all traces of Frenchness removed.

When French products do well in America, the Americans feel threatened. Nobody in Britain has ever resented the success of Perrier – we have actually let a British comedy award be named after Perrier! – but not very long ago there was a firm in Texas that bottled water under the brand name of Artesian and chose as their slogan: 'Kick Perrier in the derriere!' It is a sobering thought that down in Texas there are educated people who are not only in awe of Perrier but think that it rhymes with derrière...

British attempts to use French in advertising are crass in a different way. We seem to think that by putting *le* or *la* in front of an English word, we can make it sort of more French. 'Le crunch' was a slogan for an apple. 'Le shuttle' was a slogan for, well, the shuttle. 'Le car' was a slogan for a car, which was even more clumsy, as 'le car' is actually the French for 'the bus', but that sort of thing would never bother the British.

The French, oddly, can be creative with English words in a way that English itself cannot. For instance, I have seen the word *co-recordman* used in a French sports report. It meant 'someone who is the co-holder of a world record'. A native English-speaker could never use English like that, but the French writer didn't know that and so he got away with it.

He was also lucky to be writing at a time when the import of English was not frowned upon, because the French sometimes love the novelty of foreign words and welcome them, and sometimes hate their invasive nature and promptly put up the trade barriers. It's all ebb and flow with the French. I once worked with a French film crew in France, and was told by them that there had recently been a crackdown on the use of English jargon during filming.

'We had always started a new take with the command 'Action!' just as in English, but someone decreed that from now on it would have to be a French word, *Moteur!* So the next day on the first take someone yelled 'Moteur!' and nothing happened. Everyone said, 'Moteur? *Qu'est-ce qu c'est? Comprends pas...*' and so we went back to the American word because nobody accepted the French word.'

The French still import English words, like 'home' and 'sprint', and the British still import French words like en suite, déjà vu, genre and auteur – where would English film criticism be without the word noir? – but the difference is still that the British do it without reflection and the French worry endlessly over it. I have on my shelves a thick dictionary of 'Anglicismes' published by Robert, a compendium of English expressions taken into the French language and given a new home there, everything from *Jamesbonderie* to *Kick*. I cannot imagine any publisher in the English-speaking world even considering producing a compendium of French expressions in English.

British menus may again be filling up with French expressions – jus, noisette, medaillons, coulis, etc. etc. – while our en suite bathrooms fill up with bidets, and our beds fill up with duvets, but the British happily adapt to foreign terms by hardly even noticing that they are foreign, in the same way that it would probably surprise most Britons to learn that curry is also eaten in India.

I noted, by the way, that the work 'kick' is listed among other *Anglicismes*. 'Kick', incidentally, does not mean 'kick'. It should do. The French have no good word for 'kick'. They say *donner un coup de pied à*, or 'give a blow with the foot to'. How useless. What you need is a single powerful word for 'kick'. How can any modern language not have a single word for 'kick'? No wonder French never caught on as the world lingua franca. (What *le kick* actually means is a 'kick starter'. What a waste of a good word.)

I feel it might be churlish in the circumstances to sign off with an insult to the French language, so I am leaving the last word to the French humorist Alphonse Allais. I thought I knew his writings well, but the other day for the first time I came across his admirably terse summation of England:

Angleterre: une colonie normande qui a mal tourné.

Which one might translate as:-

'England – an old Norman colonial possession which went downhill very fast.'

Miles Kington

A Tale of Two Cultures

France–Britain, Britain–France: history, ideas, literature, theatre, painting: culture. Encounters, influences, convergences, sometimes insults, often a long road travelled together.

Since the Normans famously crossed the Channel in 1066, France and Britain, Britain and France have shared a strange passion. Wars, and the most cordial of misunderstandings, have aroused mistrust and irony. Yet the Channel has been no more than a stretch of sea that writers, musicians, philosophers and artists have from time immemorial crossed so easily that innumerable links, affinities and mutual influences have developed between the two countries in the field we are reduced to calling 'culture'. They have been rich and numerous enough, even at times of mutual mistrust, to obliterate much ill-feeling.

Let us not wallow here beneath the *pons asinorum* of the strange linguistic destiny of the Route du Roi, the Quichenotte or the Boulingrin (bowling green). Nor should we go back again to the Normans. But to consider the multiple comings and goings in the two cultures in the present century, we need to look at the more recent past. From the sixteenth century onwards one can see how readily these influences spread. It is true – and there is no point in hiding the fact – that both countries were flooded from elsewhere by the great light that illumined their cultural life. It was Italy, ancient and later modern, that from the Renaissance onwards played the key role of spiritual, intellectual and emotional capital of the Western world, including France and Britain. This continued to be so even when Henry VIII and half of Germany abruptly broke with Rome. Travelling to Italy, which soon became the Grand Tour, was a quest, a voyage of discovery and initiation. Going to France or Britain had nothing of this spiritual experience: it simply meant crossing the Straits of Dover. But the interplay that developed between the two countries was perhaps rather more subtle.

At first, it was French culture that seemed to be a major influence on Britain. Characters in Shakespeare's plays spoke French. Tales of lost love were set in the royal court of Navarre. Anne Boleyn admired Marguerite of Angoulême, and it seems that Queen Elizabeth translated Marguerite's *Le miroir de l'âme pécheresse*. And while the British public knew little of Robert Garnier or Tristan L'Hermite, Christopher Marlowe wrote and acted in *The Massacre at Paris*. On the opposite side of the Channel, there was barely any notable trace of the real intellectual revolution that was taking place in Britain. Although in 1605 some English actors played *The Merry Wives of Windsor* in France, Shakespeare remained virtually unknown there. In a valuable study published in 1996 under the auspices of the French Foreign Ministry, André Zavriew gives a convincing explanation. British travellers to Italy crossed France and brought back something French: the French went directly to Florence, Rome, and Naples. John Florio translated Montaigne into English, but Elizabethan philosophers and poets were not yet sold in Paris. The French seventeenth century, imbued with every kind of classicism, also left its mark on literature and the theatre in Britain. Poussin, to be sure, was as much Italian as French, but connoisseurs throughout Britain took him into their homes. Dryden, Pope and Congreve were all steeped in Racine, Boileau, Molière and the fables of La Fontaine.

With the eighteenth century, everything changed. For almost two hundred years, influences flowed the other way. Voltaire's *Lettres anglaises* date from 1734, and although they deplore Shakespeare's 'lack of taste' they discuss him at length. They also speak of Congreve. Meanwhile, La Place, Le Tourneur and Ducis translated Shakespeare – or, rather, adapted him to 'French good taste'. Thereafter, the pace quickened, and a whole section of French thought took its inspiration from Britain. Philosophers clearly read everything that it produced. The French novel, still in its infancy, followed the English models of Richardson and Fielding. Swift's *Gulliver's Travels* became a French best-seller, as did his *Tale of a Tub*, nowadays little read. And Laurence Sterne invented what became the modern novel, in Britain and in France.

There were endless such influences. With Walter Scott and Byron, the nineteenth century quickly confirmed them. Madame de Staël may perhaps have brought Romanticism from Germany, but it originated in Britain. The genius of Walter Scott and the life of Lord Byron attracted matchless devotion in France, influencing the whole Romantic century and what came after.

Of course, the British read French philosophers, learned from the Enlightenment and translated Choderlos de Laclos as they later translated Stendhal. Influence was not all one-way. But the prevailing current seems to have been from London to Paris. At first sight, at least, things look simple. The two countries took turns to pollinate each other with ideas, images, styles and feelings.

In the present century the situation seems much less clear, but contacts between the two cultures are now perhaps more intimate.

Two names from the early twentieth century aptly illustrate the interchange from which so many have drawn such pleasure and profit: Oscar Wilde in Britain and André Gide in France. Each was thoroughly imbued with the culture of the other country. Each lived amidst a circle of friends who crossed the Channel. Oscar Wilde, British (or Irish) to his fingertips, wrote and published in French one of his best known works, *Salome*. It would be hard to imagine, by contrast, anyone more French than Gide. It was certainly not his Protestantism that linked him with Britain, but Gide was in permanent communion with English literature. He translated Shakespeare and Joseph Conrad. It was his translation of *Hamlet* that Jean-Louis Barrault brought to the Paris stage, two centuries after Voltaire had translated Hamlet's 'To be or not to be' speech.

'Influence' here is not the appropriate word. On the one side there is Gide's *Les nourritures terrestres*, on the other Wilde's *The Ballad of Reading Gaol*. The works of the Frenchman and the Irishman were read in both countries, and still are. But even if we have perhaps over-simplified the patterns that prevailed from the sixteenth century until the post-Romantic era, there is a certain affinity between Wilde and Gide, as between many others, that transcends both sexual orientation and intellectual comparisons.

At the distance of half a century, similar affinity can be found when André Gide explained, as late as 1944, all that he owed to the Francophile and francophone British critic Raymond Mortimer, who introduced him to a little-known book that meant a great deal to him: James Hogg's *Confessions of a Justified Sinner*. I dislike the expression, but Raymond Mortimer, like Oscar Wilde and André Gide, was a go-between. His library of French books was a fine example of what would now be called an 'installation'. In a large room looking out on the garden, most of a whole wall was filled with numbers of the white-covered *Nouvelle Revue Française*. But these had been so much read, re-read, consulted, loved, opened and shut again that their spines, side by side on many shelves, had turned into paper snowflakes, the white dust of a memory far more lasting than the volumes that had filled it.

At all times, and throughout the past hundred years, writers have openly acknowledged influences from across the Channel. The great generation of French poets that included Baudelaire, Verlaine, Mallarmé and Villiers de l'Isle Adam was for many British poets a breath of fresh air, dispersing Victorian stuffiness. T. S. Eliot confessed that the poetry he needed to help him use his own voice could be found only in France. He cited two names: Laforgue and Corbière, he wrote, were more our masters than any English poet at that time.

The influence was not all one-way. Can Henry James be considered an English novelist as well as a British resident? At all events, Paul Bourget showed disconcerting naïveté when he used some of James's short stories as the basis for his own semi-fantastic tales in French. A more significant figure in this regard was André Maurois, a writer somewhat neglected today, who enjoyed a huge reputation between the wars. Much of his fame rested on studies of English subjects and biographies of major British writers such as Shelley, Disraeli, Browning and Byron, but as a passionate Anglophile he also salted his work with innumerable British images, clichés and jokes, most notably perhaps in his gently ironic *The Silence of Colonel Bramble*, inspired by his service as an interpreter with British Forces in World War I.

However, whatever the reciprocal influences and however great the cross-Channel 'traffickers', these are merely exceptional cases.

A group of British writers paid an eloquent tribute to Marcel Proust in the special number of the *Nouvelle Revue Française* published just after his death in January 1923.

In Britain we have always looked to France in the hope of seeing her add some new masterpiece to those she has ceaselessly lavished on the world. But it was with unaccustomed interest and excitement that we began to read the work of Marcel Proust. We felt that a new and great French writer had appeared... Our impression went further. In *À la recherche du temps perdu* Marcel Proust seemed to us to have rediscovered not only his own past but our own, so much so that he restored us to ourselves and gave us back the life that we had known and experienced ... but enriched, embellished, and magnified by the alchemy of art. We followed avidly the development of this great work. The news that its author had come to the end of his career is felt by us as personal grief.

Eighteen authors signed this text. Among them were Arnold Bennett, Joseph Conrad, Roger Fry, Edmund Gosse, Aldous Huxley, Lytton Strachey and Virginia Woolf. It showed what Proust's work had meant to several generations of leading British writers. One of the signatories to the *NRF* text was Charles Scott-Moncrieff, famous for his masterly translation of *À la recherche*. Not for nothing is the annual award given in London for translation from the French called the Scott-Moncrieff Prize. Some thirty years later, another British critic and translator, Terry Kilmartin, set out to revise and improve Scott-Moncrieff's work. Since then yet another translation has been published, this time collective. It seems as though Britain can never let Proust go. In the meantime, the standard biography of Proust throughout the world, including France, has been that by the British George Painter. Finally, Anthony Powell's immense series of novels, *A Dance to the Music of Time*, displays its Proustian pedigree with far greater subtlety than Paul Bourget showed in echoing Henry James. Proust's work has, in fact, gradually attracted in Britain a growing circle of admirers and disciples, whether literary practitioners such as writers and critics or simply enlightened amateurs. There is a real network of Proustians that since the 1923 *NRF* declaration has never ceased to expand. They share what Goethe called 'elective affinities'.

In France, in a very different key and probably for quite different reasons, the name of Virginia Woolf has likewise attracted an ever wider following. Its intensity and passion owe much to the feminist dimension of her work – so much so that its popularity threatens to eclipse the extraordinary and purely literary power of all her writings, including such novels as *To the Lighthouse* (1927). Is this regrettable? Virginia Woolf saw herself as a writer in society, discussing the situation of women in Britain or the rise of fascism, at a time when many writers, British and French alike, also addressed similar themes and dangers. And since the end of the 1960s ardent 'Woolfian' networks, essentially but not exclusively feminist, have arisen everywhere, especially in France. Woolf's novel *Orlando* (1928), made into a film and admirably played on the stage in France by Isabelle Huppert, has by now acquired almost as much symbolic value as Artemisia Gentileschi's 'Judith Slaying Holofernes'. Virginia Woolf, of course, showed compassion, not cruelty.

Her worldwide fame also raises what may be an essential point. Cross-Channel affinities and cultural influences by no means exclude those from either nation that have also affected the wider world. H. G. Wells and George Orwell are good examples. Although Wells' social concerns are now almost totally forgotten in France, his *The Time Machine* (1895) and other futuristic fantasies greatly influenced a whole literature or quasi-literature of science fiction. Similarly, George Orwell is remembered in France not so much for his *Homage to Catalonia* (1938), still less for *The*

Road to Wigan Pier (1932), as for the two books he published just after the war: *Animal Farm* in 1945 and *1984* in 1949. The admonitions of these two works, no longer denouncing the dangers of fascism but warning of the totalitarian order that became Stalinism, had considerable success with French intellectuals. But while in 1984 it was a French magazine (the *NRF*) that published an issue with *1984* as its title, re-assessing Orwell's predictions, his writings were read and discussed throughout the world. Still more, as the work of a convinced and militant Socialist, they were very soon used – not only in France and not necessarily wrongfully – as an intellectual weapon in the battle against communism after the Iron Curtain had cut Europe in two.

Shortly before his death, George Orwell married Sonia Brownell. When she died at the end of the 1970s, Sonia Orwell had been much maligned as a 'wicked widow', but a recent biography of her by Hilary Spurling has done her better justice. For most of her life, she found herself at the cross-roads of French and British culture. The critic and essayist Cyril Connolly recruited the young Sonia Brownell to work on his magazine *Horizon* just after the war. She already had many friends in the British intelligentsia, being close to artists such as Lucien Freud and Francis Bacon, and for nearly thirty years she played an essential role in intellectual relations between Britain and France. Closely linked to Maurice Merleau-Ponty, she was also a friend of Michel Leiris, Jacques Lacan, Roland Barthes and Marguerite Duras. But apart from her work on *Horizon*, it was her personality that counted. Disliked by some, feared but admired by many others, she was, like Raymond Mortimer, a kind of beacon, an outpost of 'French' Britain. Of course, she too was exceptional. But her network, filled as it was with great friendships and furious enmities, was one example of many relationships that in the second half of the twentieth century linked writers and philosophers from Britain and France. Another example, with more clearly tangible results, was the publishing house of John Calder, which notably introduced the French *nouveau roman* to British readers. John Ardagh, a fellow contributor to this book, has for more than twenty-five years played the same role of interlocutor, as has Anthony Sampson.

There is obviously no need to alternate instances of reciprocal influence. But, as modern counterparts to André Maurois between the wars, one might cite Diane de Margerie, Vivienne Forrester and Christine Jordis, whose *Gens du Tamise*, published in 1999, opens with a quotation from Valéry Larbaud, that Gide-like connoisseur and admirer of British life: 'In all the 200 years since Europe discovered Shakespeare, it has not ceased to pay attention to what is written in England.' Few Europeans, and few French people, can claim as justly as Christine Jordis to have taken up the mantle of Larbaud, the author of *Ce vice impuni, la lecture*, and of *Queenie*, the prettiest of his *Enfantines*. Larbaud's Britain is an entity in itself. Here, one might venture the perhaps infantile generalisation that in those days it was writers such as Gide and Larbaud who were the counterparts of Conrad and James Hogg, while in France today it is women, in the wake of Virginia Woolf, who are the most fervent admirers and exponents of English literature as a whole.

The instances just cited should not eclipse other fields of thought that have flourished in the same climate on either side of the Channel. But here too it would be improper to speak of influence, such as can be traced in earlier centuries. To return to 'France in Britain', Jean-Paul Sartre and Albert Camus enjoyed immense success in Britain in the post-war years. But their success, like that of existentialist and subsequent French philosophers, as well as of 'commitment' in the novel, was a world phenomenon. In the same way, the French *nouveau roman*, structuralism and their successors also aroused passionate controversies in Britain: yet here too the effects were worldwide. In Britain, too, perhaps more than elsewhere, it would be hard to detect these influences outside the universities. Although derivatives of the *nouveau roman* were published in London, they soon petered out. Professors of French literature, however, made their daily bread – and jam – from the same controversies, especially in the United States. And university teachers, set to dissect the works of Alain Robbe-Grillet or Nathalie Sarraute (may they forgive this inappropriate conjunction), had still not abandoned their prey. Long after the *nouveau roman* had practically ceased to exist in France, hapless students were still being crammed on the subject in Britain, California and New York. English writers, meanwhile, were subject to a very different influence, that of the North American novel.

Perhaps because zealots for the *nouveau roman* so loudly proclaimed its revolutionary nature, everywhere and especially in Britain, they overlooked what was noted at the beginning of this chapter – the equally novel narrative procedures adopted by Laurence Sterne at the end of the eighteenth century. Nor should one neglect Ivy Compton-Burnett, whose *Brothers and Sisters*, published in 1929, began a new way of writing that Nathalie Sarraute was one of the first to recognise in France. In the face of the quasi-terrorism that some people on both sides of the Channel have sought to impose on the novel, it is a particular pleasure to be able to link the two great names of Compton-Burnett and Sarraute.

The gap, or mutual incomprehension, that divided universities from the common reader could have seemed almost touching in French eyes. But it led British readers, and publishers, to neglect for too long whole facets of French fiction that were not the 'new novel' made sacrosanct by its most faithful devotees.

More serious attention is owed to those who in the 1960s gave French philosophy a leading role. Merleau-Ponty has already been mentioned. But the names of Roland Barthes, Michel Foucault and Jacques Derrida are no less crucial – so much so that their work often reached an audience outside the university sphere, in their heyday being published on the literary pages of the *Sunday Times* or the *Observer*. One might recall here the active role of Jean-Marie Benoist, a professor in London for a considerable time. It is this connection, perhaps, that the vague word 'influence' may be more confidently used. There is no doubt, anyway, that the holy trinity of Barthes, Foucault and Derrida played and continues to play as important a role in British intellectual circles as the great American linguists and semiologists. In the opposite direction (to resume the alternation), it has to be said that Karl Popper and Ludwig Wittgenstein are still little known in France outside academic circles.

Perhaps, in discussing France and Britain in the twentieth and twenty-first centuries, we have so far dwelt too much on literature and philosophy. The theatre would have merited more space. There, too, the least that can be said is that the two countries have affected each other, with varying degrees of intensity. In the heyday of Harold Hobson, the celebrated former doyen of British critics, the British press and the London public gave standing ovations to Jean-Louis Barrault's visits and had real veneration for Edwige Feuillère. At that time, Laurence Olivier enjoyed the same prestige in France. In the 1950s, above all the British theatre virtually invaded the French stage. One could certainly then speak of 'influence'. There were many famous names: John Osborne, Arnold Wesker, James Saunders, Harold Pinter, Edward Bond, Tom Stoppard. Playing the game of reciprocity, one might cite Ionesco, then Robert Pinget and René de Obaldia – without of course counting Samuel Beckett as a French playwright. Nevertheless, the place of Pinter or Edward Bond on the French stage is far greater than that of French plays in Britain 25 years ago. Half a century ago, admittedly, Peter Brook staged *La petite hutte* in London. But Pinter and Bond have powerfully revived what some narrow-minded French critics used to dismiss, a few decades ago, as 'the theatre of the text' – in contrast to the subtle improvisations of France's allegedly brilliant directors.

Another domain in which very strong influence flowed, this time from Paris to London, is even further removed from the purely literary scene. This is surrealism, and especially surrealist painting. Here again, friendships and affinities played an essential role. A leading personality such as

Roland Penrose, himself a painter, but also an art critic and an admirer of beautiful women, poetry and great paintings, was the intermediary whereby the surrealist miracle burst upon Britain. Omnipresent, a friend of André Breton and of André Masson, married first to the writer Valentine Penrose and then to the photographer Lee Miller, Penrose certainly worked on both sides of the Atlantic: but it was on either side of the Channel that his role as a go-between was essential. From the dawn of surrealism until the great exhibition mounted by Michael Kustow at the Institute of Contemporary Arts (ICA) in the 1970s, the greatness of Roland Penrose can be seen on a whole facet of the history of art in Britain.

Finally, at the risk of being accused, perhaps rightly, of compiling a kind of catalogue, we must also consider music. To do so is to stress a surprising paradox. In the first half of the twentieth century, there were close links between the two countries. Mary Garden and Maggie Teyte, the first great incarnations of Mélisande, were British. But in the second half of that century, a strange development took place. Two radically different forms of music arose on either side of the Channel. One need cite only two names: Benjamin Britten and Michael Tippett. They, and especially Britten, are today considered among the greatest of twentieth-century composers. Yet in France then, although Britten was certainly played, 'official' music doctrine, established by 'the other music' in the sacred triangle of Paris, Baden-Baden and Milan, refused them freedom of the city. Britten's music, like that of Shostakovitch, was violently rejected, if not spurned, by the fiery young Pierre Boulez. At the same time Boulez himself was acclaimed in Britain, notably thanks to William Glock, who opened for him the doors of the BBC.

But, still more than Boulez, it was Olivier Messiaen who in the last twenty years of his life became a virtual superstar in Britain. Today, Benjamin Britten's work is played everywhere in France, and Boulez has retained his status in Britain. Whence and whither has the wind of influence blown? Might one venture that at the beginning of the twenty-first century Britten and Britain have won the day?

At all events, to end on a note without controversy, there is one field in which London, Liverpool and the whole United Kingdom have triumphed in France for more than thirty years. That is popular music. Its triumph is uncontested. What real weight have the famous French names that can be set against the Rolling Stones and the Beatles? Even if American rock music played some part in their success, the word 'influence' comes into its own when applied to British pop culture in France.

May we be forgiven for this more than subjective survey, citing a handful of names that have played some part in most of our lives. We return to the word 'affinity' and to those elective affinities that have forged so many links and shared feelings between our two cultures – between 'mine' and 'theirs'; between the two 'ours'. We have underplayed the over-used word 'influence', which connotes dominance. We have avoided the fashionable expression 'complicity'. We have shunned the promiscuous term 'cross-breeding'. The notion that remains is that of dialogue between cultures. Today that word is applied most often to relations between Western culture in general and the rest of the world. Rarely, however, has it seemed so appropriate as to relations between Britain and France. It was dialogue – in the columns of the *Times Literary Supplement*, the *Observer*, and the *Sunday Times*; in Sonia Orwell's London drawing-room; and before that in encounters with Raymond Mortimer, Cyril Connolly and others now forgotten – that revealed to both Britain and France the riches of each other's literature, theatre and ways of life. In conclusion, because I am writing here on the French side of the Channel, may I mention a few names, some of them already cited. This brief and partial roll of honour is by way of homage and thanks. All these men and women lived in London, in Britain, or elsewhere in the United Kingdom: some still do. Anthony Sampson, George Steiner, Andrew Sinclair, Joanna and Terence Kilmartin, Sonia Orwell, Francis Bacon, Stephen Spender, Stephen Bann, Patrick Woodcock, Roland Penrose, Jean Gimpel, Raymond Mortimer, Harold Hobson, William Glock, Ivy Compton-Burnett...

Jean-Pierre Angremy

French Culture in Britain

In 1946 the University of Oxford, having honoured several states-men and military leaders who were associated with the war, decided to make a meaningful gesture towards culture. This would take the form of awarding an honorary doctorate to a French writer: a decision that was greatly welcomed. The Oxford authorities con-sulted widely as they considered to whom they should award this prize. Consequently, although supposedly confidential, the shortlist became known and discussed. It consisted of three authors: Paul Claudel, André Gide and François Mauriac.

Claudel's poetry and drama were not well known in England, and those who were acquainted with his work found it powerful but diffi-cult. That he had written an ode to Marshal Pétain did not help his cause, however much he had subsequently expressed his support for de Gaulle. Oxford high tables reported the story that when Claudel was French ambassador to the United States in 1930, he was irritated at an official dinner by a lady who continually asked him questions about his writings. Eventually an exasperated Claudel put an end to the questioning, saying, 'Madame, quand je suis à table je mange'; the Oxford high tables asked themselves if they wanted to have him as their guest.

Gide had many supporters who believed strongly that he was of great literary stature, the most important writer in France. But his opponents, regarding him as a figure of the past, also maintained that his creative output had never been completely successful, and this argument won support (bolstering the mainly unspoken feeling that such a prize at such a time should not be awarded to a self-publicised homosexual). There remained Mauriac. His novels were well known and had many admirers. His war record, especially his association with Resistance movements, was impressive. It was felt that he was an intellectual and a writer who, in the best French tradition, was playing a role in French society. He was awarded the honorary doc-torate and he gave a public lecture that was a great success.

But the choice of Mauriac did not meet with complete approval. The supporters of Gide continued to press his case and some months later, in May, he too was given an honorary doctorate. Admirers of Georges Bernanos claimed that he was far superior to Mauriac. There was talk of Jean Cocteau. But the atmosphere was changing.

French literature and thought became linked to new names and new ideas. Jean-Paul Sartre and Albert Camus were the authors who attracted attention. Their novels and plays told of the Occupation and the Resistance and presented new ideas, a new philosophy. It became impossible to speak of France without referring to them and their associates. The story of Sartre's play *Huis Clos* became well known, as did *La Peste*, the novel by Camus. Another feature of the war that should be remembered was the poem by Paul Éluard, '*Liberté*'! Many at school liked to recite it, and there was a gramophone record available that some schools made use of.

Naturally, the full extent of British contact with French literature was largely dependent upon translations. The history of these English translations is complicated. Certain of Honoré de Balzac's novels, such as *César Birotteau* and *Eugénie Grandet*, were available before 1860, but Balzac's *Complete Works* were not translated until 1886. Gustave Flaubert was not well known but *Madame Bovary* has been translated several times, including a recent version. During the nineteenth century Victor Hugo, Alexandre Dumas and George Sand had been household names, and in the 1930s Scott Moncrieff's translation of Proust was highly respected (although Proust has never been a best-seller, a new translation of *À la recherche du temps perdu* appeared in 2002). A novel that achieves real fame in France is virtually certain of rapid translation. Françoise Sagan's *Bonjour Tristesse* (1953) is an example of this. The award of the Nobel Prize for Literature to Claude Simon in 1985 encouraged the translation of twelve of his novels. A controversial work may also encourage translation, as was the case of Michel Houellebecq. His three novels were rapidly available in English and recommended for Christmas reading in 2002. There are examples of French works being translated in America and this having little impact in England. Thus an English translation of Alphonse Daudet's *La Doulou* (a Provençal word for 'pain') appeared in 2003, the publishers unaware that an American version appeared in 1934. Several of Maurice Blanchot's works have been translated and published by the Station Hill Press in the United States but have scarcely circulated in England. If Marcel Pagnol is best known for his films, his prose works are also well known in England because of the excellence of the translations.

One example of a decline in British knowledge of French literature comes from the schools. It used to be the case that when pupils were taking French for Higher School Certificate or 'A' Levels (to use pre-war and post-war terms) they would have to read a work of French literature, either a classic of the past or a more modern classic. This has ceased to be the case in all schools. It is interesting to reflect that when the works of Théophile Gautier were recently published in the Pléiade edition, it was thought necessary to remind the French public that he had written novels. Many who took the Higher School Certificate examination in the 1930s and 1940s were only too aware that he had written *Le Capitaine Fracasse*.

British awareness of French art can be demonstrated in many ways, but a simple and straightforward method is to mention some of the famous art exhibitions that have been held in London. In 1936 there was the International Surrealist Exhibition at the New Burlington Galleries. This was not exclusively French, since the works of 60 artists from 14 different countries were shown, but the emphasis was mostly on France, and talks were given by André Breton and Paul Éluard. The Tate Modern's 2001 exhibition, entitled *Desire Unbound*, also gave a large space to French work, having a central space dedicated to *L'Amour Fou*. Poetry was placed at the heart of the exhibition with a display of manuscripts, drawings, photographs and books.

In 1995 the Hayward Gallery organised a large exhibition, *Landscapes of France: Impressionism and its Rivals*. This displayed works that were a cross-section of the landscape paintings shown at the annual Paris salons between 1860 and 1890, many of them being taken from provincial collections and exhibiting artists who are largely forgotten. The exhibition also showed works by their Impressionist contemporaries Claude Monet, Paul Sisley, Camille Pissarro and Berthe Morisot. There was thus a contrast within the exhibition between the large salon pictures, demonstrating *la vraie France*, and the more experimental and personal images of their more famous contemporaries. But the diversity of the painters was as nothing compared to the diversity of the scenes that they painted. This showed *La France profonde* in all its variety and strength.

The Royal Academy's 2002 exhibition was called *Paris: Capital of the Arts 1900–1960*. It was remarkable by its scope, beginning with the very great names: Pablo Picasso, Maurice Utrillo, Paul Derain, Marc Chagall, Modigliani, Pierre Bonnard and proceeding through a series of rooms where great names were also present, until it came to the 1960s, where one was shown an extraordinary mass of poster and advertising art, junk art and anti-art.[1]

The organisers of the exhibition were criticised for this. It was said that they had set out to show the decline of Paris as the capital of the arts. The implication was that Paris had been replaced, most probably by New York. More precisely, while the years until 1940 were undoubtedly those when great art had flourished, and while it was natural that the war years when France was occupied were difficult even for Jean Dubuffet, Alberto Giacometti or Georges Braque, the 1950s and 1960s saw a certain decline that increased as years went by.

But this attitude was not everywhere accepted. Critics pointed to artists of interest, such as Wilfredo Lam or Victor Brauner. But essentially what one saw was the British conviction that France is still the centre for everything that is artistic and cultural.

French music has always occupied an important place in Britain. In the mid-twentieth century two orchestral conductors, perhaps the two most famous, were particularly devoted to music by French composers. Sir Thomas Beecham regretted that the normal orchestral programme in Britain was too overloaded with German music ('Teutonic', he liked to call it). Berlioz was his favourite composer, and he once said that he would give all the sonatas of Bach in exchange for one act of an opera by Massenet. Sir John Barbirolli was a great lover of Debussy and there is a story told about him conducting the Hallé orchestra at a concert in Wigan. They played *L'Après-midi d'un faune* and at the end, after an unusually long silence, the audience, deeply moved, applauded tumultuously. Barbirolli wept with emotion. 'The piece that was booed when it was first played in Paris,' he said, 'it's now applauded, applauded in Wigan!'

For those in Oxford at the end of the war, one of the most moving moments was a recital by French artists of the songs of Henri Duparc. It was a magnificent symbol. With peace came French musicians, playing and singing Duparc.

Douglas Johnson

---

1   Of course, not all of these artists were French.

British Writers in France

'Avignon!' wrote Lawrence Durrell, 'the putrescence of its squares ... it was rotten, fly-blown ... There was not a corner of it that we did not love.'

British writers who have lived or travelled in the French provinces have mostly been critical Francophiles, from Arthur Young to Graham Greene. But some have been frankly Francophobic – like the truculent Tobias Smollett, whose journal (1766) reads like a parody of today's bigot, as he inveighs against the cooking, plumbing, transport and has endless rows with *aubergistes*. Arriving at Boulogne, his beloved books were impounded: 'I know of no country in which strangers are worse treated.' And the Boulonnais he found 'very ferocious, much addicted to revenge'.

The cheerful Laurence Sterne then derided Smollett as 'Smelfungus' in *A Sentimental Journey*, in which he eagerly described his own flirtation with a pretty lady in Calais. Among later writers in the area, Edith Sitwell in *Façade* gave a surreal glimpse of Le Touquet, while Ruskin adored the Gothic glories of Amiens Cathedral and wrote a book about it. He particularly liked, on the south transept, the statue of 'a Madonna in decadence' with her 'gay soubrette's smile'. Wilfred Owen came to Artois as jaunty patriot, but steadily declined into weary pessimist, aghast at 'the riddled corpses round Bapaume'.

Further south, Alsace, Burgundy and the Lyonnais are a virtual void of British writing. But it comes thick and fast in Provence, as you'd expect. Somerset Maugham spent 35 years in his villa on Cap Ferrat, near a zoo where the chimpanzees held tea-parties. He hated gate-crashers who treated him as a tourist sight, saying to one: 'What d'you think I am, a monkey in a cage?' He set some stories on the Riviera, notably *Three Fat Women of Antibes*, about expatriates on a thwarted diet.

Cyril Connolly stayed at Haut-de-Cagnes in the 1930s, and set his one novel there, *The Rock Pool*, a tale of pagan decadence among the rich foreign community. The New Zealander Katherine Mansfield spent periods in Menton and Bandol, which she loved. But she too was shocked by the expats: Monte Carlo, she wrote, is '*Real Hell* ... a continual procession of *whores*, pimps, governesses ... old, old hags ... rich fat capitalists.' D. H. Lawrence too passed his final years in Bandol, then Vence, where he died and now lies in its cemetery.

After writing some fiction set on the Côte, Graham Greene enjoyed a serene old age in his villa at Antibes but in 1980 he was stunned by reality when the Nice criminal mafia began to persecute the daughter of some close friends, and the local judiciary did not dare to act. Greene, furious, tried to use his prestige to help the family. He returned his Légion d'Honneur and wrote a famous bilingual pamphlet, *J'Accuse*. In it, he advised would-be settlers to 'avoid the region of Nice, which is the reserve of some of the most criminal organisations in the south of France'. He accused them in detail of drug-dealing, murder, and taking over the casinos and the building industry. Jacques Médecin, the notorious right-wing mayor of Nice, retorted that Greene was the tool of a political plot to discredit him.

Two centuries earlier, Tobias Smollett was another Briton who much preferred the Riviera to its inhabitants. He was 'inchanted' [*sic*] by Nice, whose countryside was 'all cultivated like a garden'. But his usual cantankerous self was revolted by the garlic, and he found the people 'uncultured and inhospitable'. 'Most of the females are pot-bellied', and 'the great poverty of the people is owing to their religion', as they give half of their substance to 'mendicant friars and priests'.

Further west, Lawrence Durrell expressed his joy in the sensuous Provençal world in his lovely novel *Monsieur or the Prince of Darkness*. He settled at Sommières (a village west of Nîmes), where he died. To the north, at Le Monastier near Le Puy, R. L. Stevenson in 1878 bought his donkey Modestine, and they began their zig-zag hike along a route that any tourist can follow today on foot or by car, with a good map. This Protestant Scot was beguiled by the Trappist monks of Nôtre-Dame-des-Neiges, who greeted him with silent warmth. At one inn, he shared the only bedroom with a young married couple; at another, the waitress had 'the heavy nonchalance of a performing cow, her great grey eyes steeped in amorous languor'. Finally, at St-Jean-du-Gard, RLS sold the faithful but now ailing Modestine.

Over in the Basque country, Pau once had one of the largest English resident colonies on the Continent: here Dornford Yates lived, and described their doings in his 'Berry' novels (*c.*1920–45). To the north, Cognac was the setting for *The Voyage*, a rather bad novel by that arch-Francophile Charles Morgan, now half-forgotten in Britain but still vaguely admired in France.

In our own day as in the past, it is remarkable how few of the many English novels set in France are about the French and their lives: nearly all deal with expats, which perhaps is understandable, as French life is not easy to portray in depth. Honourable exception should be made of some recent stories by Sebastian Faulks and Julian Barnes – and maybe of the parables by Joanne Harris (*Chocolat*) who is half-French. Or, in non-fiction, Peter Mayle, with his genuine feeling for French life.

Of all British writers about provincial France, surely the finest is Arthur Young, a gentleman farmer and agronomist whose journeys in 1789–90 – to Brittany, Bordeaux, the Jura and elsewhere – happened to coincide with the Revolution. His enthralling book *Travels in France* has been out of print in Britain for far too long and is better known today in France itself. A sensible liberal, he was shocked at the poverty and the desperate state of agriculture (as compared with prosperous and well-ordered England at that time). Brittany in particular he found 'a miserable province, full of wild and very poor people'. And he blamed, rightly, the evils of absentee landlordism and the dreadful governmental system of the *ancien régime*. Few of today's English writers have understood France so well.

John Ardagh

The Auld Alliance

The centenary of the Entente Cordiale is rightly being celebrated, but that royal initiative was certainly not the first of the ties of diplomacy that bind together our two nations. As we pause to reassess these links we should remember the much older relationship between Scotland and France – the Auld Alliance. I press the claims of the Auld Alliance despite the fact that at various points of its history that alliance manifested itself in joint military enterprises, not always defensive, against England. For the cultural legacy of the Auld Alliance, and indeed the readiness of Scots to look outward to continental Europe, has, to our mutual enrichment, long outlasted the strategic and dynastic manoeuvrings of English, French and Scots kings and queens.

In October 1295, John Balliol of Scotland and Philip IV of France concluded a treaty promising each other military assistance. The treaty itself was short-lived, but it came to signify the beginning of the relationship between Scotland and France that has come to be known as *La Vieille Alliance*.

The fighting qualities of Scots were highly respected in medieval Europe, and the French relied heavily on the professional soldiers from Scotland after their defeat at the Battle of Agincourt in 1415. In 1421, at the Battle of Bauge, an army of Scots dealt out a significant defeat to the English, thus buying France valuable breathing space and helping to save the country from English domination. Honours and rewards were heaped upon the Scots by the grateful French.

Scots continued to serve in France: they aided Joan of Arc in her famous relief of Orleans, and many went on to form the Garde Écossaise, the fiercely loyal bodyguard of the French kings. A third-generation descendant of one, Béraud Stuart of Aubigny, was captain of the Garde Écossaise from 1493 to 1508, and a hero of France's Italian wars. To this day he and other Scots heroes of the Auld Alliance are celebrated in Beraud's home town of Aubigny-sur-Nère in an annual pageant.

The Auld Alliance was much more than a marriage of diplomatic convenience. French influence on Scottish life and language from the early Middle Ages was considerable. The Scots language, and even Scottish food, still reveal that impact; there is evidence that the traditional Scottish dish of haggis came to Scotland via France and may even take its name from the French *hachis* (minced beef). Trading links proliferated, and despite the Alliance being a mainly military instrument, it also brought more tangible benefits, as Scots merchants were given first choice of the finest French wines.

On Wine Quay of Leith (which is now the home of the devolved Scottish administration), French wine was rolled up the streets to the merchants' cellars behind the waterfront. The wine was especially popular for the now famous Scottish Hogmanay celebrations. William Dunbar (1460–*c*.1520), the famous court Makar (poet) for King James IV, wrote about the wines available in Edinburgh in his poem 'Dunbaris Dirige to the King':

> To drink withe ws the new fresche wyne
> That grew apone the revar Ryne,
> Fresche fragrant claretis out of France,
> Of Angeo and of Orliance . . .

Despite the attractions of other beverages, the appeal of French wine among Scots remains strong to the present day.

Scottish and French merchants were given immunities from the duties and taxation that other foreign merchants paid by claiming dual citizenship (a right that was available to any Scot or Frenchman). This was unique in its day and evidence that Scotland has traditionally seen itself as a part of Europe. By the time of Mary Stuart's reign (1542–87) many French people had settled in Edinburgh in an area still known as 'Little France' (where the new Edinburgh Royal Infirmary is now situated).

As today, education provided a great link with the wider world. Student exchanges with France started in the Middle Ages, with many Scots enrolling at the highly esteemed Universities of Orleans, Bourges and Poitiers. On returning to Scotland they spread their experience and knowledge and made a particular impact on the Scottish legal system, which, to this day, still shows signs of French influence. The exchange of ideas and expertise was not one-way, however: from the date of its foundation to the time of the Reformation, several of the Rectors of the University of Paris were Scots. These exchanges had a huge influence on Scottish intellectual society. The willingness of the Scots to open their minds to the ideas circulating around France, and the rest of Europe, were a major reason for the Scottish Enlightenment, and Edinburgh becoming known as 'the Athens of the North'.

The ethos behind the Auld Alliance did not perish with the Union of the English and Scottish crowns, or even with the failure of the Stuart pretenders who turned first to France when forced into exile. In learning, in the arts, and in many other walks of Scottish life, an openness toward French ideas, culture and world view remains evident.

The Auld Alliance is still recognised both in Scotland and in France. Indeed, Scots Saltires were even spotted at the Euro 2000 Final amongst the French *Tricolores*.

Scotland and France remain partners in trade. France is Scotland's largest export market by volume for Scotch whisky, with the French managing to consume almost 154 million bottles in 2001. But there is more to Scottish exports than our national drink: office machinery, radio, TV and communications equipment, and chemicals also find their way to France, highlighting the diverse range of industry in modern Scotland. Over £3.3 billion worth of Scottish goods are exported to France, proving that the partnership is as important today as it was in the past.

Today France and the UK are joined together within the European Union. The centenary of the Entente Cordiale is an opportunity to celebrate all the benefits that Franco-British relations have brought to each nation. As we build an ever more cohesive Europe it is right and proper to exalt the fact that Scots, French and English can live together with mutual respect and harmony, learning from each other to the enrichment of our cultures.

Helen Liddell

A French Shrine in Britain

How many people would guess that on the borders of Surrey and Hampshire there is a corner of a foreign field that is forever France? When Napoleon III died in exile in Chislehurst in 1873 he was first buried there, but when, six years later, his only son was killed (fighting for the British against the Zulus) the grieving Empress decided to build a mausoleum in their joint honour. A site near Farnborough Hill was eventually picked as a worthy setting, and in 1881 the Empress moved nearby to watch her *basilique impériale* and an adjoining monastery rise from the ground. The architect was Gabriel Destailleur, who at the same period was building a Buckinghamshire retreat for Baron Ferdinand de Rothschild. The basilica, wholly French in its splendid soaring interior and in the lavish marble of its funerary crypt, derives from various churches in the Loire and one in the Sarthe; while St Michael's monastery, which was finished later by the Benedictine monks who came to live there, looks much older as it is a high-class copy of the medieval mother-house at Solesmes.

The Empress' intention was that the monks should pray in perpetuity for the souls of her husband and son – and eventually her own, for her corpse too was duly entombed in Aberdeen granite in 1920. In the land of the Protestant Reformation, St Michael's must be one of the few centres in Britain dedicated to such a specific task, although these days the monks also run a retreat house, a small farm and a printing press, sell honey and candles, and welcome a devoted public (some of whom come down from London) to hear the monks chant the offices of mass in Latin Gregorian chant.

The Benedictines who settled there in the 1890s were all French, and for many decades the Abbey was not only an oasis of French prayer but of French living: French newspapers and even bread were delivered daily from Portsmouth! In the early days, during the contentious separation in France between Church and state, it was expected that many more brothers would cross the Channel to join them. This never really came to pass, and by and by the monks, in spite of their imperial endowment, made their tacit peace with the French Republic: a few younger men from the Abbey went to fight for France in World War I.

By 1947 the French monks were much reduced in numbers. Benedictines, unlike those in some other orders, choose to join their particular abbey for life, and it was increasingly difficult to tempt French novices to settle permanently in an alien land. They had already been joined by some brothers from Gloucester, and in that year the first English Prior was appointed. The English singing style supplanted the French one – rather to the disgust of the ageing French who, accustomed to a genteel, nasal style of chant, complained that the more robust English 'sang like dogs'. The classic language of Franco-British/Anglo-French insult . . .

Today the brothers are all English-speaking. The Father Prior is a relatively young man and presides with humour and intellectual acumen over a small but dedicated community. Whatever the original basis for their presence there, he feels that the monks create a valuable reservoir of traditional prayer and spirituality in a world in need of such things. To turn in at the inconspicuous gate on a main road between an office block and a roundabout, and to find yourself driving beneath overhanging trees, is to enter into another dimension.

Gillian Tindall

X

The Entente Today

Today, close relations between Britain and France extend from diplomacy and defence to trade and travel, scholarship and sport. The participants seldom refer to the Entente Cordiale – they implement and embody it, sometimes in unexpected ways.

A View from the Quai d'Orsay

On a summer's day in London, on 30 June 1981, having just become diplomatic counsellor to the new President, François Mitterrand, who had come to power little more than a month before, I began my task as note-taker for his first meeting with Margaret Thatcher, organised alongside the marriage of Prince Charles and Diana. I noted their remarks, the cry of the seagulls through the half-open windows of No. 10 Downing Street, and also the deliberate courtesy with which both leaders met. They had decided to like each other – Mrs Thatcher because she had not appreciated the way in which she had been treated since her accession to power in 1979 by Valéry Giscard d'Estaing, François Mitterrand because he was deter-mined to use all his charm and persuasion to prevent the great liberal powers, and especially the Anglo-Americans, from spurning or ostracising the first left-wing president of the French Republic, the incarnation of the Union of the Left! Some days later, in Ottawa at his first G7 meeting, François Mitterrand would make his first approach to Ronald Reagan in the same spirit. This mutual sympathy, this personal goodwill, endured – despite almost constant political disagreements – until Mrs Thatcher resigned nine-and-a-half years later. And François Mitterrand then said, to Jacques Attali and several others of us: 'She was an opponent, but at least she had a vision. Finally, I got on very well with her.'

An opponent? The word is not too strong. In nine years, what did they agree about? Few subjects: about the Falklands, a little about the Russian gas pipeline, and partially about Gorbachev and the Gulf War. In 1982, against Claude Cheysson and most of the Socialists, François Mitterrand had at once sided with Great Britain against the Argentine military men who had annexed the Falklands, and Mrs Thatcher had thought him 'splendid'. He had not acted out of Anglophilia – or not much – but because the 1930s had given him a permanent, visceral repugnance to any change of frontiers by force. He was to show this later by his firmness against Libya's incursion into Chad and Iraq's invasion of Kuwait. In 1982–83, neither France nor Britain had shared America's anxiety that the Russian gas pipeline then under construction might make Europeans dependent, and both had found unacceptable Washington's claim to impose a unilateral, extra-territorial embargo on the firms concerned. The unilateralist temptation already! Both François Mitterrand and Margaret Thatcher returned a positive verdict on Mikhail Gorbachev and his policy, whereas Reagan, Bush, and Kohl long remained hesitant and wary. As early as December 1984, having received Gorbachev at Chequers while he was still only in charge of (I dare not say 'responsible for') Soviet agriculture, Mrs Thatcher declared 'We can do business with him' – because his pragmatism overrode ideology. Mitterrand, during his trip to the USSR in June 1984 at the time of Chernenko, had been impressed by Gorbachev's frankness and lucidity when he met him at dinner at the Kremlin. Finally, in 1990, Mrs Thatcher and Mitterrand agreed with George Bush in at once deciding that Iraq's annexation of Kuwait could not be tolerated, even if afterwards they might at times differ on the means and timing of Kuwait's liberation.

These convergences of view were not negligible. But alongside them were essential disagreements – on Europe, on strategy and disarmament, and on Germany.

On Europe, from 1979 to 1984, Mrs Thatcher never stopped renegotiating even more favourable financial terms for Britain's membership of the Common Market than had been obtained in 1972. It was the period of 'I want my money back'. An Iron Lady in domestic politics, against striking unions, the Labour Party and the IRA, and in foreign affairs against the Argentinians, Europe and the USSR, for five whole years she acted like an inflexible accountant, deaf to appeals on behalf of Europe's general interest, blocking any progress by the Ten. Even after the election of François Mitterrand in May 1982, five successive presidents of the European Union, from 1981 onwards, were thwarted by her obstinacy until the Fontainebleau European Council in June 1984, when Mitterrand and Kohl, whose growing complicity she rightly feared, finally forced her to accept a compromise, after 'frank discussions' in the elegant surroundings of the Château des Valois. Mitterrand saw this as 'a certain softening of Britain's stubbornness'. Nor was the compromise bad for British interests. Eighteen years later, in the autumn of 2002, when President Chirac declared that it might be reconsidered, Tony Blair got on his high horse: it was out of the question! At the time, the compromise pulled Europe out of its rut and made possible the extraordinarily rapid advance that lasted almost ten years, from the recruitment of two new member states to the Treaty of Maastricht, including the Single European Act and the single market. All this took place with or without Great Britain or even despite Britain, but always after constant, exhausting negotiations.

As regards strategic affairs and disarmament, the second part of the 1980s was a Calvary for Mrs Thatcher. Despite her warlike energy she had to look on, powerless, as NATO's old Cold War strategy, to which she had been so attached, was gradually dismantled. More and more, she feared that Gorbachev, despite her appreciation of him, would tempt the West towards radical and premature disarmament. She was torn between her absolute fidelity to the Atlantic Alliance and her total rejection of the Utopian anti-nuclear dreams that were seducing part of American opinion, and even perhaps President Reagan himself. She was stupefied, at the seven-nation summit in Venice in 1987, to hear François Mitterrand roundly condemn the pernicious 'graduated response' doctrine of NATO in which she implicitly believed but which, thanks to de Gaulle and his successors, had never been France's doctrine of deterrence.

But it was the reunification of Germany that gave Mrs Thatcher the cruellest and most lasting nightmares. Helmut Kohl had the skill to pursue, through all the obstacles, a course that was at the same time hoped for, unexpected, and feared – and in a way that at last was sincerely approved by all Germany's partners. George Bush backed it while making sure that it did not impugn NATO, and François Mitterrand on condition that it did not impede the building of Europe. Mrs Thatcher, who wanted neither German reunification nor a political Europe nor a single currency, and who was obsessed by fear of 'greater Germany', was *incapable* of accepting François Mitterrand's policy, and was condemned to defensive activism and vain alarm, regarding Gorbachev and Kohl as deceitful, Mitterrand as misguided, and Bush as too compliant. It was during this rearguard action, with her back to the wall, and without prospect of reprieve, that on 22 November 1990 she lost power, supposedly a victim of the poll tax controversy, but rejected by her own parliamentary party, which after eleven years could no longer bear so exhausting and imperious a leader.

Mitterrand and Mrs Thatcher may have appreciated and respected each other, may have pleased and attracted each other, all smiles and velvet glances; they may have agreed on one point or another – and they met again and lunched together on 3 June 1992. But they *never* shared a common project. When, indeed, since the end of World War II have these two former empires, these two old nation-states, done so? Facing the same sense of decline, they have drawn opposite conclusions, still dominant after 47 years, from their joint failure at Suez to their respective attitudes towards the United States on the one hand and towards Germany and Europe on the other.

During the years when François Mitterrand and then Jacques Chirac had John Major as their partner, from 1990 to 1997, these structural data did not change. It was simply that Major proved a more amenable partner, who shared Mitterrand's lucidity about the irreversible effects of the unexpected break-up of former Yugoslavia and was less hostile to the Maastricht process than Mrs Thatcher would have been. From 1995 to 1997, relations between Major and Chirac seem to have been examplary. The picture altered, up to a point, with the legislative elections in Britain and France in May 1997 that brought Tony Blair and Lionel Jospin to power.

In June 1997, when I became foreign minister in Lionel Jospin's government, under the presidency of Jacques Chirac, circumstances had changed. In London there was now a prime minister who hoped his country would adopt the euro, and who in any case wanted his country to play an important role in Europe. He was not troubled by the weakening of Franco-German relations after the retirement of François Mitterrand and Helmut Kohl. Given the agnostic, pragmatic views of Europe held – in different ways – by both Jacques Chirac and Lionel Jospin, Franco-British relations on this subject no longer had any reason to be systematically opposed. The period covered most of President Clinton's second term of office and the first six months of George W. Bush's presidency – but not the frenzied disagreement on the Iraq war in the winter and spring of 2002–3. It was a time of pragmatism, when relations at the summit were friendly and relaxed, without particular affinities or especial difficulties, with nuances and differences about dates or priorities, with varying positions *vis-à-vis* the United States, but with no or very few painful disagreements.

During those five years, my relations with my counterparts Robin Cook and then Jack Straw were marked by the affairs of Kosovo and the Balkans, by Africa, by the questions of Hong Kong, India and Pakistan, by the Near East, and throughout by continual negotiations on an infinity of subjects among foreign ministers in the 'General Affairs Council' of the European Union.

Robin Cook's powerful personality was evident from the first. It was said that he had been a reluctant supporter of Tony Blair's 'New Labour' and that neither had forgotten the controversies that had divided them; that on certain economic and social subjects Robin Cook was midway between Tony Blair and Lionel Jospin; that Robin Cook had been more prepared to become chancellor of the Exchequer, the post finally filled by

Gordon Brown, than foreign secretary. Some claimed that with a more telegenic appearance the brilliant Robin Cook might have been able to challenge the dazzling Tony Blair for leadership of the party. Many things were said, in fact. But they were eclipsed by the energy, convictions, negotiating skill and sense of humour of the new man at the FO, who was as Scottish as he was British. Cook's first concern, as he had promised Labour militants, was to persuade the member states of the EU – with the support of the new French government – to adopt a code of conduct for arms sales. At first, the British wondered how that would accord with French 'cohabitation' between a left-wing premier and a right-wing president. But it was the question of the Balkans that quickly brought us into daily cooperation – or, more precisely, that of Kosovo. It was with Klaus Kinkel, then German foreign minister and very aware of this problem, that in the spring of 1998 I paid my first ministerial visits to the region, in particular to Serbia and Croatia. The Dayton Agreements of late 1995 had not settled the fate of Kosovo, and Serbo-Albanian tension was fast becoming explosive in this province of the Yugoslav Federal Republic, where three-quarters of the population spoke Albanian. Several of us foreign ministers decided to raise the problem in the 'contact group' that since 1993 had fortunately brought together the foreign ministers of the United States, Russia, France, Great Britain, Germany and Italy. There, Robin Cook and I found ourselves almost constantly agreed on the goals to seek and the steps to be taken. And when at the end of 1998 we concluded that the many diplomatic efforts were getting nowhere, we both had the idea of giving a spectacular last chance to a peaceful solution to the Kosovo problem. This took the form of the Rambouillet Conference, which we jointly chaired. (It could have been done with Joschka Fischer, the German foreign minister, since October 1998, in the new German government, but at that time he bore the heavy burden of presiding for six months over the European Union.) For more than a month, in the ancient château, we ceaselessly multiplied the contacts, the meetings, the efforts on both sides, regularly seconded by other foreign ministers from the contact group while Igor Ivanov thoughtfully followed and Madeleine Albright deployed great energy. This conference was essential, showing Western public opinion that everything politically and diplomatically possible had been tried to solve the problem without the use of force. Unhappily, Milosevic never showed the least intention of shifting his policy by a single centimetre. The rest is history.

Likewise, in December 1998 at the Franco-British Summit at St Malo, famous for its pioneering and creative compromise on European defence, Robin Cook and I issued statements announcing that France and Great

Britain intended to go beyond their traditional antagonism in Africa (which dated from the Fashoda incident) and work closely together. From then onwards, with approval in principle from Lionel Jospin and hesitant agreement from the Élysée Palace, I made progress. Robin Cook said he had the support of Tony Blair. I think in fact that he found in Africa some of the scope that Tony Blair and his more and more presidential staff gave him more grudgingly in areas such as transatlantic relations, Europe and the Near East, where the prime minister perhaps thought him too close to the continental Europeans, and in any case the French, or too independent.

So Robin Cook and I went to West Africa on 10 and 11 March 1999, swapping aircraft, to Ghana and the Ivory Coast, where we brought together for the first time French and British ambassadors in Africa. The African heads of state, so long accustomed to putting up with, or exploiting, European rivalry in Africa, were uncertain whether to believe in this new policy, and whether to find it welcome or worrying. They greeted it prudently and waited to see what promise it held. For my part I believe that we should not disengage from Africa but that we cannot return to purely national policies there. We have everything to gain from pooling the efforts of those European countries for which Africa is significant. In order to involve the respective bureaucracies, often hesitant or sceptical, we asked the French minister for cooperation, Charles Josselin, and his British counterpart Clare Short, no great Francophile, to pay a similar joint visit. This they did in April 2001, going to Guinea and Sierra Leone.

The friendly cooperation I enjoyed with Robin Cook, deepened during long conversations at the Quai d'Orsay, at la Celle Saint Cloud, in White-hall, and at Scheveningen and elsewhere, was intense and, I think, productive – without compromising the ever closer relations I was then forming with Joschka Fischer. I should add that, oddly enough, our cooperation on many subjects, of which I am citing only the most important, was not affected by the Community bargaining that took place at that time, including that which marked the European Council in Nice. This may seem strange. After all, foreign ministers are supposed to be always on duty, in charge of all the European questions that arise in the annual Council of General Affairs. The answer is that by common accord we drew a distinction between the sometimes opposing positions we had to defend in Community debates and the diplomatic tasks we sought to pursue together apart from Community disagreements. Exhaustive and seemingly endless discussions such as we had seem to me a fruitful way of working out a common European view and, one day, a real European foreign policy, whereas a majority vote on it in a 25-nation Union would stifle debate, would create no consensus and, in serious cases, would not be respected.

After winning the election of 7 June 2001, Tony Blair made his home secretary, Jack Straw, foreign secretary in place of Robin Cook, whom he put in charge of relations with Parliament, an important post in the British system.[1] It soon became clear that the new foreign secretary, who was very close to the prime minister, had as his first task to make sure that there was perfect harmony between the policy of the Foreign Office and the wishes of Downing Street. Hence his extreme prudence on a number of delicate subjects, especially from the point of view of Anglo-American relations, if only in the revival of the 'contact group' at a time when Tony Blair was busy, before and after 11 September 2001, re-establishing with George W. Bush a relationship as close as he had enjoyed with Bill Clinton.

The likeable Jack Straw and I worked on a large number of subjects without meeting any particular problems. Finally he too agreed to visit Africa with me. We decided to go together to the region of the Great Lakes, which was in the grip of interminable and bloody regional hostilities with many implications, and where Franco-British disagreements about the causes of the conflict, the role of the different states in its genesis and its prolongation, and the way to put an end to it, were still very much alive and were still being used by English-speaking Africans against French-speaking Africans and vice versa. With a view to this visit, Jack Straw and I worked hard with our respective officials[2] to reach common elements of analysis, language and solution. The previous summer, I had visited the region as a representative of France. Now, with my British counterpart, I again met the sophisticated heads of state of Ruanda, Burundi, Uganda and the Democratic Republic of the Congo, and appreciated their efforts, in this new and disturbing situation, to reconcile those aspects of their statements that they normally kept distinct, depending on whether they were talking to the French or the Anglo-Americans. This led them to reconsider some of their positions. I think Jack Straw, like me, was fascinated by this experience and its results. I am convinced that our joint efforts, and the message they conveyed to the protagonists in the conflict, contributed to the subsequent improvement of the situation, and I am glad that they are continuing.

During this period, the good relationship of Tony Blair, Jacques Chirac and Lionel Jospin was aided by the fact that there were no fundamental differences between them, and that no crisis – apart from the painful BSE affair – forced them to confront each other. In this intermediate phase of

---

1 Robin Cook resigned in the spring of 2003 because he disagreed with Britain's military involvement in the war in Iraq.

2 On my side, essentially Georges Serre, now ambassador in Kinshasa.

Europe's development, Tony Blair was as European as one could expect a British prime minister to be: no one could reproach him on that score. There were many potential European discords, but they remained latent. The debate within the European left about Tony Blair's 'Third Way', and Lionel Jospin's doubts on the subject, did not weigh upon *governmental* relations between France and Britain, but it was certainly with one eye on it that President Chirac several times mischievously expressed his sympathy with Tony Blair's policy. All this was always friendly on a personal level. It was before the George W. Bush revolution and above all before the war in Iraq. In sum, rather sadly, it shows that Franco-British relations are no longer, by themselves, *the determining factor*. They can be more or less good, more or less tense. It is better that they be good. But they are dependent on the global situation, on the relations of each party with the United States, with Germany, and on the attitude of each *vis-à-vis* the European process and the policy of the United States.

What is to be done in the present world by countries such as ours whose intellectual and political heritage is so great? Each of us, at present, is facing the challenge separately, in its own way. Yet there is something that the French and the British could do together – and that no one else could do in their place. It is to conceive the lineaments of Europe as a power in partnership with the United States in a way that would be serene and acceptable to *all* Europeans – Atlanticists as well as partisans of 'European Europe'. This would mean concessions by both – but the prize would be worth it. Germany would of course be an integral part of the synthesis. However, the French and the Germans alone cannot overcome the dis-agreement of principle about what Europe should be and do in the world. This disagreement essentially divides the French and the British and those who are close to them. It was vital to revive Franco-German relations. That became possible after the two countries' elections in the spring and autumn of 2002 – whatever the results. It happened. But experience in 2003 showed that the revival was no longer enough to bring all Europe in its wake, and that it could even lead to British counter-moves. It is indeed the conceptual difference between Britain and France that lies at the heart of the present European dilemma about what Europe should be and do in the world. It is this difference that must be tackled. The British and the French need to hold a 'super St Malo' in close coordination with Germany and in the interest of Europe as a whole.

Hubert Védrine

Defence

After centuries of hostility and murderous conflict, the 1900s – with rare exceptions – were marked by the growth of deep friendship and real armed comradeship between the military of Britain and France. In all likelihood, their long rivalry may in the end have created the conditions for reconciliation by leading each of them, over time, to understand and respect the other. By the end of the nineteenth century, in fact, they had so much in common that mutual understanding had become possible. They had both become capable of fighting on land and at sea; they shared comparable skills and regulations; they had developed similar military training and traditions. Both had acquired extensive colonial experience and considerable knowledge of the world at large.

In the lengthy battles of two world wars they fought side by side. Despite France's grievous situation in World War II, shared hardship linked the two armies – as witness the graves of countless British soldiers killed on the soil of France.

At Suez in 1956, France and the United Kingdom, together with Israel, rapidly mounted a large-scale combined operation that remains an object lesson for staff colleges. Militarily, it was a swift success. It was halted, and troops were withdrawn, at the abrupt bidding of the Soviet Union and the United States. That episode in our shared military history shows how well our armed forces worked together, but its outcome revealed our two countries' inability to resist threats from the two nuclear superpowers. Both Britain and France recognised their military weakness. Each, however, chose its own way of ensuring its security.

The United Kingdom gave priority to its transatlantic relations and linked its security with that of the United States. It developed military cooperation that continues to this day, especially in the nuclear field and as regards intelligence. It unequivocally supports the Atlantic Alliance. France, while remaining true to its Allies, was determined to remain captain of its own fate: it therefore established its own independent nuclear deterrent. Its withdrawal from NATO's integrated command arrangements, moreover, isolated its armed forces in Europe until the end of the Cold War. Yet, even during that long period of separation, relations between the French and British military remained very friendly. The two navies both adopted the Exocet sea-to-sea missile, and they established discreet but effective cooperation on naval security, since each had the same role in its country's deterrence. Britain and France together developed and built the Gazelle and Lynx helicopters. They produced the Jaguar fighter aircraft at the beginning of the 1970s. Despite this success – and their converging needs – France withdrew from the European fighter project in 1985. However (and this is less well known), French forces gave immediate assistance to their British colleagues when the Falklands War broke out. It was perfectly natural: French airmen had not forgotten how much they owed to the Royal Air Force.

The end of the Cold War marked a new stage in the strengthening of links and exchanges between the British and French armies. Several characteristics distinguish them from their neighbours and ease their mutual relations. Both countries retain strategic ambitions outside Europe, and as a result accept budgetary and research burdens of roughly the same order. Both have defence industries, nuclear weapons, comparable military capability and similar experience of outside engagement. During the past fifteen years, Britain and France have undertaken more joint decisions and actions than ever before, opening the prospect of gradual long-term integration. Some of these are worth recalling.

Since the end of 1989, the respective general staffs have held regular, frequent meetings on strategy, arms procurement and nuclear affairs. These have very quickly dispelled a certain number of past misunderstandings, and on most subjects have revealed remarkable convergence of views. They have since led to a very fruitful strategic dialogue between the two Ministries of Defence.

Thirty-five years after Suez, the first Gulf conflict revived fraternal collaboration in this theatre of war.

In June 1991, the British defence minister agreed to back France's proposal to set up a European satellite centre at Torrejon in Spain. Its first director was British, followed three years later by a Frenchman.

In 1992, the British joined the French forces under the UN flag in the former Yugoslavia. Their joint peace-keeping efforts brought together their respective services and especially their land forces, which had recently had little contact. Despite the differences between a professional and a conscript army, the troops found they had much in common in terms of resources, military capability and behaviour. In particular, they showed the same courage and unrivalled ability to settle in and secure the safety of the local population. This experience, which has lasted more than a decade, has forged solid links of friendship based on great mutual esteem. One natural result, today, is the adoption of a policy for the joint use of land forces.

In 1993, France set up its own Special Operations Command, modelled on the British SAS. From 1994 onwards all its professional training enjoyed help from the British, who gave full access to their experience. During this period, interchange between the armies was greatly intensified. In London in 1996, the air forces produced a joint policy for European aviation. The Franco-British Air Group was set up at the same time, with its headquarters at High Wycombe; two years later, it was enlarged to include Spain, Italy, Belgium, the Netherlands and then Germany. This structure, which prefigures what could become the staff headquarters of a European air force, shows how Franco-British cooperation can contribute to building Europe in the field of defence. In 1999, during the NATO operations in Kosovo, the Royal Navy placed a ship under the operational control of the French aero-naval group. It was more than just a symbol. And the Royal Air Force operates from a French air base at Solenzara in Corsica.

Exchanges about arms procurement have also been fruitful. They reached decisions about cooperation on the two fleets' new sea-to-air missiles as well as Cobra anti-artillery radar for the battlefield. The first European cruise missile programme – Storm Shadow or, for the French, SCALP – was begun after the establishment of the MBDA industrial group. The results were remarkable: all the missiles launched by the Royal Air Force during the first Iraq war were successful, although Storm Shadow had only just been put in service. In 1999, France backed the United Kingdom's initiative and joined the Meteor long-range air-to-air missile programme, while Britain played a decisive role in launching the A 400 M military transport aircraft. Finally, the two countries have just decided to study together the development of a new kind of marine engine for warships.

There are still greater prospects for further joint action. Thanks to French and British pressure, the L.o.I. (Letter of Intent) agreement signed by six European countries will provide a structure for industrial cooperation on military research, development and production: it settles the questions of jointly establishing technical specifications, deciding on intellectual and industrial property rights, transferring technology, safeguarding trade and exporting military materials. Meanwhile, the growing consensus between the respective military authorities, coupled with the fact that their missions were close to each other and their resources were mutually complementary, now makes it possible to envisage the pooling of military capabilities, beginning with forward planning, where both countries have very similar capacity.

So the armed forces of Britain and France are in a position to plan their future together, but they will do this only if they are backed by a clear political will continuing what was decided at St Malo in 1998.

Jean Rannou

The Narrowing Channel?

François Mauriac wrote in 1961 that 'The *entente cordiale* was a master-piece of diplomacy, completely artificial.' With regard to the original Entente of April 1904, this was largely true. The British and French governments concluded a complicated set of agreements whose details have been forgotten because they were matters we now prefer to forget – notably the distribution of territory and influence in Africa, Asia and the Pacific between two imperial powers. Yet in another sense Mauriac's remark was quite mistaken. The phrase 'entente cordiale' has acquired a life of its own. In 1994, on the 90th anniversary of the 1904 agreement, the two Foreign Ministries issued a joint brochure to mark the occasion, bathing the relations between the two countries in a roseate glow. In 1999 the Franco-British Chamber of Commerce published a similar pamphlet, *Britain and France. Partners for the Millennium*, with forewords by the prime minister and the president of the Republic. Prime Minister Tony Blair invoked the values and outlooks shared by the two countries. President Chirac looked ahead to the centenary of the Entente Cordiale, and observed that 'This expression has today become the very symbol of our friendship.' The phrase itself has indeed proved to be a public relations masterpiece. Who can possibly be against a 'cordial understanding' between two neighbouring countries? The words are so vague that they can include a whole variety of contacts, and conceal a multitude of differences. What do they mean today? Can we say that the Channel (which sometimes looms larger than the Atlantic in the maps of the mind) is growing narrower?

On one point there is no doubt. People are swarming across the Channel in increasing numbers. In 1990 there were 6,859,000 visits from the United Kingdom to France; in 1995 (the year after the opening of the Channel Tunnel) there were 9,645,000; in 2000 there were 11,903,000. In the opposite direction, in 1990 there were 2,297,000 visits from France to the UK; in 1995 there were 3,184,000; and in 2000 there were 3,087,000. British visits to France outnumber those in the opposite direction by about three to one. It is true that many of the British visits are only shopping trips to the hypermarkets of Calais or Boulogne, but the average stay in France is lengthy – seven nights in 1998, as against only two to three nights by French visitors to Britain. Strikingly, the figures for business visits tell rather a different story. In 2000, there were 1,557,000 British business visits to France, and 1,065,000 French visits to the UK – a ratio of 1.5:1, as against the 3:1 for all visits. Britain is more attractive to the French as a business proposition than as a holiday destination.

Among the British visitors to France are the growing numbers of those who buy property there, either as holiday homes or to live permanently. House agents and magazines specialise in the French property market. Television programmes are devoted to the attractions of buying a house in France, and a new type of purchaser comes from a wide range of British society. The TV programmes follow a plumber from Liverpool, a brick-layer from Devon, or a sub-postmaster from the Home Counties – a far cry from those who lived in Nice or Cannes 'when the Riviera was ours'. Moreover, the house-buyers are attracted by the whole experience of living in France. The phrase 'quality of life' is much used, and in heartfelt tones. Britain has markedly less appeal to French holiday home-buyers, largely because the British climate has such a poor reputation in France. But French nationals are working in Britain in increasing numbers. In 1998 it was estimated that about 200,000 French nationals were living in the UK, and of those who took the trouble to register with their local French Consulate, the vast majority were young (average age 28). In 2001 the Consulate-General in London estimated that about 110,000 French were living in the city, although only 75,000 had registered their presence. They stayed for four or five years on average, found London extremely expensive, and sometimes found difficulty in understanding the natives. 'On a l'impression de se heurter à une carapace qu'on ne peut pas briser' was one comment, echoing many others down the years. And yet a London posting by a French company has become attractive. The Channel Tunnel and the Eurostar train have made England 'la plus proche des terres lointaines' – which was once an advertising slogan for Corsica.

France and Britain are also important commercial partners. UK exports to France amounted to £18,575 million in 2000 (9.88 per cent of all British exports) and in 2001 to £19,529 million (10.19 per cent). In the other direction, French exports to the UK were valued at 31,897 million euros in 2000 and at 31,807 million euros in 2001. In 2001 France was the third largest market for British exports and the third largest supplier of British imports, after the United States and Germany. For France, the United Kingdom was the second largest market for French exports (after Germany) and the fourth largest supplier of French imports. These figures tell us a good deal about the collective result of business decisions, but offer no firm guidance to the general state of relations between the two countries. After all, in 1913 Britain and Germany were each the other's second best trading partner, but they still went to war in 1914. And what seemed for some time to be a highly promising commercial venture, the opening of eighteen Marks and Spencer stores in France, ended in tears and recrimination in 2001, when they were all closed abruptly, to the dismay of their employees and customers. Commerce is a fickle jade.

Trade in ideas and culture may be a better measure of relations between France and Britain. The two peoples have long been conscious of sharing a common cultural inheritance. For the British, France remains a synonym for culture and enlightenment. The remarkable new Musée d'Orsay, the vast extension to the Louvre, with its imaginative pyramid, and the ambitious if ill-starred enterprise of the Opéra Bastille – all command British admiration. The French press, for its part, shows a keen and eclectic interest in British culture. From October 2000 to March 2001 there was a film festival at Beaubourg, showing some 200 British films and eliciting the somewhat grudging tribute in *Libération* that British film production 'n'est pas si indigne'. At the end of 2001 the film of *Harry Potter* was greeted with glowing reviews, and in *L'Express* with the observation that: 'Il y a chez Harry Potter un peu de Sartre, un peu de Kierkegaard, également' – a point that most cinema audiences may have missed. There was widespread admiration for London's new ventures – the transformation of Somerset House, the showpiece of Tate Modern, and the new Great Court of the British Museum. Even restaurants receive favourable mentions, and *Libération* devoted a sympathetic full-page article to Jamie Oliver and the phenomenon of 'television chefs' – although the author noted derisory comments about 'un rosbif qui vient nous donner des leçons de cuisine'. (Another example of the continuity of an old stereotype!) Novels by Martin Amis and Jonathan Coe caused a reviewer to recall that the 'Angry Young Men' of the 1950s had wanted to break free from a stifling, hidebound England. Now that task was done. There were no more taboos, traditions or values to fight against. 'A vrai dire, il n'y a peut-être plus d'Angleterre du tout. Ces écrivains errent dans les décombres.' This makes painful reading for an Englishman, but the author was certainly taking English literature seriously.

One long-running cultural issue seems to be drawing to a close. The official defence of the French language continues, but with an unhappy sense that the battle is being lost. Legislation to check the advance of English in France remains on the books. Conferences of francophonie in the world continue to be held, and conferences of francophone Africa have been enlarged to include English-speaking countries. But despite these defences, the tide keeps flooding in. For French popular music to be exported, the singers have to perform in English. English is the language of science, the internet and above all of the United States. Moreover, French parents *want* their children to learn English – in 2000, 89.7 per cent of pupils in secondary schools chose English as their first foreign language. Jack Lang once rashly exclaimed that if he were a dictator he would forbid teaching English in primary schools. He was in fact only minister of culture, and even his hypothetical *diktat* would surely have been ineffective. The advance of English is probably inevitable, and need do no grave harm to the French language, which has its own resonance and character. It is surely wise to recognise, as writers such as Henriette Walter and Christine Geoffroy have done, that the two languages are akin, have lived together for a long time, and will go on influencing one another.

By simply getting along together, living and working in one another's country, and through cultural contacts and understanding, the British and French peoples were probably closer together at the turn of the twentieth and twenty-first centuries than at any earlier period. Certainly on the British side, the flood of holidaymakers and house purchasers betokens an interest in and affection for France different in kind from, and far wider in scope than, the upper-class and intellectual Francophilia of earlier years.

Culture and the movement of people count for much, but the Entente Cordiale has always been primarily a matter for governments. It was governments that brought about the Entente of 1904 and then guided its development. Current relations between governments display more dissonance than *entente*, and more friction than cordiality.

In 1999, in his introduction to the pamphlet *Britain and France*, Blair claimed that the two countries were committed partners in the European Union. He forbore to add that their degrees of commitment have differed widely. That same year *The Economist*, in a 'Survey of France', came nearer to the mark. In France, 'Europe is still the answer, no matter what the question . . . the British see Europe as a threat to their national power, the French see it as a multiplier of theirs.' While British attitudes to European integration have varied from one government to another and one

individual to another, it remains true that France is more deeply committed than Britain to the European idea.

The French set out to build Europe from 1950 onwards, partly as an
end in itself, pursuing the vision conjured up by Victor Hugo, and also in
pursuit of French interests, the chief of which was to find a satisfactory
answer to the German question. Germany was to be so bound into Europe
that it would no longer be dangerous, and so closely attached to France as
to make the two countries the motive force of European integration, as
they have been since the Treaty of Paris in 1951. The couple's harmony
was disturbed by German unification in 1989, which brought a sudden
increase in the country's population and a marked growth in self-
confidence and assertiveness. The French coped with this by moving more
quickly towards integration, through the Treaty of Maastricht and the
introduction of a single currency, the euro. Some problems remained, and
in 2001 there were a number of Franco-German differences and misunderstandings, notably when Chancellor Gerhard Schroeder adumbrated
the establishment of a European constitution modelled on German federal
lines, but met only a reticent response from France. Even so, when faced
with a plain question about the Franco-German couple in an interview
with *L'Express* in November 2001, the French minister-delegate for
Europe replied firmly, 'Il est irremplaçable' – although he added that it
would no longer suffice on its own.

This affects Franco-British relations, because Britain is outside the
charmed Franco-German circle. French newspapers are quick to seize on
any appearance of British moves to inveigle themselves into the circle, or
perhaps set up a new axis outside it, with Rome or Madrid. When Blair
met Schroeder on 29 January 2001, his visit was regarded as a manoeuvre
to weaken the Franco-German couple, and was at once followed by a specially summoned Franco-German summit at Strasbourg. When Blair went
to see the Italian Prime Minister Silvio Berlusconi in February 2002, and
concluded a joint 'action plan' in preparation for an imminent European
economic conference, this was seen by some of the French press as another
manoeuvre against Franco-German leadership – claims that were given
substance by a junior minister at the British Foreign Office, who said on
the eve of the visit that it was neither desirable nor feasible for Europe to
be led by France and Germany.

These were tactical and often only superficial difficulties. But behind
them lay deeper differences between France and Britain over Europe. At
bottom, France is committed to Europe in a way that Britain is not. The
French press rightly sees Blair as a genuine 'European' in a country where
significant sections of public opinion remain either indifferent or hostile to

European integration. France has been a leader in the adoption of the euro, from which Britain has so far opted out. Even a British government that is broadly in favour of accepting the single currency has so far hesitated to put the matter to a referendum. This question may well have long-term consequences for Franco-British relations, not as a result of having different currencies (the two peoples are used to that), but because of the issue of political principle of which the euro is a symbol. How far are the British prepared to go in the direction of European integration?

Moreover, if Europe is to be built, it must be on the basis of some political principle, and here again France and Britain hold divergent views. Despite some moves towards more regional autonomy, the French political model has long been one of administrative centralisation, which goes back as far as Jean-Baptiste Colbert in the seventeenth century. The British model is based on precedent, custom and pragmatism. There may be room for some compromise, although it is hard to find. Otherwise, in the long run one model is likely to prevail over the other, with a good deal of ill-feeling along the way.

There is a further problem. The whole European project is in part designed to combat the economic, political and cultural predominance of the United States. On the launch of the euro as a currency in public use, *Le Monde* carried a cartoon depicting a flight of euros as fighter aircraft, climbing to attack a flying dollar sign. The inference was almost painfully obvious. Britain holds a very different position. Successive British prime ministers from Churchill onwards, with the exception of Heath, have tried to *avoid* choosing between Europe and the United States, and to maintain close links with both. But in times of crisis, if a choice is necessary, the British have repeatedly clung to the American connection.

This has been strikingly true in recent years, notably in regard to Iraq and Afghanistan. In 1991 both Britain and France joined the USA in the Gulf War against Iraq. But since then Britain has worked closely with the United States in maintaining economic sanctions, and taking occasional military action, against Iraq. In February 1998 the United States demanded access to all Iraqi weapons sites for United Nations inspectors, and tried to recruit international support for military action in support of this demand. Britain supported the Americans and offered prompt military assistance, despatching an aircraft carrier to the Persian Gulf, while France (along with Russia and China) tried delaying tactics in the Security Council, and despatched an envoy to Baghdad to hold talks with the Iraqi government. Three years later, in February 2001, with the issue still rumbling on, American aircraft attacked military targets near Baghdad. British planes joined in the attacks, while the French Foreign Ministry issued a statement expressing its incomprehension and anxiety. The contrast was plain – and still is.

The events of 11 September 2001, when al-Qaida terrorists assailed the United States on its home territory, brought out the differences between Britain and France more sharply still. The British government pledged immediate and total support. When the Americans began bombing and missile attacks against Taliban targets in Afghanistan on 7 October, British forces took a minor but well-publicised part. When the land campaign against the Taliban began in November, the British made a substantial contribution. Meanwhile, although President Chirac was the first European leader to visit President Bush after the attacks on 11 September, he also expressed reservations about military action. The French government offered military support, but reserved its position on the actual means to be employed. Eventually, Chirac was able to announce that French warships (in the plural) were engaged, but he was only just correct – there were two, a frigate and a fuel supply ship. On the diplomatic front, the British prime minister threw himself into a flurry of activity, under the half-admiring gaze of the French press. Claude Imbert wrote in *Le Point*: 'Blair caracole de Washington à Karachi en vice-président d'une alliance atlantique impromptue.' *Le Nouvel Observateur* wondered who was 'le véritable leader de l'Occident blessé', Bush or Blair? *Le Monde* headlined 'La croisade de "Tony Coeur de Lion"'. The impression throughout was of a remarkable revival of the Anglo-American alliance, with France as no more than a cautious auxiliary. The contrast was not lost on the Americans. When President Bush thanked his various allies, Britain came first, with France bringing up the rear.

In the crisis over al-Qaida and the war in Afghanistan Britain and France had a common problem, because each included in its population a substantial Muslim minority, some of whom sympathised with al-Qaida. Neither country seemed sure how to deal with this situation, and each tended to accuse the other of being too lenient towards the militants. British newspapers suspected that French caution in the war in Afghanistan was due to fear of offending Muslims in France, while the French press claimed that London provided a safe haven for Islamic terrorists. On the broad issue of how best to deal with their Muslim minorities, Britain and France adopt different approaches. British governments follow a policy of multiculturalism, encouraging separate communities to retain their own identities and languages, and supporting the concept of faith schools. The French maintain, at least in principle, that the Republic is one and indivisible, its language is French, and state schools are secular, allowing no place for religious symbols, whether the Christian cross or the Islamic *hijab*. The issue is of serious long-term importance for both countries. Dealing with it cooperatively will greatly tax their imagination and skill.

Political relations between Britain and France have been plagued by two other problems, comparatively minor in the whole scale of international affairs, but of great importance to those involved: illegal migration from France to England, and the French refusal to accept exports of British beef.

The issue of illegal immigration to England has taken a new form since the opening of the Channel Tunnel, and raises strange echoes of Victorian fears. In 1882 the British government closed down an early project for a tunnel, partly through fear of French soldiers passing through unobserved to invade England. In 2001 this fear was revived in a different form. Illegal immigrants were boarding Eurostar trains in Paris with tickets to Calais, and going straight through to London. Refugees from the Red Cross centre at Sangatte were breaking into Eurotunnel terminals and stowing away on freight trains to England. Between January and July 2001 Eurotunnel intercepted some 25,000 persons trying to enter the United Kingdom illegally, and estimated that another 5,000 had passed through undetected.

The two governments achieved some degree of cooperation in dealing with these problems. British police and immigration officials were allowed to operate at the Gare du Nord, and French at Waterloo. But the Sangatte camp remained a constant irritant. Eurotunnel criticised the French authorities for being lax in their security measures, and the company (with the support of the British Home Office) applied to the French courts to close the Sangatte camp, but twice had their applications rejected before agreement was reached in September 2002. Meanwhile, the French press and government ministers pointed out that it was the advantages offered by the British social security system, and the weakness of British control over immigrants, that made England so attractive to refugees. It was a story that was still running, with ill-feeling on both sides, while this chapter was being written. If there was ever a practical case for the Entente Cordiale to get to work, this was surely it, but it remains to be seen what can be achieved.

The problem over beef arose from the outbreak of BSE (bovine spongiform encephalitis) in Britain, and the fear that the disease might be transmitted to humans. France, along with other European countries, placed a ban on imports of beef from the United Kingdom to avoid a risk to public health. In July 1999 the Commission of the European Union decided that exports of British beef could safely be resumed, but the French government maintained its ban on the ground that its own experts were not yet certain that there was no risk. In December 2001 the European Court of Justice ruled that France was acting illegally in maintaining its ban. Eventually, in July 2002, fines were demanded from the French government, but the French still insisted that they must wait for the advice of their own experts. It came two months later, was positive, and shortly afterwards took effect. Nevertheless the issue seriously affected British cattle farmers, many of whom believed that French motives were protectionist rather than scientific or medical. The French for their part distrusted the way in which the British had dealt with the problem of BSE, and thought the British public veterinary system was inadequate. While no more than an irritant in terms of scale, the dispute caused much ill-feeling.

One of the key elements in the Entente before 1914 consisted of military and naval staff talks, which were kept as secret as possible. A marked feature of current Franco-British relations is a degree of cooperation between the armed services both closer and more public than in earlier times. Since 1997 the chiefs of staff and their deputies have met twice a year. The military staffs hold annual talks; the navies work together on several projects; and a Franco-British Air Group was established in 1998. The existence of these contacts, of course without the details, is published freely on the Ministry of Defence website.

At the same time, the two countries have taken a leading part in proposals to set up a European Rapid Reaction Force, to be made up of some 50,000–60,000 troops, capable of taking autonomous action in the event of crises in which NATO is not involved. This idea took shape at a Franco-British conference at St Malo in December 1998, although its actual progress has been painfully slow. The original intention was to have a small force in readiness by December 2001, but this proved impossible, and at the time of writing the target date was 2003. One reason for this delay has been the problem of working out the exact relation between the new force and NATO, and the impression prevails that Britain is rather more anxious than France to ensure that the Rapid Reaction Force should not undermine the tried and trusted North Atlantic alliance. The old question of relations with the United States thus continues to haunt the British and French. Even so, the military aspects of the Entente display a closeness and cordiality that would have been highly welcome at certain times in the past.

What is the state of the Entente today? Politically and militarily, Franco-British relations are much less important than they were when the Entente was first concluded in 1904, or at any time up to World War II.

Then, relations between the two countries could influence the fate of Europe, and sometimes the world. Now they are subsumed in the politics of the European Union or transatlantic affairs. This means that, while irritants still exist, they are less important than was once the case, and their effects are smaller. When Britain and France quarrelled in the 1920s and 1930s, they wrecked the Paris peace settlement and opened the way for Hitler. Today, when they take different lines over Iraq or the war in Afghanistan the effect is marginal, because they do not take the major decisions. The same is true when the two countries cooperate successfully. The British and French staffs work closely together, but the forces they represent are small in number compared with those of the United States. British and French troops have tried to keep the peace in Bosnia, but the problems of Bosnia (and the whole of the former Yugoslavia) are beyond solution by Britain and France.

In these circumstances, other elements in relations between the two countries and the two peoples assume greater importance. The old stereotypes have plenty of life left in them, sometimes because they represent an element of truth. The press in both countries enjoys a fight with the old enemy. From a British point of view, Jonathan Fenby wrote that 'the easiest way to knock off a quick column or headline is to bash the Frogs'. French newspapers still refer to 'perfide Albion' and 'les rosbifs'. But these exchanges have the air of an old but not yet worn-out joke with little relevance to actual events, and the two peoples take their cross-Channel contacts in their stride.

The Entente today is very different in character from that of a century ago. Britain and France are far less important in the world, and the state of the Entente is of no great significance on the global stage. Politically, the two countries rub along as neighbouring states do – not as well as some, but much better than many others. On a personal and cultural level, they are very much at home with one another – almost certainly more so than in 1904. The Entente, never completely artificial, has in some respects become quite natural. Yet over all aspects of Franco-British relations there hangs the nagging question of the degree of British commitment to European integration. On that question may well turn the political future of the Entente Cordiale.

The above chapter was completed in September 2002. Since then, the 40th anniversary of the Franco-German Treaty of 22 January 1963 has been marked by solemn ceremonies, including a joint cabinet meeting at the Élysée and a joint session of the two parliaments at Versailles, at which President Chirac declared that France and Germany would be the centre of gravity of the new Europe. It seems at present unlikely that the centenary of the Entente will be greeted in the same elaborate fashion. France and Britain were sharply divided over the war on Iraq, which began in March 2003. The British government committed itself fully to the support of the United States in the war, and sent strong British forces to take part in the fighting. France on the contrary opposed the war, and French relations with both Britain and the USA were badly strained. The uneasy triangular relationship between Britain, France and the United States again produced a crisis. As often happens, a conflict of policy was accompanied by personal friction, with a confrontation between the two foreign ministers at the Security Council, and a distinct coolness between Blair and Chirac. Some British newspapers were highly critical of France and the French; but at the same time the French Embassy in London reported a large and sympathetic postbag – some of it in French.

Such disturbances are not unknown in the history of Franco-British relations. Fashoda preceded the original Entente. Britain and France quarrelled over Turkey in 1920–22, and over Syria from 1920 to 1945. Poincaré reduced Curzon to tears. Relations between Churchill and de Gaulle were sometimes explosive. De Gaulle's two rejections of British applications to join the EEC were severe, even disdainful in tone. Relations between France and Britain have had a long and volatile history. If, as we approach the centenary of the Entente, the road is somewhat rocky, that is not unusual. Yet the two countries and their peoples will arrive at April 2004 to find that they are still neighbours, with a good deal in common.

Philip M. H. Bell

A Renault in London

If General Charles de Gaulle were to return to London in 2004, he would find a city (and country) very different from whence he led his campaign to liberate France at the time of the Occupation.

Finding a Renault in London in 1940 must have been rather difficult. Most of Renault's production at the time was designated for German use. It was alleged in 1945 that Renault had produced 32,887 vehicles for Germans during the Occupation and only 1,697 for French customers. In 2004 de Gaulle would find no such shortage. The 'Papa? Nicole!' publicity campaign for the Renault Clio in the UK in the 1990s was highly successful. Nowadays, France's top export product to Britain is motor vehicles, as indeed is Britain's to France. The main difference between the two is, of course, that while the French continue to make cars of their own, the British tend to export cars that others have made for them. The British car industry was once the strongest in Europe. High spending on research and development has ensured that Renault and Peugeot have not suffered a similar fate: Renault has recently increased its European market share, with sales of French cars accounting for approximately one-fifth of total car sales in Western Europe.

Today, France is Britain's third largest export market (after the US and Germany), accounting for 10 per cent of British exports. Britain is France's second export market (after Germany), and France's exports to Britain likewise account for about 10 per cent of French exports.

Were de Gaulle to visit his local supermarket in London, he would be astonished at the influence of French food in particular – cheeses and yoghurts, fruit, vegetables and salads, mineral water and wine – on British eating habits. Long scorned for our supposed lack of culinary skills, the British have shamelessly adopted the foods and practices of other cultures. French retailers now dominate the European food industry, with Carrefour-Promodès in first place, accompanied by Intermarché, Auchan and the irrepressible Leclerc in the top ten. British retailers do not fare badly either, with Tesco in third place and Sainsbury's in tenth.

Were de Gaulle to turn on a tap in his London lodgings, the water might well be French-owned. In 2002 Vivendi Entertainment bought Southern Water, taking the company's share of the English and

Welsh water market to 10 per cent. Vivendi already owned North Surrey Water, Tendring Hundred, Three Valleys and Dover water suppliers. The Orange mobile phone network de Gaulle might use to make a telephone call is also French, Orange being acquired by France-Télécom five years ago. A French waste company, such as Sita, rather than local council workers, might collect the general's rubbish.

And were de Gaulle to turn on a light, the electricity lighting up his room might also be French: the culmination of the bold decision taken in 1955 to develop nuclear power. Little was done until France was roused into action by the Yom Kippur war. At the time the amount of primary energy imported into France was 76.3 per cent of consumption, as against 47 per cent in Britain. So successful was France's nuclear programme that in the mid-1980s it began exporting electricity to 'oil-rich' Britain. Électricité de France (EdF), the state-owned electricity monolith, has since bought up London Electricity, as well as the supply arm of Sweb, Seeboard, and generation assets such as Sutton Bridge power station. EdF now supplies 4.5 million customers with electricity in the south of England. In fact, EdF has purchased the rights to control the flows of electricity throughout Europe, buying up the interconnectors that link France to the UK, as well as France to Spain, and so on. This is a far cry from the situation that obtained in 1974, when French dependence on imported energy left the country reeling. The contrast with Britain, which has benefited since 1975 from North Sea oil, now beginning to run out, is stark. British Energy, privatised in 1996, was by 2002 on the brink of bankruptcy and facing administration.

On leaving London to return to Paris, the general might choose to travel by Eurostar. After a century or so as a 'pipe dream', the cross-Channel passenger train company began operating in 1994. It currently has 80 per cent of the leisure travel market between Paris and London. In 1986, at the time of the inaugural ceremony for the Channel Tunnel attended by President Mitterrand and Prime Minister Thatcher, some British people feared that it might provide a channel for rabies to enter Britain – about which the British are paranoid, at least in French eyes. Such fears have proved groundless. Few suspected, on the other hand, that the tunnel would become a conduit for thousands of asylum seekers to enter Britain illegally. The strategically positioned Sangatte refugee camp, just one mile away from the opening of the tunnel, fuelled this particular trade in unwanted immigrants, making for an *entente* that has been at times somewhat less than *cordiale*. Closure of the camp was agreed in 2003.

In 2000 Concorde, the joint Franco-British supersonic airliner, a potent symbol of Franco-British cooperation in the post-war period, suffered a major setback when one of its planes tragically burst into flames on take-off at Roissy, after which all Concorde planes were grounded for a year. Initially, any thought that this might be the end of the road for Concorde seemed to be unfounded. Like a Phoenix rising from the ashes, Concorde resumed operations the following year, though not for long. In October 2003, after 50,000 supersonic flights, Concorde was grounded for good.

Airbus, on the other hand, the leading aircraft manufacturer owned jointly by BAE SYSTEMS and EADS, has enjoyed better fortune. In 2001, Airbus achieved a 61 per cent market share in terms of value and 53 per cent in terms of units, selling 375 aircraft and delivering 325 aircraft around the world (*The Airbus Way*, 2002), keeping the upper hand over its American rival Boeing. Despite the downturn in the global air travel business that followed the terrorist attacks of September 11th, the future looks bright for Airbus, with the new A380, the 555-seater, double-decker plane, set to make its first commercial flight in 2006. The wings for the new A380 are over 36 metres long, the longest ever designed for a commercial aircraft. Built in Broughton in Wales, in a new £350 million factory the size of twelve football pitches, they will be shipped to the Airbus headquarters in Toulouse by barge. Work on the new aircraft is likely to safeguard 100,000 aerospace jobs in the UK for the foreseeable future.

The British and French are sometimes said to have a 'love–hate' relationship – illustrated by the 'row' between Jacques Chirac and Tony Blair in October 2002 over the funding of the Common Agricultural Policy, or by the illegal ban, now lifted, imposed by France on British beef in response to BSE.

But the reality is somewhat different. In the words of the French writer Michel Tournier, 'les petites trahisons font les grands mariages'. Despite occasional bickering, trade ties between the two nations are becoming ever stronger, year on year, to our mutual benefit.

Mairi Maclean

Immigration and Integration

After World War II the reconstruction of Europe made it necessary for Britain and France to attract a substantial number of immigrants to meet the needs of their expanding economy. Both countries imported immigrants from colonies and former colonies as a result of their privileged links with those territories, while France also received significant numbers of Southern Europeans. This process took place within the context of an open immigration policy, without any state planning as such. Companies recruited workers in countries of origin or as a result of spontaneous arrivals on the national territory.

Neither the society receiving them nor the migrants themselves at this stage conceived this phenomenon as a migration of settlement: it was viewed as temporary labour migration. The word used in Germany, *Gastarbeiter*, expresses the conception of immigrants in France and Britain in the very initial stages. There was an underpinning assumption that immigrants do not stay or just assimilate of their own accord; no measures were taken by the receiving societies to integrate them and they fended for themselves. They remained marginalised partly as a result of their installation in *bidonvilles* and hostels (France) or in derelict areas of inner cities (UK).

One notes a British peculiarity and exception in Europe: Commonwealth immigrants became British citizens on arrival as a consequence of the 1948 British Nationality Act, which derived from a nostalgic conception of the Empire. This does not mean that the movement was construed as a migration of settlement, but it gave them the political clout to modify their situation as time went on; fairly early on in Britain immigration became a political rather than a purely economic issue as it was in France. The metamorphoses of the Nationality Laws in France meant that immigrants acquired the rights of citizens at a later stage.

On the asylum front the Geneva Convention introduced a selective and liberal regime of access and integration in both countries within the context of the Cold War.

While the control of 'coloured immigration' had been initiated in the 1960s in Britain, the 1970s saw the closing of doors to immigration in the whole of Europe as a result of the oil crisis and the economic recession, with the exception of family reunion and asylum.

Asylum policies subsequently became restrictive with the end of the Cold War and the preparation of the Single European Act.

Immigration limitations were paired with an integration programme for those who were settled. It became clear to all concerned that one was then dealing with an immigration of settlement. Both France and Britain initially developed a programme aiming to redress social disadvantage through general social policies: in France measures focused on housing with the creation of the SONA-COTRA and the Fonds d'Action Sociale; in the UK the 1968 Urban Programme and the 1977 Inner City Policy proposed the regeneration of deprived areas largely occupied by immigrants. In France initiatives continued to involve general policies addressing all disadvantaged groups, whereas Britain adopted specific policies targeting ethnic minorities. A race relations paradigm became established through racially motivated immigration regulations (the patriality concept introduced in the late 1960s) and anti-discrimination legislation and policies (1965, 1968 and 1976 Race Relations Acts). The aim was to redress 'racial disadvantage' with a good number of policies and institutional structures, which included the powerful independent Commission for Racial Equality (CRE). Local authorities also took on special responsibilities in this area with budget lines devolved from a national level.

The immigrants, who have come to be called ethnic minorities, were the main motor of changes in policy through their involvement in mainstream politics, the mobilisation of their associations and communities and finally as a result of riots raging through the main British cities in the 1980s (1981, 1985). In France local government initiatives were limited and so was the involvement of immigrants. Some degree of mobilisation nevertheless took place, with the flourishing of immigrants' associations when changes in the legislation in the early 1980s made it possible to bring them under the 1901 law on not-for-profit associations. SOS Racisme and France Plus campaigned against the Front National and against discrimination. Small-scale riots took place and *La Marche des Beurs* gained national support.

In the French scenario, the official Republican Jacobin ideology prevailed: perception driven by an assimilationist approach construed equality and difference as mutually exclusive, while cultural diversity was officially deemed detrimental to integration. In Britain, on the other hand, multiculturalism and the recognition of communities were adopted as public policy. Research certainly shows that the existence of ethnic communities does not preclude and may sometimes facilitate integration, and that discrimination remains the main obstacle to satisfactory settlement in both countries.

In the new millennium both France and Britain are confronted with serious challenges, which have not yet been tackled satisfactorily.

A dramatic demographic curve and an ageing crisis make it imperative for France and Britain to import great numbers of immigrants for the survival of their economies and the payment of their pensions. The neo-liberal economic project and the demise of the welfare state aggravate this situation.

On the European level a restrictive asylum policy is being harmonised while anti-discrimination legislation is strengthened through Article 13 of the Amsterdam Treaty and two European Union Directives, respectively on Race and on Employment. This contributed to the expansion of anti-discrimination legislation in France and Britain. For a short while France even set up an independent body resembling the British Commission for Racial Equality: *Groupe d'Études et de Lutte contre la Discrimination* (currently disbanded). At the same time an anti-immigrant attitude emerged, leading to a recurrent hostile discourse on the part of politicians and media. Immigrants and asylum-seekers are portrayed as scroungers, delinquents, terrorists, criminals – in short, as a danger to our culture and society. This applies equally to those of the 'second/third generation' born and brought up in France and Britain. What is proposed is a stringent asylum policy combined with a temporary immigration programme, often implemented by stealth without satisfactory conditions of settlement. Meanwhile settled minorities and youths of immigrant origin also bear the brunt of discrimination and animosity. Muslims are a main target of prejudice, further exacerbated by events on 11 September 2001 in the USA.

France and Britain are subjected to a commonality of influences: the presence of substantial ethnic minority populations, the acceleration of European integration, the globalisation process generated by the neo-liberal economic project and its cortege of privatisations. Both countries have been significantly transformed as a result of their immigration history in the last century. While they lost their vast empire they witnessed the installation of former colonial populations in substantial numbers on their territory. Those brought with them a kaleidoscope of cultures which today contribute to the questioning of a mythical homogeneous national culture. Immigrants have made noticeable contributions to the fabric of French and British society in the economic, social and cultural domains. Despite differences in their political cultures vis-à-vis immigrants, the two countries are facing similar issues regarding their integration and exchange notes to learn from each other; this process is strengthened through European Union policies. In France and Britain we are facing a reformulation of our society and we are coming to a cross-road; the continuation of current policies promises social fractures and instability not to mention ethical and human rights questioning.

This approach involves serious problems: grave social differences and a possible move to the extreme right are in the offing whilst a well-thought out transparent policy of immigration and integration could help reception societies and populations of migrant origin to reap great benefits.

Danièle Joly

The Tunnel

In September 1987, when I received an invitation to become chief financial officer of Eurotunnel, it took me about ten seconds to accept. It was the fulfilment of one of my most cherished dreams, to be part of this extraordinary Anglo-French project physically linking Great Britain to mainland Europe. By the time I stepped down nine years later, regular commercial services were running through what, when I arrived, was downland and undersea rock.

In 1985 this latest, and last, relaunch of a 200-year-old project was in the best power-political traditions of the Entente Cordiale itself – Thatcher needed a *quid pro quo* to offer Mitterrand for his support for the British budget rebate battle.

But operationally, if it was to work at all, it would have to be a real-time test-bed for binational cooperation – or its absence. One part of the solution was to create Eurotunnel as a combination of two parent companies, one French, one British, quoted in indivisibly twinned shares and with a unified operating and management structure. Executives were originally based partly in Paris but mostly in London, later moving to Calais as the main operations centre and to Folkestone.

Cartoonists from both sides of the Channel had a ball devising new takes on Anglo-French rivalries, and certainly (until we got to know each other better) national stereotypes, closely reflecting our respective education systems, played powerfully. Examples: the French can only think in threes, the Brits think without any structure at all; the French are more likely to keep you out of trouble, but the Brits will get you out of it once you're in it, and so on.

Endless arguments raged: should our public reports be written in one language and translated into the other, or should they be written simultaneously from an agreed brief, or should one version be read, turned face down and rewritten in the other language? However, we were responsible to stock exchange authorities and bankers who went berserk at the idea of anything other than the strictest of translations. Joint jurisdiction – here as elsewhere – meant compliance with both sets of national requirements on corporate reporting, employment, health and safety, environment, and on and on. Sometimes good, more often just expensive.

Internally, communications were very much easier. We were all expected to be able to follow discussions and presentations in either language and thus be free to make our own contributions in whatever language we felt most comfortable in. It worked even at the joint board level, and outside the formal working environment conversations would switch easily back and forth without any obvious pattern.

The project's travails are well enough known. It was indeed, and appropriately, 'the best of times, the worst of times'. But it was brought to completion. The Channel Tunnel will remain for decades to come, maybe for centuries, a monument to rival any built by Eiffel or Brunel. For all who took part in it, the national stereotypes were softened, mutual suspicion was progressively replaced by mutual respect and friendship and what remains is an abiding source of pride and shared memory.

High among those memories: the first breakthrough, when a smart French worker, with his soundbite at the ready, stepped through to meet a totally unprepared British tunneller; the great celebration lunch under the channel, when 800 guests sat down at white linen-clad tables in recognition of Brunel's similar event in the Rotherhithe Tunnel to persuade his creditors that work really was going ahead (*plus ça change...*); the formal opening, when prodigious negotiations were required to permit the two trains carrying the Queen and President Mitterrand to approach each other end to end on the same track against every rule in the rule book. A notable *entente* for sure, and, as often as not, *cordiale* as well.

But what of the larger picture? Has it truly helped to bring Britain closer to mainland Europe (or vice versa – see how careful one has to be?) The answer surely has to be yes. For the 20,000 passengers a day who use it, for the 3,000 trucks and the 19,000 Eurostar passengers, the Channel Tunnel has quickly become an accepted part of our daily lives – whatever did we do before it?

Graham Corbett

Entente Cordiale Scholarships

'There may have been misunderstandings and causes of dissension in the past but that is all happily over and forgotten.' That was the view of British–French relations expressed by King Edward VII in a notable speech in Paris on 1 May 1903, during the visit which paved the way for the Entente Cordiale. The century since then has shown that the causes of real dissension, which brought wars in the past, were indeed gone. But differences and misunderstandings have persisted. You find them in conversations about the other country on both sides of the Channel, and sometimes in parliamentary debates or in arguments between the two governments.

This impression was confirmed for me by experiences in Britain and France during my first months as ambassador in France in early 1993. Ambassadors don't stay many years in the job; indeed 'HE' or 'SE' might stand not for 'His Excellency' or 'Son Excellence' but for 'Highly Ephemeral' or *'Strictement éphémère'*. So I had to move quickly if I was to do anything during my three and a half years in France to try to reduce the ingrained suspicion that can arise between the British and the French.

The problem arises from past rivalry and current ignorance. Today many people in each country know more of the other than ever before. But some of those love particular things, say the châteaux on the Loire or a farmhouse in Périgord or the ease of starting a business in Britain or the excitement of working in the City of London, yet do not learn much about wider subjects such as the motives that underlie the foreign policy or the attitudes to agriculture of France or Britain. Serious differences arise between the two countries from time to time, as over Iraq in 2003. But even lesser arguments tend to flare up beyond their real significance because of a readiness on either side to impute the worst motives to the other or just through lack of knowledge of the other's approach to the subject in hand.

That was the background to the founding in 1995 of the Entente Cordiale Scholarship scheme. It was announced by President Chirac and Prime Minister Major, who said 'Young people in our two countries represent our shared future. The more they learn about their near neighbour as they advance in their education, the more they can contribute to the enlightened partnership and growing opportunities, which we are now developing in an enlarged Europe.'

The scheme brings outstanding postgraduate students from Britain and France to study for a year on the other side of the Channel, at an age when friendships and impressions are formed for life. Most of the scholars do a master's degree or research towards a doctorate. Many of them intend to go later into politics, the public service, journalism, business, banking or university teaching. All are gifted and some will become influential as they advance in life. I hope that this will mean that decision-makers in Britain and France in the future will increasingly include people who know the other country well. Knowledge is the executioner of prejudice, and more balanced views at senior levels on both sides of the Channel should result. That benefit comes on top of the inherent benefit of providing additional opportunities in higher education in the two countries. The scheme is now in its seventh year. So far 250 scholars have benefited from it, about half French and half British. They come from a wide range of universities on either side of the Channel and they study a wide range of subjects. The money for this – about £10,000 a year for each student – is raised from the private sector and foundations, who deserve much gratitude. The French government is financing two British scholars in 2003–4. The administration of the scheme, including the selection of scholars, is managed free of charge by the British Council on the French side, and the Service Culturel of the French Embassy in London on the British side. So the benefactors know that the money they give will be spent on scholars and not on administration.

Already some of the alumni of this scheme hold jobs which give them influence. Past British scholars are now working at the Foreign and Commonwealth Office, and one is about to join the Department of Transport. One used to work at the British Council in Paris and now for the president of the Committee of the Regions of the EU in Brussels. Another is a borough councillor in Camberwell. Past French scholars include one working at the Victoria & Albert Museum, and a freelance journalist working in London, previously arts correspondent for *Le Figaro*. Another is working as an assistant to a *député* at the Assemblée Nationale, another as a medical consultant to Médécins Sans Frontières. Another completed a PhD in quantum physics at Cambridge University and is now general manager of a company that produced a guidance system for partially sighted people.

So the Entente Cordiale Treaty of 1904 has an echo in a scheme for young people in the twenty-first century. The positive effect on the mutual psychology of Britain and France should grow as the century advances.

Sir Christopher Mallaby

Vive Le Sport!

France taught Britain to cook and Britain taught France to play. This seems a pretty fair exchange, although the course of cultural reciprocity rarely runs smooth. Take the summer of 1789, for example. The British ambassador, the philandering third Duke of Dorset, chose to raise French morale with an exhibition cricket match on the Champs Élysées. However, 'events' intervened and he had to scuttle back to Dover just in time to stop his team, which included his gardener, the fearsome bowler 'Lumpy' Stevens, from embarking. But for this, cricket might not be the barrier to mutual understanding that it is to this day. Conversely, had the British decided to allow men to race bicycles on the open roads, the subtle manoeuvrings of the *peleton* might attract the same attention in Britain as they do in France. Tom Simpson would be a hero in his own country just as he is in France, a victim not to drugs and alcohol but to the terrible suffering of the Tour de France and the peculiar torture of the Mont Ventoux. British sport and Continental sport remains very different. Few Britons could stomach bullfighting or the shooting of small birds in the *chasse communale*. Until recently winter sports were a closed book to most Britons, although it was an Englishman, Arnold Lunn, who invented alpine skiing as a competitive sport.

It would be wrong, however, to harp on the differences. We may not share some things, but we do share many things. By the late nineteenth century traditional French sports – *jeu de paume* and *la soule*, Breton folk football – were in decline, although 'boules' and skittles remained strong as did *pelota* in the Basque country and bull-running in Provence and the Landes. Bourgeois youth needed something new, less aristocratic than hunting on horseback and more fun than the paramilitary German gymnastics, which French nationalists were promoting to avenge Sedan. *Les sports anglais*, a term that lumped together athletics, football, rugby and rowing amongst other sports, became suddenly fashionable in the 1880s as an enjoyable way to pursue the goal of national revival. Anglomania swept the privileged Parisian youths, who joined the Racing Club or the Stade Français. Pierre de Coubertin was the most famous of these young men. At the Sorbonne in 1894 he founded the modern Olympic Games modelled on the public school sports of Victorian Britain.

Ten years later another Frenchman, Charles Simon, frustrated by British insularity, founded the Fédération Internationale de Football Association (FIFA) to run the game around the world. The British may have invented modern sport, but it was the French who organised much of it internationally.

At first France struggled to match the superior skills of their British counterparts, especially in athletics, though in Jean Bouin, a bank clerk from Lyon, they found a champion who won in England and almost took the gold in the Olympic 5,000 metres in 1912. His death at the front in 1914 made him a national hero, and many a *stade communal* bore his name between the wars. Boxing produced an even more gifted figure. Georges Carpentier famously knocked out the British champion 'Bombardier Billy Wells' – an event regarded as so astonishing that a song 'Bom Bom Bom Bombardier, Got knocked out by Carpentier' became a music-hall hit. Carpentier eventually succumbed to Jack Dempsey in 1921 at Madison Square Garden in the first million-dollar match, the result of which was relayed instantly to a large Parisian crowd. This signalled the beginnings of a shift from a purely British focus in French sport, which led the boxer Marcel Cerdan to try his luck in America and to die in an air crash on the return journey – an event that prompted Edith Piaf's greatest love song, *Hymne à l'amour*.

If boxing challenged British stereotypes of the French, tennis reinforced them. Britain also had to bow the knee to France in the more genteel sport of tennis as the 'Four Musketeers', Cochet, Lacoste, Brugnon and Borotra, the 'bounding Basque' as the British loved to call him, dominated Wimbledon and the Davis Cup for much of the 1920s. But here France's first sporting heroine must take pride of place. Those who saw the young Suzanne Lenglen defeat the doughty English champion, Mrs Lambert Chambers, the lantern-jawed daughter of an Ealing clergyman, never forgot her astonishing agility and the impressions she made on the *couture* of the court.

In team sports it was through rugby rather than football that France and Britain forged a special relationship. The Five Nations competition got off to a flying start with France beating Scotland 16–15 in 1911, although the French crowd rioted at the return match when Mr Baxter, the English referee, was thought to favour the Scots. It was not until 1927–28 that France beat Wales and England.

By this time French rugby had spread deep into the Languedoc and beyond the élite Anglophile bastions of the lycée and university. Southern rugby was fast and furious, altogether too violent for the British, who broke off contact with French rugby union in the 1930s. Vichy was a painful interlude for French rugby, and relations with the British were not fully repaired until the great French team of the 1950s, led by Jean Prat from Lourdes, won the Five Nations.

The 1950s were good for French football, too, with the marvellous attacking skills of Raymond Kopa and Juste Fontaine of Reims, who led France's sparkling World Cup team of 1958. A new pattern was taking shape. France was no longer in the shadow of Britain with its 'small state' and amateur traditions. As the twentieth century drew to a close a remarkable reversal came about. French players such as Eric Cantona, Thierry Henry and Patrick Viera were the new heroes of Old Trafford and Highbury and it was two French managers, Gérard Houllier and Arsène Wenger, who routinely lectured a grateful English audience on the art of playing the game that England had given to France a century earlier.

Richard Holt

The French in Britain

It is a strange paradox that the flow of migrating nationals between France and the United Kingdom, two countries so close in terms of population, wealth and living standards, has for centuries been occurring for mostly opposite reasons.

In the past, Britons, particularly the English, enjoyed a long tradition of venturing outside their borders in search of fortune, fame or adventure, while the French were more inclined to stay at home. Those who did leave were usually fleeing political or religious persecution or searching for freedom – the Protestants in the sixteenth and seventeenth centuries, priests and aristocrats after the 1789 Revolution, and the Free French escaping to England after General de Gaulle's appeal of June 1940.

Since the opening of borders within the European Union, and even more so after the launch of Eurotunnel, the respective migrations between France and Britain have increased dramatically, and statistics suggest a certain geographical reorganisation of the European expatriate communities across our two countries.

According to the French Ministry of the Interior, the total number of adult Britons in France by the end of 2002 was 73,626, an increase of over 24 per cent over ten years. But statistics can be deceptive. First of all, these figures refer only to those holding a *carte de séjour*, the requisite open sesame for employment in France. They do not take into account pensioners, dual-nationality passport-holders or home owners. It is estimated that Britons, who now own 3 per cent of all 'rural space' in France, including vineyards, farms and forests, have bought 600,000 houses. This would appear to result from both the huge increase in house prices in Britain and the introduction of low-cost airlines to a number of new locations in France. Even these somewhat fragmented statistics cannot disguise the shift in nature of the British presence in France, and its geographical spread is particularly telling, with a strong increase in tourist areas. While Provence–Côte d'Azur remains the first choice of destination outside Paris, the growth of the British population has been more particularly striking these last ten years in other sea-bordering areas (an increase of 78 per cent in Languedoc, 98 per cent in Basse-Normandie, 120 per cent in Brittany and 172 per cent in Poitou-Charentes).

Surprisingly, the northern industrial regions of France have hardly benefited from the opening of the Channel Tunnel (with a mere 5 per cent increase since 1992 in the Nord and Picardie regions). There has also been a steady decline in the British population in both the north-east areas, such as Lorraine and Champagne-Ardennes, and even more surprisingly in the Paris area, which – although remaining the first area of settlement, with 19,157 Britons – has seen its British population decline by 23 per cent in the last ten years.

Official statistics relating to the French presence in Britain are also fragmentary, and the British Census does not take into account the nationality of residents. Figures supplied by the French Consulates of London and Edinburgh show a total of 91,500 people registered, two and a half times the number recorded ten years ago. Most French people, especially the younger generation, do not take the trouble to register, and it is estimated that the real number of French people living in the UK is now close to 300,000. Most of them live in the London area, and they are relatively young, the average age registered at the French Consulate being 29 years.

While the British seem to be mostly attracted to the French *douceur de vivre* and lifestyle, the French see Britain more as a business proposition, a place to seek employment and improve their financial prospects. Thirty years ago, things were very different. Most of the French in the UK were au pairs or students who had married British nationals, and, to a lesser extent, teachers, cooks and the occasional business professionals.

Nowadays, besides the ever-increasing number of young people coming to improve their English, and to find a job, the biggest influx of French people in Britain is of professionals, mostly in the service industries and, more notably, the finance sector. The French have discovered that UK administrative practices and tax structure are more relaxed than at home, and so have taken advantage of this to launch all kinds of initiatives, often with great success. Over 1,700 French companies now employ close to 330,000 people in Britain.

Beyond the arrival of well-known football players and managers, there is also an increasing number of teachers (4,000 registered at the London Consulate), doctors (more than 300 registered), lawyers, engineers, scientists, hi-tech and computer specialists, as well as international corporation executives and entrepreneurs.

But while most Britons consider moving permanently to France, the majority of French coming to Britain do not expect to stay beyond three to five years. One deterrent for the French migrant is the spiralling cost of living in Britain, especially of housing. A growing number of executives have, therefore, chosen to commute daily between England and France. This is probably one reason why the majority of French in Britain do not integrate themselves more fully into the local French community, unlike their British counterparts in France, who become much more involved within an often highly structured British community.

Although France and Britain have similar numbers of expatriates, Britain has five Consulates General in France, while there are only two French ones in Britain. There are more than one hundred cultural, educational, sports and social clubs and professional organisations devoted to Britons in France. There are eight British churches in the Paris area and thirty Anglican chaplaincies across the country. In comparison, there are only two French churches – one Catholic and one Protestant – for the whole of Britain. But all this cannot compensate British nationals for the loss of their voting rights when they have lived abroad for more than fifteen years.

The British head for France for leisure; the French go to Britain to improve their prospects. This is obviously too much of a caricature, a disservice to both countries. There are indeed some wealthy French people enjoying retirement in the UK and benefiting from more lenient tax laws, while there are many professional Britons who have gone to France to work within a strong business environment, be it in aeronautics in Toulouse or as accountants and lawyers in Paris. But this parallel between the two expatriate communities could summarise the traditional dichotomy between the slightly distorted perceptions of our respective countries. Strong Protestant ethics in Britain, a hedonist image in France – each segment of our expatriate communities being attracted to the differing characteristics of its neighbour.

But an interaction between France and Britain's expatriate communities, in the sense of both opposition and complementarity of their approaches, could represent an element of progress and mediation between two fundamentally opposed conceptions and political models of modern Europe. Mutual appreciation and acceptance of our differences should be a message we take from Europe. It should herald the end of all those stereotypes and misconceptions that have blighted relations between France and Britain for too long, and that one regrettably still sees reflected in some of the tabloid press.

As an elected representative of French people in the UK and a committed European, I appreciate fully the growing interest with which most EU countries view their diasporas. However, I remain puzzled by British efforts to hamper the political rights of its expatriates, who have contributed so greatly to the influence of their country, not only in France, but also around the world. As Europe expands, it is to be hoped that the voice of the expatriate and the migrant will not be lost, but will rather grow and carry greater significance.

Joëlle Garriaud-Maylam

Tourist into Resident

Member, male or female, of *la bonne bourgeoisie rurale*:

> 'You have a house near here? . . . I did not know there were many English in the area?'
> Me, with an edge of briskness: 'I'm afraid I can't tell you about that [*je ne saurais pas vous dire*]. We mainly see our French neighbours and friends.'
> 'Ah . . . [Faint change of gear] – You have perhaps owned your house for some time?'

Well, yes, for thirty years, and for the first twenty-five of them I had this conversation, with variations, many times. In the beginning, when my husband and I acquired a small house on the edge of an obscure village in the pretty but unremarkable heart of France, a slight bewilderment tended to accompany the initial question. Motorways had not yet reached the Indre and the Cher; the phenomenon of *des résidences secondaires*, even for Parisians, was virtually unknown there. The occasional person would question us as to what we saw in an area so lacking in scenic, sun-drenched tourist attractions, and be politely surprised to hear that what we liked about it was that it was its ordinary, quintessential French-ness. As for our elderly widowed neighbour (rattling about in a farmhouse with a leaking roof, goats, chickens and a plague of dormice) our tendency to disappear again just when she had got used to gossiping with us seemed to her beyond all sense:

> 'What, off again? But you haven't eaten up all your carrots yet . . .'

That old lady has been dead many a year now, and her house, extensively done up, is a holiday home to a Parisian family with ancestral roots in the village. And yet these days, since two books of mine relating to the history of central France have come out in French, the repetitive conversation reminds me of those early ones with old Marie D:

> 'I so enjoyed your book. It made me think about my grandmother/my great-grandfather . . . You live here all the year round, of course? . . . You don't? You're going back to London soon? Oh dear . . .'

They are right, of course. Oh dear. Our emotional investment in the place over the years is such that I have evolved a parallel universe to our London one, full of just the same sort of satisfactions and responsibilities ('Must have the Alabrys to dinner ... Must draw up old Monsieur Chose's family tree as I promised him...'). All departures in either direction are a wrench, inflicting obscure if temporary damage on an intricate web of life. There is a price for everything, and this is the price of acquiring over the years, with endless self-effacement, a second identity. Sharing worries about falling lamb prices. Conspiring against the plan to put a town by-pass in an obtrusive place. Joining in the hopes that the house near the school won't be sold to Dutch people. 'One foreign family in the village is enough', I say. People laugh, but agree, complicit in my obscure guilt, my endemic propitiation.

For rural France, over the last dozen years, has been increasingly colonised. In our rolling country well south of the Loire French integrity is to a large extent protected by relative prosperity and by the lack of dramatic scenery already noted, but over the great tracts of mountainous France that are not, today, much worth farming, a declining population and a steady stream of properties for sale or abandoned to ruin has left the countryside open to a virtual foreign invasion. The cricket team and English news-sheet run in the Dordogne by British residents may seem lovable quirks – but one wonders why these dedicated Anglophiles are actually in France at all. The same question occurs to the French, although they hope that the answer will be something complimentary to do with French culture. I hardly have the heart to tell them that many of these buyers appear to be motivated solely by the relatively low prices of French real estate, over which they congratulate each other in the manner of Western coach parties shopping in a Third World bazaar. I do, however, occasionally explain that, given the relatively modest size of the UK compared with France, no cheap cottages are, alas, available in *le pays des lacs* or yet in *la Cornouailles*.

True, other British buyers are attracted to France by something less tangible than affordable real estate – by the archetypal yearning for a different way of life; but often they do not seem to realise that this insubstantial dream will survive only if underpinned by a willingness to acquire extra skills, including the ability to communicate in French. The fact is, many buy their ancient farmhouses and turreted *gentilhommières* and do them up lavishly, often with needlessly imported British labour, then lead an insulated existence among themselves, as if France were nothing but a painted backdrop, a cheese market and a restaurant or two – which it therefore becomes.

It was in the late 1980s that the trickle of foreign housebuyers in France became a flood, jumping from 2,000 to 30,000 per annum in two years; the figures included Germans, Dutch, Italians and Belgians as well as domiciled Africans and Asians from France's old colonies, but the British were said to head the list. The numbers fell again in the early 1990s, but by 1998, when more detailed statistics were being kept, there were again over 20,000 purchases by foreign nationals. In 2000 there were nearly 25,000, of which British nationals accounted for almost a quarter, with Americans, Irish, Canadians and Australians also significantly represented.

Some years ago a member of the French right wing claimed rather loudly that the English were 'slowly rebuilding the Plantagenet empire'. One may dismiss this as paranoia (many English holidaymakers have only the haziest notion that English kings ever ruled chunks of western France) but some of the indictment, though politically incorrect, was painfully sensible – 'When 80 per cent of the population of the Dordogne is English then it will not quite be the Dordogne, even if the English there are very amiable.'

The remark goes to the heart of the world problem of tourism, and indeed of more permanent settlement. Simply by being there, the outsider, however amiable and admiring, tends to destroy the very thing he has come to seek. This is particularly true when what is sought is an 'unspoilt' rural idyll, which so many of us have internalised in childhood but which, in the England of today, is far harder to find. Our history has been different and more intensively industrial than France's; the historical markers for the two nations occur in different places. Patterns of farming have survived in France that, on the English side of the Channel, have gone the way of the reaping hook and the fairies. Rural France is many things, but one of those is the dream of time-travel, the return to a symbolically pristine land before the Fall. Such countries of the heart are, alas, all too vulnerable.

Gillian Tindall

XI

France and Britain in Tomorrow's Europe

As neighbours in the European Union, France and Britain will soon have more new neighbours still. Will Europe's enlargement to the east bring new strains, or lead its core countries to draw closer together? Will the future Union be looser or more divided? Will it become a multi-speed, multi-tier entity? And if it does, how will this affect the Franco-British Entente?

Towards a New Alliance

Relations between France and Britain have not ceased to be difficult since the end of World War II. Old rivalries and recurrent accusations of bad faith, blithely orchestrated by the mass media, have certainly played their part. But a more recent and more deep-seated difference divides the two countries. While both are aware that they are no longer the world powers they were until 1939, each sees very differently its ambitions and its role on the world stage. France has chosen to meet its destiny through the union of Europe and the cooperation with Germany that is its driving force. Great Britain bases its future on its 'special relationship' with the United States. Can this divergence be overcome? If so, how? These questions are central to relations between Paris and London. They already were before the Iraq war. They are still more so today.

If the building of Europe rests on the solid foundation of Franco-German agreement, this is not because Great Britain was deliberately excluded. General de Gaulle's rejection of its first attempt to join was an exception in the long series of overtures made to Britain. It was Britain that declined the invitations extended at every stage – at the founding of the ECSC, the EDC, and the EEC, at the time of the Schengen Agreements and, more recently, when the Euro was born. Successive French presidents and German chancellors have almost all gone to London soon after being elected. They went to seek ways of possible rapprochement, either to escape a Franco-German *tête-à-tête* that was felt to be too exclusive, or to restore the balance of a European Community that Britain's absence destabilised or hindered in areas as essential as defence. None of these efforts bore fruit.

When Tony Blair arrived at 10 Downing Street, there seemed to be a new atmosphere. Britain was no longer the sick man of the European economy. Revitalised by the brisk therapy imposed by Mrs Thatcher, it was enjoying faster growth and much less unemployment than the rest of Europe. Thus strengthened, Tony Blair had the courage to commit his country to modernisation on two fronts: 'devolution', giving Scotland (and, to a lesser degree, Wales) a measure of long-sought autonomy, and a new policy *vis-à-vis* Europe. The young prime minister intended – as he clearly said – not only to integrate his country fully in the building of Europe, but also to lead the way. He realised that such an ambition implied Britain's membership of the euro, to which he was openly favourable, as well as the establishment of autonomous European defence arrangements within NATO. The basis for the latter was laid by the Franco-British Summit at St Malo in 1998.

This reorientation of British policy was all the more timely in that it coincided with a lapse in Franco-German cooperation. At the Berlin summit meeting, Chirac and Schroeder fiercely disagreed about the future of the Common Agricultural Policy. They clashed even more violently about the Union's institutions at the calamitous summit in Nice. The way seemed open for Tony Blair's ambitions. Determined to reconcile commitment to Europe with the 'special relationship' with America, he sought for his country a key role in the necessary renewal of the Atlantic Alliance.

These hopeful prospects could not resist the Iraq crisis. If Tony Blair had been content to back the United States, no one would have been surprised and the damage would have been limited. But by committing large numbers of troops alongside the American expeditionary force, and by signing – on 30 January 2003, with seven other heads of government – a letter opposing the position taken by France and Germany, he went beyond what the special relationship with Washington required. For Paris and Berlin, the conclusion seemed clear: in the last resort, come what may, Britain would side with the United States even if by so doing it compromised its commitment to Europe. Reality, no doubt, was rather different. To all intents and purposes, Tony Blair was convinced that Iraq possessed weapons of mass destruction, that they were a major danger, and that it was vital to eliminate Saddam Hussein, however British public opinion might react.

Nevertheless, the policy endorsed and supported by the British prime minister was not that traditionally followed by the United States, but the new policy initiated by George Bush under the influence of American neo-conservatism. It turned its back on what the United States had pursued since 1945. In those days, the effort had been to establish international order based on law, applied by the United Nations and its specialised agencies. President Wilson had envisaged this in 1918. President Roosevelt and his successors had made it the cornerstone of their policy.

To resist Soviet imperialism, the United States and its European allies had been obliged to pursue a policy of global military 'containment', very different from what had been hoped in 1945. But that hope had remained the long-term objective of the United States and of the West.

The failure of the Suez operation in 1956, the ensuing decolonisation, the crumbling of the Soviet empire and the removal of its threat all encouraged Europe in its endorsement of the ideas that America had championed in 1945. The old continent agreed *en masse* to the international conventions worked out under the aegis of the United Nations: the Kyoto Agreements, the International Court, the treaties limiting, forbidding, or controlling armaments. Europeans were not discouraged by the limitation or delegation of sovereignty that these involved. But today the United States rejects them.

Europe, in fact, has been becoming 'Wilsonian' just as America has been growing 'Bismarckian'! Although the United States alone now dominates the world stage, since the fall of the Berlin Wall it has not ceased to expand its military potential. With a defence budget equal to that of all the other countries in the world combined, and with new weapons over which it has the monopoly, its military preponderance is overwhelming. A huge technological gulf now exists between America and Europe. As a result, Washington is sorely tempted to eliminate by force any threat that appears on the horizon, above all if it affects the security of the United States. The tragedy of 9:11 greatly strengthened this tendency. Little by little, the USA has withdrawn from international agreements signed during and after the Cold War, and has opted for a 'unilateralism' of which the Iraq crisis is a fair measure. Lacking authorisation from the UN Security Council, it formed an *ad hoc* coalition of countries favourable to its armed intervention, not hesitating to divide Europe, whose union it had hitherto encouraged.

Does this mean that the two sides of the Atlantic are now so far apart as to nullify the pact that has united them since 1949? Nothing is less certain.

All public opinion polls show that Europe and the United States share the same ideals: democracy, the rights of man, the non-proliferation of weapons of mass destruction, intervention in humanitarian tragedies, free access to markets and raw materials, in particular oil, and the fight against drug trafficking, against international crime and against terrorism.

Their obvious interest is to defend these shared values together. The United States needs military bases, financial aid, troops trained to maintain order, and more generally the political support of Europe on the world stage and notably at the United Nations and in the Third World. Europe, for its part, has learned the painful lesson that solving problems often requires the use of force, and that its own resources are not enough for it to do without the United States. This was its sorry experience in the tragedies accompanying the disintegration of Yugoslavia.

So the Atlantic Alliance has lost not one jot of its value. But it must not turn Europe into a mere appendage. To avoid this depends more on Europe than on the United States. It is Europe's task to become a politically and militarily credible partner. Divided, the Europeans will never be heard in Washington. United, their influence is and will remain considerable, above all if they make the effort to establish a military force – modest, no doubt, compared with America's resources, but autonomous and able to intervene in distant theatres.

Europe will have great difficulty in achieving such political union and military capacity without the active participation of Great Britain. Will Britain realise that the future of transatlantic relations, to which it is rightly so attached, requires its unstinting and unequivocal commitment to the building of an integrated Europe? Will it accept the delegation of sovereignty in foreign policy and defence that it has hitherto rejected?

Jean François-Poncet

The French for Entente Cordiale

There was a time when the French Republic and the United Kingdom dominated the sea, from the coast of the Mediterranean to that of the Pacific, and the land, from Africa to the Indo-Chinese peninsula.

Competition between them was always keen, sometimes bitter, and occasionally bloodthirsty. But, as they developed their power overseas, they came to realise the growing danger from a great continental power. In the disastrous war of 1870, the German empire brought France to its knees.

France and Britain were old enemies: they had confronted each other throughout their history, and rivalry had been part of their national consciousness. It was how they had learned to know each other and to co-exist in Europe. The German newcomer disturbed their policy and worried them – all the more so when it began to nurse ambitions overseas.

So they decided to combine forces, as far as they could, to hold in check the power that sought to dominate the European stage. Thus was born the Entente Cordiale. It was a union of ancient nations more than of democracies, despite the gilded version of history passed down by our great-grandparents.

The events that followed, however, gave substance to the legend. Defeated Germany began to suffer appalling convulsions. The Weimar Republic, which the French and British had thought to build upon the ruins of war, survived no more than fifteen years, and the National Socialist regime revealed the hideous face of unknown demons. With that, myth became reality: the Franco-British Entente became truly an alliance for democracy.

But World War II left France humiliated and Britain exhausted. There was now another great power, without which Paris might have remained under the Nazi heel and London might have been crushed. Up-and-coming America had saved the two countries, but now it was about to divide them.

Throughout the nineteenth century, the London press had shown nothing but scorn for Uncle Sam. After World War II it was quite otherwise. The new *entente*, between Britain and America, had been forged in combat – D-Day, the battles of France and Germany – and at summit meetings, from Casablanca to Yalta, in the absence of France.

From then onwards, Great Britain liked to imagine the United States as a somewhat fractious child which in the long run would follow the wise advice of its erstwhile mother country. But it was the child that delivered a fatal blow to these imaginings. One autumn day in 1956, US President Dwight D. Eisenhower put an end to the Suez expedition that France and the United Kingdom had mounted together. This also forced British Prime Minister Anthony Eden to resign. And it made the two nations' peoples and their leaders realise that they were no longer the superpowers that they had thought themselves.

Eden's successor was Harold Macmillan. He had declared twelve years earlier: 'We are the Greeks of this American empire.' Henceforward, British prime ministers busied themselves with remaining in the good books of the presidents of the United States. Some did so out of opportunism, bearing in mind what had happened to Anthony Eden; others because convinced that the fate of London was bound to that of Washington. This was the case with Margaret Thatcher, and may be so today with Tony Blair. France, meanwhile, maintained its grudge against the United States.

When General de Gaulle returned to power in 1958, he became convinced that the United Kingdom had for ever 'chosen the open sea'. Perhaps also remembering slights he had suffered during the war, he turned to Germany and made it France's major partner in the unification of Europe.

Between the reign of General de Gaulle and that of Margaret Thatcher, however, a more modest statesman briefly occupied 10 Downing Street. This was Edward Heath, and he had firmly chosen Europe rather than the open sea. Georges Pompidou was not instinctively drawn to the Germans. Thanks to him and to Edward Heath, the United Kingdom joined the European Economic Community, then known as the 'Common Market'. Since then, the Community has greatly changed. It has imposed itself, becoming a little more political and a little less economic. At each stage along the way, Great Britain has seemed about to get off the train, then has 'jumped in the last carriage', to quote François Mitterrand's metaphor. But Britain still hesitates between Europe and the illusion of its 'special relationship' with the United States.

For their part, French leaders are well aware that in matters of defence their only 'serious partner' in Europe is the United

Kingdom. In European and other theatres of war, whether in the republics of former Yugoslavia or of Africa, British and French soldiers find themselves side by side. If an aircraft is to be built, either military or civil, it cannot be effective unless manufacturers from both countries are involved. Many people in France today are hoping that the mist will clear from the eyes of London's leaders, that they will abandon the dream of being able to influence America, and that Britain will make fast to the continent and stop drifting in the Atlantic.

Before World War I, the Entente Cordiale was born from the appearance of a new power on the European stage. It has suffered, most recently, from the inability of both our countries to deal with the arrival on the world stage of the United States, now the only superpower.

When Britain and France finally come to terms with America's place on our planet, when Britain sees that America cannot be influenced by persuasion alone, and when France realises the need to be stronger to stand up to the giant, then perhaps the Entente Cordiale will be reborn. Only thus will Europe be able to be heard in the world: only thus will the United States be induced to appear to listen.

Dominique Bromberger

Envoi

There will always be an element of tease and rivalry in the relationship between France and Britain. To take a mild pleasure in each other's small setbacks, to emphasise the superficial differences between us, is part of the give and take of life in our two countries. It is born of our history and is quite compatible with the lesson, also resulting from history, that our fundamental interests are virtually identical. From time to time this friendly competition and rivalry degenerates into real irritation and bad-tempered tension. The British press moves more quickly than the French into this mode, perhaps because in the present phase of our history Britons possess less innate self-confidence than the French. There is no lack of opportunities for those who wish to convert teasing into tension. To take one example, for three hundred years now the French and British have differed on the philosophies of free trade and protectionism. The most eloquent defence of protectionism as a creed that I have ever heard was given to me many years ago by a mayor of Paris called Jacques Chirac when I called on him at the Hôtel de Ville.

Paradoxically, the absolute and evident need for Britain and France to collaborate more closely than ever on matters of immigration and crime inevitably leads from time to time to arguments on particular issues, such as the camp for asylum seekers at Sangatte. The colonial rivalries in Africa during the nineteenth century have not entirely disappeared, as witness the very different treatment accorded by the British press to the French intervention in the Ivory Coast and to the similar British intervention in Sierra Leone.

But the most important tension stems from the attitude of our two countries to the United States as the only superpower in the world. At each moment of difficulty in transatlantic relations the French press take up the ancient cry of General de Gaulle that Britain must choose between the two sides of the Atlantic. In practice such a definitive choice is unreal and impracticable. Britain and France, like Germany, Italy, Spain and all other European countries, each have their own relationship with the United States. It happens that the British relationship, because of history, language and culture, is closer than that of other countries. Some British make the mistake of supposing that the Anglo-American relationship is built on a specially strong rock of shared values and mutual affection. More closely inspected, history shows that the Anglo-American relationship is founded on the continued usefulness of each country to the other. At moments when Britain was not particularly useful to the United States, as in the immediate aftermath of World War II, or when Britain was actually damaging those interests, as at the time of Suez, the relationship evaporated quite quickly. It is certainly in the interests of Britain and of Europe, including France, that the Anglo-American relationship should continue to be friendly and strong – just as it is in the interests of Britain and Europe as a whole that the Franco-German relationship should continue and prosper. Diplomacy is not a zero-sum game in the twenty-first century. The outbreak of angry rivalries between important partners tends to embarrass and damage us all.

Both Britain and France look out on the world as a whole. They do not find it surprising that at any given moment parts of this world will be in tumult. They do not find it alarming that our own countries should be required from time to time to deploy military force to deal with such tumults. They do not shrink from the knowledge that such intervention will result in casualties. The armed forces of both our countries are increasingly configured on the same lines. They think, equip themselves, and train in terms of the rapid deployment of forces of volunteers. In Bosnia the French and the British provided the backbone of the international force, while the Germans and Americans for different reasons lamented and criticised from afar during the greater part of this tragedy. Miserable though that experience was, it has now led to Europeans assuming a senior role in the Balkans. The Americans retain, as is important, a significant interest, but because of their preoccupations elsewhere they are content in Europe's backyard to leave the main burden to Europe. This would not have been possible without constructive British and French leadership. That is how the transatlantic partnership should operate if it is to have any chance of success.

Contrary to what is sometimes dreamed in Paris, we as Europeans are not constructing, and have no hope of constructing, a rival to the United

States, calculated by any of the measures of military or economic capability. The failure of Europe over the last five years has been our slackness and incoherence in building a valid partnership with the United States. Britain cannot be content with the uneven Anglo-American partnership resembling one of those early bicycles christened in Britain the penny-farthing because of the huge disparity between the size of the two wheels. France cannot be content with occasional tactical initiatives that simply illustrate the divisions and relative ineffectiveness of Europe compared to the superpower. Both Britain and France have a fundamental interest in a European/American partnership in which Europe is neither a rival competing with the Americans for power nor an incoherent collection of satellites, scurrying to echo the latest decisions emanating from the White House. The main failure of British and French foreign policy in the last few years has been lack of success in building that European partnership across the Atlantic.

That failure became disastrously clear with the disagreement over Iraq. Both the French and British governments can be criticised for harsh remarks made at moments of tension. British ministers blamed the French for the lack of persuasiveness of our own diplomacy in the Security Council. President Chirac dismissed in a patronising manner the views of the new members of the EU. By our disagreement we created a temptation for the Americans. Instead of favouring European integration, the Americans might switch to a tactic of divide and rule. They might calculate that it would be easier to rely in each future enterprise on those European governments that on present form can be relied on to follow their lead regardless of circumstances; they might again ignore others who doubt or oppose. Such a decision to rely on ad hoc coalitions of the willing rather than a Euro-American partnership would in the end serve no one. The Americans would find themselves inadequately supported, and the Europeans permanently divided. The remedy lies with the governments of Europe, but particularly with Britain and France. The differences in our approach are less significant than the interests we share. The statesmen of our two countries realised this in 1904 and acted accordingly. Their successors must do the same.

Douglas Hurd

Postface

'Cross Channel Currents; 100 years of the Entente Cordiale'. This title indicates our desire to examine frankly the way that our entente has developed and the deep impact it has had on our mututal relations. In deciding to publish this book, we remain faithful to the spirit of the founders of the Franco-British Council, President Georges Pompidou and Prime Minister Edward Heath.

In 1972, when the United Kingdom joined the European Community, it wanted, in parallel with governmental action, a body representing civil society to meet and promote cooperation between the two countries in the framework of the building of Europe.

The Franco-British Council, for its part, has worked for thirty years for better understanding and rapprochement between France and Britain.

Its structure and its workings remain flexible. It consists of two sections, one British and one French, each comprising some thirty leading figures representing different sectors of national life.

Supported by both governments, which have not been sparing with their aid, the Council has tried to diversify its partners and its resources and so reflect the full spectrum of civil society on both sides of the Channel.

Those taking part in its meetings include members of governments, civil servants, academics, research workers, journalists and many others, each with full freedom of expression.

Its gatherings, its seminars and its reports bear witness to the importance of its work. If it has not invariably managed to reach unanimous conclusions, it has been able to clarify viewpoints and chart the way to future agreements.

In its first phase, the Council gave priority to the development of inter-governmental relations, greatly intensified by Britain's membership of the European Community. It made a notable contribution to this relationship by running large-scale conferences in the presence of the two countries' premiers and other ministers.

Very soon, the Council developed activities of its own in parallel with inter-governmental contacts. International questions naturally had an important place in its programme. Africa, the Middle East, and the future of the European Union were the subject of far-reaching debate, as were defence, security and conflict resolution.

In 1995, for instance, a seminar on Africa revealed broad areas of agreement in the analysis of the situation and on attitudes to adopt to difficult problems.

The Council has conducted an in-depth examination of the points of view of both states *vis-à-vis* the construction of Europe. Its meetings have made possible a fruitful debate on monetary union, institution-building and foreign and security policy.

It goes without saying that economic questions have also been discussed, whether to do with currency, industry or trade. At the request of French participants concerned with financing small and medium-sized business and industry, information has been pooled on both side's sucessful experiments. Management, competitiveness, pensions and funding the health service – all are subjects where experience on one side has helped the other, sometimes involving recommendations to the public authorities.

The Council's most important contribution to Franco-British relations has undoubtedly been in improving the two societies' understanding of each other. Where else would one find the like of its studies on education or the role of the media? Its reports are a mine of information that has often enabled experts to know each other better and pursue together their further reflections.

Among the numerous meetings devoted to education, that on history teaching in secondary schools was especially important. It was in fact the first such venture undertaken by the two countries. Carefully prepared, in particular by a poll of what British and French pupils knew and by a study of their textbooks, this seminar produced proposals for improving the curriculum.

Whether the subject be the training of future élites, nursery education, or more recently violence in schools, teachers and organisations active in these fields have profited from exchanging views with their counterparts.

As former colonial powers, the two countries have received as immigrants large-scale Muslim communities. So the Council has thought it useful to consider Muslims in France and Britain, as well as immigration and integration policies.

At a time when traditions are being disrupted by cultural globalisation, and in reaction to that some people are seeking to protect their identity within communities of language or religion, the Council has tried to measure the strength of both countries' cultures to resist these challenges, as well as the gradual emergence of a European cultural consciousness.

In 1997 at the Abbey of Fontévraud, some fifty leading figures debated at length the idea of European culture, the role of the state, the place of language and the relationship between culture and economics. A book was published as a result. Further publications were devoted to the financing of culture in the two countries and to the promotion of academic mobility.

A special study by the Council was devoted to those two great international organisations, the Commonwealth and Francophonia. Leaders from both came to give evidence and made it possible to evaluate what they involve for Britain and France respectively. The results have been brought together in a recently published book.

Disagreements over the Iraq crisis have shown that the Council has lost none of its relevance and usefulness. Its task is to pursue its goals in reliance on the values our two countries share: the practice of democracy, the rule of law, in international as well as domestic affairs, pluralism, tolerance and mutual respect.

Allegiance to these values, a long tradition of intellectual interchange and reciprocal influence have created between us a community and a capital of friendship which it is our duty to preserve and make fruitful. The work of historians, along with the judgement of statesmen and the evidence of all those involved in this book, shed light on this evolution, throwing into relief the high points, the misunderstandings to overcome, the lasting obstacles, and the results achieved.

Our traditions and our interests may sometimes lead us to take up different positions. While seeking to minimise these differences, we must accept them, and seek to avoid polemics which harden attitudes and hinder the search for reasonable solutions. In a word, we must respect each other, and to do this we must accept what we are. But, in this field, as in others, much remains to be done.

We are delighted that the British and the French have worked actively together recently in the Convention that has drawn up a Constitution for Europe. We hope that this cooperation will continue and grow.

We are convinced that France and the United Kingdom can offer the world irreplaceable experience, knowledge and human vision. We also believe that Franco-British *entente* will enable our two countries to help build a solid European Union and to maintain their place and the values they stand for in Europe and in the world.

Jacques Viot and Lord Radice

Contributors

Christopher Andrew is Professor of Modern and Contemporary History at Cambridge, and is a specialist in international relations and the history of intelligence. Among his books are *Théophile Delcassé and the Making of the Entente Cordiale* (1968) and *The Mitrokhin Archive. Vol. 1: The KGB in Europe and the West* (1999) (with Vasili Mitrokhin).

Jean-Pierre Angremy (known as Jean-Pierre Rémy) is a diplomat, writer and member of the Académie Française. He was Cultural Counsellor at the French Embassy in London, Director of the Académie de France in Rome and President of the Bibliothèque Nationale de France. Among his numerous books, some concern England, such as: *Cordelia ou l'Angleterre* and *Londres, un ABC romanesque et sentimental*. He has also published a biography of *Berlioz* (2002).

John Ardagh is a freelance journalist and broadcaster. His books include *France in the New Century*, Viking (1999) and *Writers' France*, Hamish Hamilton.

Jean-Jacques Becker is a writer and Professor Emeritus at the Université de Paris X-Nanterre. He is Vice-President of the Société des Amis de Clemenceau. In 2002 the Académie Française awarded him the Grand Prix Gobert for his complete work, which mainly concerns the First World War.

Philip Bell is an historian and author of many historical works, including *A Certain Eventuality: Britain and the fall of France* (1974), *France and*

Britain 1900–1940: Entente and Estrangement (1996), *France and Britain 1940–1994, The Long Separation* (1997), *The World Since 1945: An International History* (2001).

Jean-René Bernard worked with Georges Pompidou as Inspector-General of Finance from 1962 to 1974. A former Joint Secretary-General of the Presidency of the French Republic, he acted as economic and financial adviser to the President of the French Republic. He was also French Ambassador to Mexico and to the Netherlands, and President of the Crédit Industriel et Commercial. Since 1997 he has been a member of the Conseil de la Politique Monétaire of the Banque de France.

Dominique Bromberger is a journalist who has worked for French radio stations and TV channels (Radio France, TF1, Arte) and has been a correspondent in England and Washington. His publications are *L'itinéraire de Pahan au château d'Alamut et au-delà* (1978), *Le grand manège* (1993) and *Aller et Retour* (to be published in 2004).

Isabelle Bussy studied at the universities of Paris and Cambridge. A specialist in twentieth-century history, she is presently working on Franco-British relations, and is the co-editor of *Voices from Wartime France, 1939–45: Clandestine Resistance and Vichy Newspapers from the British Library, Colindale* (2002).

Graham Corbett was Chief Financial Officer of Eurotunnel plc and Eurotunnel SA from 1987 to 1996.

Dr Martyn Cornick is a Reader in Contemporary French Studies and Head of the French Department in the University of Birmingham. He publishes widely on French intellectual history and on Franco-British representations, and is editor of the review *Modern & Contemporary France*.

Dr Anne Deighton is at Wolfson College, University of Oxford. She has been *Professeur invité* at the Universities of Paris I (La Sorbonne) and Paris III (La Sorbonne la nouvelle). She has published widely on European integration, British foreign policy since World War II, and on issues relating to European security.

Jean Dhombres, is a mathematician and lecturer at the École des Hautes Études en Sciences Sociales. He has written, among other books, *Func-*

tional Equations in Several Variables (Cambridge University Press, 1989) and *Gian-Carlo Rota, Selected papers and commentaries* (Birkhauser, Boston, 2003).

Maurice Druon, novelist and essayist, served as Minister for Culture in 1973–74. He was a member of the French Resistance and in 1942 escaped to London, where he worked with La France Libre. In 1943, with his uncle Joseph Kessel, he wrote *Le Chant des Partisans*, the song of the Resistance. He was elected *Secrétaire perpétuel* of the Académie Française in 1985. Among his many books are the cycles of the *Grandes familles* (*The curtain falls*) and of *Les Rois Maudits* (*The Accursed Kings*). He is a Grand officier de la Légion d'honneur and Knight of the British Empire.

Professor David Dutton teaches Modern History at the University of Liverpool. His books include *Anthony Eden: A Life and Reputation* (Arnold, 1997) and *The Politics of Diplomacy: Britain and France in the Balkans in the First World War* (I. B. Tauris, 1998).

André Fontaine is a journalist and former director of *Le Monde*. He is now adviser to the Director of *Le Monde* and writes editorials. He was a member of the Institut Français des Relations Internationales. In 1976 he was elected International Editor of the Year by the revue *Atlas* (New York). He has written many books, including *Un seul lit pour deux rêves* (1981) and *Après eux, le déluge, de Kaboul à Sarajevo* (1995).

Hilary Footitt is Honorary Research Fellow at the University of Stirling, and Chair of the University Council of Modern Languages. Her book, *War and Liberation in France: Living with the Liberators*, will be published by Palgrave Macmillan in 2004.

Jean François-Poncet, French Foreign Minister from 1978 to 1981, is Sénateur for Lot-et-Garonne. He is also President of the Forum d'Initiatives Franco-Indien. He writes editorials for *Le Figaro*.

Joëlle Garriaud-Maylam is the elected representative of the French in Great Britain and Ireland at the Conseil Supérieur des Français de l'étranger.

Robert Hanks is a Lecturer in modern European history and international relations, University of Toronto, Canada. His doctoral dissertation was entitled: 'Culture versus Diplomacy: Clemenceau and

Anglo-American Relations During the First World War' (University of Toronto, 2002). His article 'Georges Clemenceau and the English' appeared in *The Historical Journal* 45, 1 (2002).

Richard Holt is a Research Professor in the International Centre for Sports History and Culture, De Montfort University. Among his publications are *Sport and Society in Modern France* (1981) and *Sport and the British: a Modern History* (1989).

Sir Alistair Horne is an Honorary Fellow of St Antony's College, Oxford. Author of many books about France; notably his trilogy *The Price of Glory: Verdun 1916; The Fall of Paris: The Siege and the Commune 1870–71; To Lose a Battle: France 1940* and *A Savage War of Peace*, about the Algerian War. His most recent publication was *Seven Ages of Paris*, published in 2002. He is also the biographer of Harold Macmillan (2 vols, 1894–1956 and 1957–1986). He is currently working on *A Short History of France* to be published in 2004. He was knighted in 2003 for services to Franco-British relations.

Lord Hurd retired as Foreign Secretary in July 1995, after a distinguished career in Government spanning sixteen years. After positions as Minister of State in the Foreign Office and the Home Office, he served as Secretary of State for Northern Ireland from 1984–85, Home Secretary from 1985–89 and Foreign Secretary from 1989–95.

Roy Jenkins, active in British politics for half a century, entered the House of Commons as a Labour member in 1948 and subsequently served as Home Secretary and Chancellor of the Exchequer. In 1977–81 he was President of the European Commission. In 1987 he became Chancellor of Oxford University and took his seat as Lord Jenkins of Hillhead. He also served as President of the Royal Society of Literature and was awarded the *Légion d'Honneur*. Among his many books was a highly acclaimed biography of Winston Churchill. He died in January 2003.

Douglas Johnson is Professor Emeritus of French History, University of London. He has been honoured with the *Ordre National du Mérite, Commandeur des Palmes Académiques* and the *Officier de la Légion d'Honneur*. He has written many books on France and Europe.

Danièle Joly is professor of Ethnic Relations and Director of the Centre for Research in Ethnic Relations, University of Warwick.

H. Roderick Kedward is Emeritus Professor of History at the University of Sussex. Honoured in 1989 by the French Government as *Officier de l'Ordre des Palmes Académiques*, he has researched and written extensively on Occupied France. Two major books on Resistance in the south of France were based on oral history as well as archival documentation. Published by Oxford University Press (*Resistance in Vichy France*, 1978; *In Search of the Maquis*, 1993) they have both been translated into French: *Naissance de la Resistance dans la France de Vichy* (Champ Vallon, 1989; *À la recherche du Maquis*, Cerf, 1999). The Maquis book shared the 'Prix Philippe Viannay – Defénse de la France' in 1995. He is currently concluding a *History of 20th Century France* for Penguin.

John Keiger is Professor of International History and director of the European Studies Research Institute at Salford University. A specialist in French foreign policy, his books include *France and the Origins of the First World War* (1983), *Raymond Poincaré* (1997) and *France and the World Since 1870* (2001).

François Kersaudy, Professor at the Sorbonne (Paris 1), is a specialist in contemporary diplomatic and military history. Among other books, he has written *De Gaulle et Churchill, la mésentente cordiale* (Perrin, Paris, 2001); *Winston Churchill, le pouvoir de l'imagination* (Tallandier, Paris, 2000); *Churchill contre Hitler, Norvège 1940* (Tallandier, Paris, 2002).

Miles Kington is a humorous columnist who has contributed to *The Times* and the *Independent* for many years. He has also written many books including an attempt to bring the two countries together with the *Parler franglais* series.

Keith Kyle, a Fellow of the Royal Historical Society, was Visiting Professor of History at the University of Ulster from 1993–99 and author of *Suez* (1991) and *Suez: Britain's End of Empire in the Middle East* (2003). In 1956 he was the Washington Correspondent of *The Economist* and subsequently worked for BBC TV and the Royal Institute for International Affairs.

Paul-Marie de La Gorce is a writer and a journalist. He has been a television commentator on various radio and TV programmes. He is a former advisor to the French Prime Minister. He is also Director of the Fondation Charles de Gaulle publication. *Le Dernier Empire* (1996) and *De Gaulle* (2000) are the latest of his many historic works.

Jean-Marie Le Breton, diplomat, was French Ambassador to Portugal, Bulgaria and Romania. He has a doctorate in philosophy from Oxford University and was a Visiting Fellow at the university. He is Secrétaire-Général of the French Section of the Conseil franco-britannique. He has published *L'Europe Centrale et Orientale de 1917 à 1990* (Nathan, Paris, 1994).

Helen Liddell was Secretary of State for Scotland from January 2001 to June 2003. She was Minister for Energy and Competitiveness in Europe at the Department of Trade and Industry from July 1999.

Mairi Maclean is Professor of European Studies at the University of the West of England, Bristol. She has published widely in the field of French business and comparative European business, and on the French author Michel Tournier.

Sir Christopher Mallaby is Chairman of the Entente Cordiale Scholarships Trust. He was Ambassador in France from 1993–96 and before that in Germany. He is now Managing Director at UBS.

Dr Richard Mayne is a writer and broadcaster. Educated at St Paul's School and Trinity College, Cambridge, he was Personal Assistant to Jean Monnet, a senior official of the European Commission, and for six years its UK representative. He has been Director of the Federal Trust, a Council member of Chatham House, a visiting professor at the University of Chicago and an honorary professorial fellow at the University of Wales, Aberystwyth. He has written extensively on France and Europe, and is an *Officier de l'ordre des arts et des lettres*. His historical works include *The Community of Europe, The Recovery of Europe, The Europeans, Postwar* and *In Victory Magnanimity, In Peace Goodwill: A History of Wilton Park*.

Pierre Messmer is a former French Prime Minister and a member of the Académie Française. He is also Chancelier of the Institut de France. During World War II he joined the Forces Françaises Libres. He is chair of the Institut and the Fondation Charles de Gaulle. He has written *Après tant de batailles – mémoires* (Albin Michel, 1992), *La Patrouille perdue* (Albin Michel, 2002), *Ma part de France – entretiens avec Philippe de St-Robert* (Editions Xavier de Guibert, 2003).

Marc Michel is a professor emeritus at the Université de Provence. He is a historian and has written several books on Africa, including *Les Africains*

CONTRIBUTORS

et la Grande Guerre (Karthala, 2003). He is editor of the publication *Outre-mers*.

John Newhouse, from 1998 to 2001, served as senior policy advisor on European Affairs to Strobe Talbott, US deputy secretary of state. From 1980 to 1998, he was a guest scholar at the Brookings Institution, and served as a staff writer for the *New Yorker* magazine from 1980 to 1994. He is an expert in arms control and diplomacy, having spent 1977–79 as assistant director of the US Arms Control and Disarmament Agency with responsibility for East–West matters, including Strategic Arms Limitation Talks. He is the author of a number of books, including *Europe Adrift, War and Peace in the Nuclear Age*, and *Cold Dawn: The Story of SALT*.

William Philpott is a Lecturer in the Department of War Studies at King's College, London, and a member of the British Commission for Military History. His publications include *Anglo-French Relations and Strategy on the Western Front, 1914–1918* (1996).

The Rt Hon Lord Radice is Chairman of the Franco-British Council, British Section, and Chairman of the European Economic Committee of the House of Lords. He was a Labour MP from 1973–2001 and is the author of a number of books including *Offshore: Britain and the European Idea* (1992), *The New Germans* (1995) and more recently *Friends and Rivals* (2002).

Jean Rannou is General of the Armed Airforces (2è S). He is a former fighter pilot, and former Chief of Staff of the Airforce.

Gillian Tindall is a novelist, biographer and historian. Her many works include *Célestine: Voices from a French Village*, and *The Journey of Martin Nadaud*. She is a *Chevalier de l'ordre des arts et des lettres*.

Robert Tombs is a Reader in French History at Cambridge, and the author of *France 1814–1914* (1996). He is presently working on Franco-British relations.

Raphaële Ulrich-Pier is a former student of the École Normale Supérieure, and has a doctorate in History. She is the author of a thesis on René Massigli (1888–1988), *The Biography of a Diplomat* (Paris 1, 2003).

Maurice Vaïsse is Professor of International Relations at the Institut d'Études Politiques de Paris and vice-chairman of the publishing committee of French diplomatic documents. His latest publication is *La grandeur politique étrangère du Général de Gaulle 1958–1969* (1998).

Paul Vallet was born in Washington, DC, in 1970 and graduated from the Institut d'Études Politiques de Paris, and from Tufts University's Fletcher School of Law and Diplomacy, before undertaking his doctoral work at Wolfson College, Cambridge, on '*The origins and development of an Anglo-French Entente, 1902–1914*'. He lectures in history and international relations at the Institut d'Études in Nancy.

Hubert Védrine was French Foreign Minister from 1997 to 2002. He worked closely with Président François Mitterrand from 1981 to 1995. He was diplomatic adviser, spokesman and then Secretary-General for the Élysée. He is manager associate of the Hubert Védrine consultancy. He is the author of *Les Mondes de François Mitterrand, à l'Élysée 1981–1995* (Fayard, 1996) and *Les Cartes de la France à l'heure de la mondialisation* (Fayard, 2000).

Jacques Viot was French Ambassador in Canada and Great Britain. He is President of the Alliance Française and President of the French section of the Franco-British Council.

Index

casualties, Algerian War 68; Napoleonic Wars 67; World War I 50, 62, 67
Cerdan, Marcel 269
Ceylon 147, 148
Cézanne, Paul 136
Chaban-Delmas, Jacques 170
Chagall, Marc 221
Chalfont, Lord 174
Chamberlain, Austen 29, 76
Chamberlain, Joseph 64
Chamberlain, Neville 31, 83, 84, 85, 94, 96, 100, 118, 136
Chambers, Mrs Lambert 269
Channel Tunnel 71, 77, 246, 257, 262–3, 269
Charles, H.R.H. Prince 233
Charlot, Monique: *L'Angleterre 1945–1980* 193n
Chechnya 193
Chemin des Dames, Battle of 50, 56
Cheysson, Claude 233
China, Attacked by Japan 82
Chirac, Jacques xii, 192, 198, 199, 200, 236, 238, 240, 245, 251, 254, 255, 258, 265, 282, 288, 289
Chou En Lai 175
Churchill, Clementine 121
Churchill, Randolph 93
Churchill, Winston xv, 9, 23, 28, 84, 88, 90, 91–8, 100, 101, 102–5, 108, 109, 111, 112, 113, 116–21, 133, 145, 155, 192, 193, 194, 196, 255; *Complete Speeches* 118n; Fulton speech (1946) 193; *Great Contemporaries* 117n; *History of the English-Speaking Peoples* 194n; *The Sinews of Peace* 194n; Zurich Speech (1946) 166
'civilising mission', France's 148
Claudel, Paul 219
Clemenceau, Georges xiv, 19, 28, 51, 52, 63, 64–6, 71, 117, 118
Clerk Maxwell, James 38
Clinton, President Bill 199, 236, 239
Cobra radar 243
Cocteau, Jean 129, 219; *Orphée* (film) 129
Cochet, Henri 269
Coe, Jonathan 247
Colbert, Jean-Baptiste 250

'cold war' 152, 185, 283
'collective security' 74–5, 81
colonialism 5, 6, 141
colonial rivalry 4, 7, 153, 288
Combat (Resistance group) 124
Common Agricultural Policy (CAP) 167, 170, 198, 258, 282
Commonwealth 141, 147, 167, 293
Compton-Burnett, Ivy 215, 218
Concorde 258
Confrèrie Notre Dame (Resistance group) 125
Congo crisis 152
Congreve, William 210
Connolly, Cyril 214, 223; *The Rock Pool* 223
Conrad, Joseph 211, 212, 215
Constant, Benjamin xiv
Constantinople Convention (1888) 4
'controlled interference' in liberated France 134–5
Cook, Robin 236–9
Cooper, Alfred Duff 133
Corbett, Graham 263
Corbière, Tristan 212
Corbin, Charles 104
Cormeau, Yvonne 128
Cornick, Martyn 129n
Corot, Camille 136
Corp, William G. 122
Cot, Pierre 100
Côte d'Azur, British on 92, 98, 118, 223–4, 271
Coty, President René 23
Couve de Murville, Maurice 169, 174–5, 197; *Une politique étrangère* 175n
CRE (Commission for Racial Equality) 260
Crowe, Sir Eyre 30
culture 5, 209–18, 219–22, 223–5, 247
Cunningham, Admiral Andrew 95
Curtis, Lionel 99, 101
Czechoslovak crisis (1938) 84–5

Dakar 88, 96–7, 107, 120
Daladier, Édouard 85, 100, 118
Dale, Reginald 185n
Dalton, Hugh 126
Dawes, Charles G. 73–4

Erhard, Ludwig 197
Esher, Lord 57, 63
Euratom (European Atomic Energy Community) 114, 160
Euro xv, 250, 281
European Coal and Steel Community 114, 160, 249
European Constitution 249, 293
European Defence Community 114, 164
European Economic Community 114, 138, 155, 157, 160, 164; Britain's financial contribution 234–5
European Free Trade Association (EFTA) 166
European Union xiii, xv, 101, 164–5, 185, 186, 192–201, 228, 248–9, 280, 291, 293; Briand proposal for (1930) 77, 82
Eurostar 257
Eurotunnel plc xi, 252, 263–4
événements (1968) 169
Exocet missiles 241–2
expatriates 273, 275–7
L'Express 247, 249

Falkenheyn, Erich von 62, 63
Falklands War 198, 233–4, 242
Fall of France (1940) 86, 88
Fallières, President Armand 18–19
Fashoda xiv, 4–5, 6, 12, 47, 144, 152, 238, 255
Faulks, Sebastian 225
Faure, Félix 5
federalism 114, 174
Fenby, Jonathan 254
Ferguson, Niall 195n
Feuillère, Edwige 216
Fielding, Henry 210
FIFA (Fédération Internationale de Football Association) 269
Figaro, Le 200n, 266
Financial Times, the 192n, 195n
Fischer, Joschka 237, 238
Flandin, Pierre-Étienne 92–3, 118
Flaubert, Gustave 136, 220; Madame Bovary 220
Florio, John 210
Foch, General Ferdinand 8, 51, 53–61, 63, 65, 117, 118

'Fogg, Phileas' 5
Fontaine, Juste 270
Fontenoy, Battle of xiv
food 14–15, 177, 223, 224, 226–7, 247, 256
Foot, M. R. D. 126; SOE in France 126n
football 270
Foreign Affairs 199n, 200n
Forrester, Vivienne 214
Foucault, Michel 216
France Libre, La 122
Franco, General Francisco 84
Franco-British Air Group 243
Franco-British Exhibition (1908) 17, 18
Franco-British Naval Agreement (1912) 9, 116
Franco-British Union proposal (1940) 23, 96, 99–108, 119
Francophonia 142, 249, 293
Franglais 207
Free France 89, 122
Frenay Henri 124
French, Sir John 49, 55–6, 65
'French Community' 142
French Union 147, 148
Freud, Lucien 214
Fry, Roger 212

Gamelin, General Maurice Gustave 118
Garden, Mary 217
Garnier Robert 210
Garriaud-Maylam, Joëlle 274
Garton Ash, Timothy 200
Gaujac, Paul 156
Gautier, Théophile: Le Capitaine Fracasse 221
Gazelle helicopters 242
Geneva Conference (1954) 138
Gentileschi, Artemisia 213
Geoffroy, Christine 248
George V, King 102
Georges, General Alphonse 93, 112, 120
Germany 5, 7, 25–35, 36–43, 70, 71, 240, 285; admitted to League of Nations 76; disarmament 80; Navy Law (1900) 5; occupation of 113; quits League of Nations 81; rearmament 196; reunification 181, 188, 189, 195, 235, 249
Ghana (Gold Coast) 149, 151

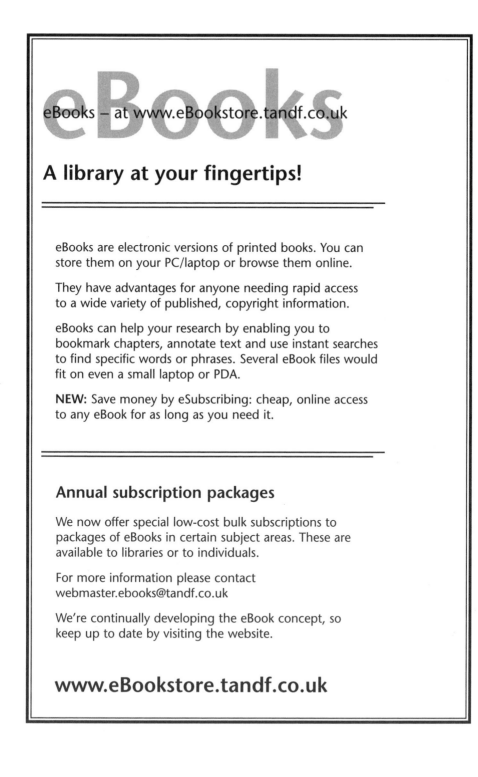